SOUTH INDIAN TEMPLES

South Indian Temples

An Analytical Reconsideration

Edited by

BURTON STEIN

VIKAS PUBLISHING HOUSE PVT LTD
New Delhi Bombay Bangalore Calcutta Kanpur

VIKAS PUBLISHING HOUSE PVT LTD
5 Ansari Road, New Delhi 110002
Savoy Chambers, 5 Wallace Street, Bombay 400001
10 First Main Road, Gandhi Nagar, Bangalore 560009
8/1-B Chowringhee Lane, Calcutta 700016
80 Canning Road, Kanpur 208004

ISBN 0 7069 0581 4

1V02S6002

Printed at Bharti Printers, K-16 Navin Shahdara, Delhi 110032

Contents

Introduction

These several essays seek to say something new about South Indian temples. Each pursues different questions or problems according to the interests of its author; all speak to only a fragment of the ramified and changing functions and meanings of Hindu temples. The essays are presented here to stimulate discussion and, it is hoped, research which reaches beyond the cumulative scholarly quest for understanding Hindu temples, a quest which is of two centuries duration.

The methods which shape and the sources which inform these essays are, to some extent, those to which all scholars have turned for understanding and for communicating their understandings of these complex institutions. But, in some respects, both methods and sources are different from those of the learned predecessors in this task. Thus, inscriptions, puranas, and early eye-witness reports continue to provide the major sources of information about temples until quite recent times Each of these kinds of evidence involve methods appropriate to their idiom, methods which historians have long used to study temples and other elements of premodern life in South India. More recently, however, legal, administrative, and census evidence have come to figure in the analysis of temples, and these sources prefigure appropriate and different methodologies. The variability of sources and methods stem from the diachronic emphases of these essays In the case of only one, the work of Dennis Hudson, is there some deviation from the explicitly diachronic focus, and here the voice of the ethnographic present does not preclude the concern with change which occupies the other essays.

Why scholars of South India, generation after generation, return to the study of Hindu temples, is a question that may be answered in simple or complex ways. The simple answer is that like the mighty mountains they are often intended to resemble to the eye, they are there; and temples have been there for over a millennium Temples command attention in being the most enduring and grand monuments in the South of India. They have inspired the architectural creativity of South Indians, as the tombs and fortified palaces of the Muslim rulers of the north of India and the Deccan did for centuries; and great religious structures moved Europeans and Mayans in a contemporary period, or the archaic Egyptians and Harappans long before. To generations of scholarly witnesses of life in South India, the Hindu Temple was a compellingly attractive subject, because it was equally attractive to the South Indians these scholars sought to understand. Nor was it only in South India that the temple was observed to exercise this attraction, as is known from the reports of early Chinese Buddhist pilgrims.

Yet, it is widely assumed that the temple came to be more important in the lives of the people of the southern peninsula of the Indian subcontinent than in the lives and cultures of those of the North. Perhaps this was, as often argued, a consequence of the hostile context created for the public worship of Hindu deities by Muslim dominance in North India after the thirteenth century. That may be true, but it may also be true that the Hindu temple, from even pre-Muslim times, occupied a different place for South Indian Hindus than for North Indian Hindus. These essays do not take up the questions of differences among the several cultural regions of India—questions of the highest potential interest—but it must at least be considered that such differences were substantial, and not simply because of the Muslim presence, but because Hindus in various parts of the subcontinent perceived the shrines of their gods in essentially very different ways. One implication of this observation is that the various viewpoints and findings in these essays should not be construed as universal characteristics of Hinduism during the medieval or modern period. A greater degree of complexity in Indian Hinduism should be anticipated in this vast subcontinental civilization, just as complexity is the clearest attribute of the temple itself in South India.

It is precisely this complexity which makes the answer to the question of why temples are objects of endless scholarly fascination, a complex one. It could scarcely be otherwise when it is recognized that many South Indian Hindu temples are centuries old, and that each of the thousands of temples has a separate past. This past begins with its being one sacred place (*tīrtha*) among numerous others, a place of sacred performances, vows and supplications for local people as well as, in many cases, for persons of distant places. Of these many sacred places, some seized the interest (whether pious or self-aggrandizing) of a powerful local personage with the resources to build a modest or even magnificent shelter or palace for the deity of the place.

The term *kōyil* in Tamil preserves the dual conception of temples as shelters for deities and for kings; the word means both temple and palace. However magnificent the structure, the essential sacredness or importance of any sacred place is not to be measured in architectural terms alone. All sacred places are important to some devotees. But, it is clear that some such places became more important than others as this may be inferred from the number of pilgrims who thronged their precincts, the celebration of their fame in the sacred songs of Siva hymnists (*nāyanārs*) or Vishnu hymnists (*āḻvārs*), and the inscriptions incised on their walls.

Careers of temples may have been long—some were established in very ancient times and are still important in the present day—or short; but, each underwent changes which have been recorded in a way deemed appropriate by its supporters in accounts of the place. These accounts (*sthalapurāṇas*) are an aspect of the pasts of temples and of obvious interest to those wishing to understand temples in South India.

Changes in the development of single temples are not the focus of the essays here. It is rather the relationship of temples to other institutions with which temples are linked. Empirically and conceptually, South Indian temples were linked to other institutions in South Indian society by multiplex strands. It is these complex and integrated relationships which give to South Indian temples a major part of their consuming interest. Temples could not but reflect, and in fact influence, the totality of relationships within local societies of South India during medieval times and in more recent times. As the most significant locus of public information through its inscriptions, its varied constituent groups, and its special relationships with locally powerful groups and at times the most powerful of all, kings of the regions in which temples were—because of all of this, temples provide the best evidence available on the most important changes in society. They also provide hints as to why such changes occurred. Temples draw our attention as perhaps the most sensitive institution for registering changes in the surrounding society, certainly in South India.

Put another way, South Indian temples summed a varied set of social, political, and cultural relationships; at any time, the social composition of temples was the outcome of numerous and diverse social actions among local and supralocal people the meanings of which were clear to all. In this sense, the temple is the complex and transitory outcome of an extraordinary range of relationships (interactions and transactions); a temple is a statement about its constituent social groupings. The reading of such dynamic social situations requires of the researcher a sensitivity which is equal to the sensitivity of the temple institution itself in registering these most complicated and often "heated" interrelations. To consider the temple in the sort of isolation or compartmentalization as modern western religious institutions are considered is to commit the same violence upon truth and reality as when the Indian village is taken as a self-sufficient isolate. The solipsistic error, in both cases, is perilous.

Compartmentalizing the temple as just another of many South Indian institutions, and viewing the temple either as a sectarian sodality or as a bureaucratic institution under its managers (*sthanattars*), certainly imperils an adequate understanding of authority and dominance in medieval and early modern South India. The presence of kingly, great chiefly, or minor chiefly personages at large and small temples may be, and often is, taken either to be the expression of personal piety of such personages or of their dharmic, protective responsibility which extended equally to other spheres of South Indian life. It is the argument of all of these essays—in one way or another—that temples were in fact the prime locus of authority and dominance issues and decisions. In no other social or cultural context were matters pertaining to authority and dominance so explicitly raised and resolved as in temples.

This orientation with respect to the temple is somewhat more explicit in the central question or problem of some of the following essays than in others. The central question in the essay by Stein is: what factor or factors account for the particular configuration of over two thousand temples during the Vijayanagara period of the fourteenth to the eighteenth centuries? Having determined that temples devoted to Siva deities declined relatively, at about the same rate that temples devoted to independent goddesses (*amman*) increased, the question of why this should have been so is considered. The answer is framed in terms of differential patterns of local dominance situations, especially whether local dominance was exercised by subcaste groups of the same larger caste category of the region, or whether by groups of different caste categories. Appadurai's central question even more explicitly turns on authority and dominance. The question which emerges from his analysis of sectarian fission among Sri Vaishnavas during the Vijayanagara period is: why were sectarian leaders and their constituencies as involved with kingly figures and temples as they were? Here, dominance patterns of realm, region and locality are engaged through the confrontation and conciliation of the diverse objectives of authoritative spokesmen from powerful warrior-groups, sectarian followerships, and temple organizations. Breckenridge's essay takes a close and graphic look at the question of authority and dominance in relation to temples. Why, she asks, was the Raja of Ramnad so intensely engaged in conflicts involving ritual and management over temples at a time, in the late nineteenth century, when his royal position with respect to British power was growing precarious or, at least, anomalous? Why were temples, and the Raja's relationship with, and participation in, them considered so vital to his interests? Her answer, framed in terms of inscriptional as well as legal evidence, focuses on the changing relationship between the social context of temples and royal rituals. In his study of the Cittirai festival in Madurai, Hudson discovers a popular myth which links two distinct temple festivals into a single event. The marriage of the deities Siva and Minakshi, celebrated in Madurai, is popularly understood to involve a nearby Vishnu deity, considered to be a brother of the goddess. Vishnu's journey (i.e. the procession of the deity) toward Madurai to attend the marriage is annually frustrated by the news that the marriage was completed before Vishnu could arrive on the scene. Hudson's question of why this popular mythology came into existence in the seventeenth century is answered by the proposal that it served as a means for the regional king, the Tirumala Nayaka of Madurai, to express his superordinate position over the Kaḷḷar devotees of Vishnu in the area. The idiom is kinship and marriage; the purpose is to express a problematic political relationship between the Nayakas and the warrior, Kaḷḷar folk of his realm. Hardy has raised the question of the meaning of the temple for Sri Vaishnava worshippers as this may be understood from the interaction of theological, cultural, and aesthetic formulations of Vaishnava hymnists and theologians of the sixth to the sixteenth centuries as well as more recent literary productions. Three principal interpretational foci are considered: the theological or philosophical conception of *arcavatāra;* the powerful emotional poetry of Sri Vaishnava hymnists (*āḻvārs*), and those mythic works (*sthalapurāṇas*) which intend to place a temple into a temporal and spatial universe and social context Each of these interpretations draws upon a different idiom and each derives from different cultural sources, but all together merge as a distinctive Tamil variant of Hinduism.

These problematic issues are distillates of the present essays. Their formulation calls upon the long-standing interest of each of the writers in the temple and society in South India. An opportunity to present versions of the papers (except that of Hardy) occurred in August 1976, during the 30th International Congress of the Human Sciences in Asia and North Africa, in Mexico City. The present collection preserves much of the discussion in Mexico City. In "Temples in Tamil Country, 1300-1750 A.D.," Stein makes use of a series of volumes of the Madras State (Tamil Nadu) census of 1961, which surveys temples of the State. From this census data, 2,035 shrines which achieved importance between 1300 and 1750 A.D. are analyzed in order to form an estimate of the aggregative pattern of temple construction and worship during Vijayanagara times. The census data are analyzed in a set of categories: the time of major construction in four periods of about a century; the principal deity (Siva, Vishnu, Ganesha, Murugan, Amman, "other") worshipped; and the spatial distribution of these shrines according to the important cultural territory, *maṇḍalam.* Appadurai's, "Kings, Sects and Temples in South India; 1350-1700 A.D.," locates the origin of recent temple politics in South India in the period of the consolidation of the Vijayanagara kingdom over the Tamils. Then, authoritative relations, which in other political traditions are divided between religious and political hierarchies, were combined in a single authority system. Sri Vaishnava temples occupied a strategic place as the locus of ritual and economic exchanges between Telugu warriors seeking to establish their dominance over Tamil country and Tamil Vaishnava sectarian leaders. The enduring legitimacy of the former in Tamil country was achieved largely through exchanges at temples. A by-product of these interactions was the division of Sri Vaishnava sectarians into two subsects, Vadakalai and Teṉkalai; these sectarian subgroups during the eighteenth and nineteenth centuries became competitors for temple control. Breckenridge deals with the crisis of a minor, South Indian kingly house, the Setupati Rājās of Ramnad, confronted with British courts and law, and the recourse of this royal house to the elaborate celebration of the Navarātri festival as a means of renewing its authority. Her "From Protector to Litigant—Changing Relations Between Temples and the Rājā of Ramnad" provides a dense description of the Navarātri festival of 1892 based on an eye-witness account. This festival has been one of the most popular public and domestic ritual events in South India for centuries; as a kingly ritual it is an elaborate and incorporative ritual performance of ten days duration. Then, through an examination of a set of temple inscriptions of the seventeenth and eighteenth centuries, the Rājā's crucial role as donor in and protector over temples in his realm is established. Finally, the intervention of British judicial institutions is examined through several court cases. Shown here is the fundamental alteration of the Raja's role in temples and the subsequent divestment of his kingly qualities.

Hudson's previous research on the Cittirai (Citra) festival in Madurai brought to his attention the popular myth of the kinship relationship of the deities Siva, Minakshi and Vishnu. Though unrelated in a formal sense, two concurrent temple festivals are merged as a single expressive event for the people of Madurai and its vicinity. In the present essay, "Siva, Minakshi and Vishnu—Reflections on a Popular Myth of Madurai," Hudson attempts to discover the meanings expressed in the festival event. This leads him to the detailed examination of the idiom of family kinship (*kulam*) in which the popular myth is expressed and the marriage of Siva and Minakshi involving Vishnu as the brother of the goddess, hence the brother-in-law of Siva. By this means, the socio-political structure of Madurai and its vicinity is homologized as a unity, but one in which there are tensions The tension of the brother-in-law relationship in the South Indian system of cross-cousin marriage provides the popular structure of meaning for understanding and expressing tensions between the foreign Telugu dynasty of Nayakas established at Madurai during the seventeenth century and the indigenous, locally dominant Kaḷḷar people. Again, kingship is seen as expressively realized in temple ritual and events involving temples. Challenges to the unity of the realm under its king are given recognition and meaning in temple ritual performance. Finally, Hardy perceives an evolving set of understandings or interpretations of the temple for Tamil Sri Vaishnavas which result from the interaction of two cultures. One is the philosophical or theological culture of Sanskrit which perceives Vishnu as placed in a local temple as a manifestation (*arcavatāra*) of that god's universal and mythic characteristics. The other is the poetic and emotional linking of the devotee to the installed god whose attributes are those of king, lover, and child. This second culture is Tamil, its hymns of devotion are based upon earlier Tamil poetry of the *caṅkam*. The full synthesis of meaning is achieved in *sthalapurāṇas* which place the temple into a mythic and thus social framework. These are complexly related elements of indigenous interpretation; they are highly variable with respect to historical conditions, on the one hand, and with respect to their expounders (*āḻvār* poets, *acharya* theologians, and *sthalapurāṇa* myth-makers), on the other hand.

It is our belief that these essays raise some new questions concerning South Indian temples in addition to addressing certain old questions in new ways. Notwithstanding several differences among these essays, in matters of scope, method, and particular focus of attention, they share a set of understandings of the South Indian temple which can be formulated in the following preliminary hypothesis. Temples play a central role in South Indian society, in virtue of their indispensability to structures of authority, at various levels. Temples come to be indispensable because of the widely shared South Indian conception that authoritative human leaders (kings both large and small, imperial and local), and the deities installed in temples, *share sovereignty*. That is to say, powerful human leaders, whether they rule empires or subcastes, in their ritual transactions with temple deities, actualize a model of rule in which neither (king or deity) is in any simple sense dispensable or dependent.

There is a temptation to propose neologisms, terms that more precisely and evocatively capture the character of sovereignty than the phrase *shared sovereignty*. "Segmented sovereignty," "partitioned sovereignty," and "reciprocal sovereignty" suggest themselves. But, each of these is deficient or extravagant in certain ways. Segmented sovereignty suggests a sameness in the attributes and dynamism of the kingly and deity expressions of sovereignty which is only partly true. For example, each has a court and each exercises sovereignty in ad hoc (administrative) rather than general and categorical (legislative) ways. But, segmented sovereignty implies so dispersed a conception of sovereignty as to distort the paradigmatic sovereignty relationship of kings and gods. Partitioned sovereignty properly denotes the divided character of sovereignty—that of a king and that of a deity—but, unfortunately, this notion implies some prior unity which has been divided and thus raises questions about origins and prior conditions which are neither important nor relevant. Reciprocal sovereignty implies process and especially transactions and thus correctly underlines the feature of exchanges as the expression and essential medium of sovereignty in the South Indian case. However, reciprocal, because it is contrastive with redistribution in much usage, obscures the crucial pooling and redistribution of resources which occur in the context and thus in the expression of sovereignty.

It may further be argued that traditional South Indian political communities are *communities of worship*, communities ultimately defined by their recognition of the shared sovereignty of their human rulers and their temple deities. This recognition is observed in the ritual contexts of South Indian temples, but it is not merely a ritual "idiom." The temple is the cultural and ideological context in which men and resources can be controlled, authority contested, and kingship revitalized.

This argument about the definition and articulation of traditional political communities in South India is less perverse than it seems. Indeed, criteria of caste, blood, territory, and language have united South Indians in a variety of ways, and for a variety of purposes. However, these conventional media for integrating South Indian political communities have two shortcomings. Firstly, they often define functional groupings which are not always explicitly or exclusively political in their nature and purpose; secondly, they define no *general* principle for the definition of political communities of different kinds, at different levels, and of different sizes and levels of integration. The hypothetical relationship of kings and deities presented here has the advantage of accounting, in principle, for the political implications of the smallest lineage temple as well as the largest temples favored and subsidized by imperial rulers and standing at the apex of a highly segmented polity. Thus, the shared sovereignty of human rulers and temple deities is the *defining feature* of premodern South Indian political communities which, according to context, depend on a variety of other principles (e.g., caste, clientage, territory, language) to ensure loyalty, recruitment, and dominance. To be sure, these essays do not by any means provide conclusive evidence for such a proposal. Such evidence would focus more heavily on donors and endowments representing a wide assortment of authoritative domains not explicitly discussed in these essays. But, these essays constitute reasonable basis for a preliminary hypothesis of this sort.

No introduction to a set of papers such as these would be complete without discussion of two further matters. First, there is a deep sense of indebtedness to scholars who have treated the subject of the relations of temples and society in South India. Though seeking new ways to extend knowledge of this relationship, these essays are clearly an extension of that cumulative knowledge and wisdom which has come from generations of scholars, Indians and others. This debt will be clear from references in each of the papers, and none of the writers believes that these papers, jointly or severally, do more than add to the rich tradition of scholarship that South Indian temples have inspired.

A second matter is to acknowledge what any reader will become aware of on even a cursory reading. There are many relevant issues which are not, or are barely, touched on in these papers. Among them are the following. No attention is given to general and comparative questions of theology, theogony and ritual. Agamic texts, manuals of temple ritual, are barely discussed, nor is notice taken of somewhat similar studies of temples in other parts of India such as Bengal, Orissa, and elsewhere. Another gap in the discussion here is that there is no explicit attention given to contemporary or near contemporary political and social activities centered upon temples in the modern, bureaucratic context of India. Still another subject upon which there has been much creative scholarship is that of temple architecture, and this subject, though implied in some of the discussions below is not considered explicitly. Again, in these papers there are no comparisons of Hindu temples in South India and other sacred places and centers such as mosques, Jaina temples, Christian churches, and those sacred places marked by stones or splashes of color on trees or walls. Finally, none of the papers carefully examines the matter of what the South Indian temple's social and material catchment area is. All temples depend not only upon enduring participation and support by some groups, but the periodic participation of others during occasional festivals; and the issue of temples in relation to community-formation is barely touched on.

The recital of what has not figured in the analyses of these papers is not meant merely to acknowledge their limited scope, but to suggest some of the many subjects to which attention should be given if this scholarly generation is to pay its dues to the fellowship of scholars who have always been attracted to the study of temples in South India.

BURTON STEIN
Philadelphia, Pa

The Indian Economic and
Social History Review, Vol. XIV, No. 1

Temples in Tamil Country, 1300-1750 A.D.*

BURTON STEIN
University of Hawaii

Introduction: Questions

This is a preliminary analysis of important structural shrines devoted to Hindu deities in Tamil country between the fourteenth and eighteenth centuries. The discussion is preliminary in a number of ways. It is, first of all, incomplete. The study does not take up the question of prevailing and perhaps changing contexts of religious practice and doctrine in South India during the several centuries under study. Nor is attention given to the prevailing and perhaps changing context of resource control and availability. On these and related matters, there is a growing corpus of published research.

The present discussion is preliminary in yet other and perhaps more important ways. It is based upon evidence of questionable validity; its methodology is based upon assumptions that are also questionable; and the principal finding on the relationship of Siva and Amman temples is too startling, perhaps, to be accepted without considerably more research.

Even so preliminary a study of temples of medieval Tamil Nadu is valuable, however, in that it seeks to identify and explain certain heretofore neglected features of what most South Indian historians have agreed is one of the most important institutions in Tamil society—the Hindu temple. It is widely agreed that in devotional (*bhakti*) Hinduism, the temple bridged social and cultural stress points in earlier centuries as they appear yet to do. Temples linked towns and their rural hinterlands; religious groupings (*sampradāyas*) lodged in temples incorporated new peoples within the context of the devotional religion, offering new conceptions of deity which assimilated different levels and kinds of religious experiences and affiliations; temples constituted an arena in which the ancient locality populations of Tamil country and the new, intermediary level of political authority of the Vijayanagara period of the fifteenth to eigh-

*First presented as a working paper entitled "Goddess Temples in Tamil Country, 1300-1750 A.D." to the Committee for the Study of Religion in South India, University of Chicago, 24-26 May 1974. Subsequent readings by Arjun Appadurai, Carol A. Breckenridge, and R. Nagaswamy have helped to clarify the argument.

teenth centuries were linked. The temple was the chief focus of all of these facets of society of the time. Yet, notwithstanding this widely recognized focal character of Hindu temples, almost nothing of an aggregative character has come to be known about temples. Where and when were structural temples constructed or enlarged beyond their often ancient and modest bases? To what deities were they devoted? Are there patterns that can be discerned and underlying processes that can be suggested about the temporal and spatial distribution of Hindu temples in Tamil country? These queries guide the present discussion.

EVIDENCE

Only the most imprecise knowledge exists about temple construction during the medieval period. Fuller understanding must await an altogether different use of inscriptional evidence than we have had heretofore,[1] together with research on the *sthalapurāṇas* and *māhātmyas* of individual temples of which we have but few Pending these developments, recourse must be had to evidence of a far less certain sort. One such body of evidence has recently become available as part of the Madras (Tamil Nadu) State Census of 1961 operation, that is, the series entitled, *Temples of Madras State.*[2] Some information on 10,542 temples[3] from the several districts of the State for which these volumes have been published has provided the basis for Table 1.

The limitations of the data upon which Table 1 is based are considerable. Not unexpectedly, coverage is a major problem. Thanjavur (Tanjore), the district with the largest number of temples in the State,[4] is not represented in

[1]Professor George Spencer of Northern Illinois University has already embarked on a scheme of computer analysis of inscriptional data; others engaged in such work are N. Karashima and Y. Subbarayalu

[2]India (Republic), Census Commissioner, *Census of India*, 1961, Vol. IX, *Madras*, Part XI-D, *Temples of Madras State*: i, Chingleput and Madras City (1965); ii, Tiruchirapalli and South Arcot (1966); iii, Coimbatore and Salem (1968); iv, North Arcot and Nilgiris (1968); v. Kanya Kumari and Tirunelveli, vi, Ramanathapuram and Madurai (1969); and vii, Thanjavur, part 1 (under the altered title of "Temples of Tamilnadu") (1971).

[3]This figure is provided in the Thanjavur volume, p. xxiv.

[4]*Ibid.*, v. 7, Thanjavur, pt. 1 provides an estimate of 1809 temples for the district. Of these, 277 are discussed; the remainder are merely reported to have been distributed according to presiding deity as follows:

Deity	*Number*	*Per cent of Total*
Siva	914	51
Vishnu	426	24
Murugan	57	3
Ganesha	127	7
Amman	173	10
Other	112	6

tables because comparable data on the chronological and taluk distribution of temples in that district had not been published, when this analysis was undertaken and completed This has required the exclusion of Chōḻamaṇḍalam from the tables presented here and thus reduces the reliability of the overall analysis of the 1961 survey data. In the following discussion, it is also to be borne in mind that not all of the temples which were actually constructed in the period from 1300 A.D. to 1750 A.D. were surveyed in the Census volumes. The criterion for inclusion in the Census survey of temples was that temples be consecrated, functioning institutions. Many temples constructed over these several centuries have been abandoned; some were destroyed. Another source of error pertains to the presiding deity of temples during the time of the survey. Except where inscriptional evidence from the medieval period exist and were consulted, there is no way of determining whether the present deity was the original one. This does not merely refer to changes in the name of the deity, from one to another Siva appellation, for example. Such name changes seem to have occurred, but for the present purposes, these would not be important whereas a change from a Siva deity to a Vishnu deity, for example, would be.

Finally, and perhaps most hazardously of all, the dating of temples was based upon architectural features primarily, and in about a quarter of the cases, this information was not known or clear to the survey personnel. Nor were the survey personnel trained to make informed judgments on the basis of such features. Architectural features were grouped into well known stylistic categories beginning with those of the Pallava period and concluding with "modern" features from the late eighteenth century on.[5]

The procedure followed in this analysis was to consider the age of temple as that when its dominant architectural features were established. On that basis, each temple was assigned to one of the four time periods of this study. Major sacred places in Tamil country, as elsewhere, were often places of ancient sanctity, and in many temples, the sanctorum (*garbhagṛiham*) may date from the Pallava period (c. seventh to tenth centuries A.D.). However, most temples in Tamil country possess an overall architectural quality which can be associated with later eras when major construction occurred. And, even if some construction was undertaken at even later times, the modal architectural character of a particular temple would change but little.

Were elements of architectural style the sole criterion for dating (as perhaps assisted by inscriptional evidence) and were each temple enumerated in the

---

It may be noted that the general proportions of the distribution resembles that of Toṇḍaimaṇḍalam, perhaps reflecting the fact that the latter area was, after the Kavērī, the principal locus of Chola authority.

[5]These features together with sketches are discussed in the first of the survey volumes to be published, vol. i, 'Chingleput and Madras City,' pp. 6-8, and again in vol. vii, "Thanjavur," pp. xxviii-xxxiv.

Census volumes appraised at its site by trained enumerators, few could cavil about the dating of these thousands of temples. However, this procedure was not followed in most cases; questionnaires and site evaluations by untrained personnel were resorted to in many cases. This error factor is compounded by the propensity of respondents and local "experts" to exaggerate the age, hence the venerability, of temples; at other times, spite or malice may have led to the opposite distortion of the age of some temples. These and other potential sources of error appear to have been taken into account by the compilers of the Census volumes on temples.

According to the summary statements for each district in the several volumes, temples whose major architectural features indicate construction between about 600 and 1750 A.D. constituted approximately one quarter of all the temples surveyed. However, based upon a detailed examination of the date presented in the volumes, this presumed proportion appears to be low: a truer estimate would be closer to thirty or thirty-five per cent of the temples surveyed falling within these dates.[6]

METHODS

To underestimate the many probable sources of error in the data displayed in the accompanying tables would certainly be rash. However, to reject the evidence provided by the 1961 Census temple survey because of its errors and incompleteness would be equally rash. For to do so means either to ignore the potential value of aggregative analysis or to revert to the usual impressionistic methodology of historical research on aggregative aspects of the question. Statistical procedures exist to assess the limits of reliability of findings involving evidence which is quantifiable, and these procedures have been followed in the present analysis. The number of temples is large enough to provide safeguards against incorrect inferences about general trends from the evidence, provided of course, that there has been no systematic error in the basic data themselves. No such systematic error in the evidence appears to exist,[7] and the statistical test for reliability and significance of the data presented in Table 1 provides the basis for proceeding with confidence in the analysis and interpretation of the evidence.[8]

[6]According to the summary statements for each district in their respective volumes (and excluding Thanjavur and Kanya Kumari for which there are no summary statements, 2,066 are stated to date from the seventh century to 1750 A.D. However, Tables 1 and 2 are based upon 2,035 temples, all of which have certain dates attributed to them and these 2,035 temples are those constructed between 1300 and 1750 A.D.

[7]This is evident both from the methodological sections of each of the volumes, and as a result of the special efforts which the present writer made to ascertain the reliability of the survey findings in 1967-68 and in 1975 while in Madras.

[8]The procedure followed for the data presented in Table 1 was as follows. For each of the taluks of the four maṇḍalams, the number of temples by deity and period were entered

The presiding deities of the temples in the present analysis are designated in slightly different form than those given in the census survey volumes. In the latter, presiding deities are enumerated as: "Siva and His consort," "Vishnu and His consort," "Murugan," "Vinayagar," "Goddesses (village deities)," and "Other Deities." For the present analysis, "Ganesha," a more common name for the elephant-faced god, "Vinayagar," has been used. In place of the designation "Goddesses (village deities)," the name "Amman" has been substituted to correspond with the actual names of the presiding goddesses enumerated in the census survey, e.g., "Sri Kaliamman," "Sri Mariamman," "Sri Badrakaliamman."[9] The designation "Amman" temples also avoids the ambiguous label of "village deities," since the survey volumes take considerable care to point out that the survey was restricted to "structural shrines" and "well-known and important temples," not the great number of shrines of a less substantial and more local nature.[10] The latter are properly distinguished as "bajanai koils" or "temples for village deities" and are far more numerous than the more substantial shrines enumerated in the survey. The magnitude of difference was estimated for Chingleput district where five randomly selected villages returned a total of seventeen structural shrines of importance and a total of fifty-three village shrines. As a result, the discussion for Chingleput concluded that, for that district, there may have been as many as 2,000 village shrines as against the 404 structural shrines enumerated.[11] Finally, the temples presided over by those designated as "Other Deities" deserve preliminary mention here. For the overall sample analyzed here, temples of "Other Deities" exceeded temples devoted to Murugan and approximately equalled those presided over by Ganesha (four per cent and nine per cent respectively). Little attention will be given to this category in the analysis below, but it is well to note here that this class of deities is limited in number for the survey region as a whole, and in any single maṇḍalam or part of a maṇḍalam a few of these "other deities" turn up consistently, suggesting localized cults.[12]

Other points of procedure in analyzing the temple survey data presented here should be made. The dating of the 2,035 temples is reported in the

---

into a computer and a three-way analysis of variance was performed. This analysis revealed that there were statistically significant effects for the differences shown among maṇḍalams, periods and deities as well as for interactions among the three. It is general trends alone which are of significance in these displays.

[9] *Temples of Madras State*, iii, "Coimbatore and Salem," Gopichettipalayam, pp. 34-36.

[10] *Ibid.*, vii, "Thanjavur," p. xxiv.

[11] *Ibid.*, i, "Chingleput and Madras City," p 9.

[12] Thus, for example, in the Krishnagiri and Hosur taluks of Salem, the god "Hanumantharoyaswami" is popular; in Tiruchengode taluk, the "other deity" frequently worshipped is "Ammamarswami"; and in Namakkal taluk, the god "Karuppannaswami" is popular; *ibid.*, v. 3, "Coimbatore and Salem." Or again, in Nilakottai taluk and elsewhere in Madurai, the gods "Ayyanar" and "Karuppuswami" are worshipped in substantial temples as well as in more modest village shrines; *ibid*, v. 6, "Madurai and Ramanathapuram."

census survey volumes in a form different from that in the present analysis. Temples are reported in the survey as so-many hundred years old. This has been converted into four time periods for purposes of convenience in display and to avoid attributing an accuracy which is not supportable from the basic data. Thus, a temple reported to be "three hundred years old" is shown in the analysis as dating from the period, 1650-1750 A.D. The second clarification pertains to temples of Madras City, returned in the first volume of the survey. These seventy-six temples have been excluded from the analysis for the reason that the factors involved in the construction of many, if not most, may be considered to result from European occupation and developments of the sixteenth and seventeenth centuries. Only two temples are returned from here for the time before 1550 A.D. when the major settlement was what is now Mylapore.[13] The Madras city distribution is strikingly and suspiciously different from that of the surrounding countryside both with respect to the periods of construction and the proportions among presiding deities.

Finally, the method followed here is to aggregate temples by the ancient maṇḍalam to which the taluks in which the temples are found belong (Map 1). The use of the maṇḍalam region is justifiable on the grounds that this territorial unit was a major cultural category through the entire period covered by the analysis. This is known from the *maṇḍala-Śatakams*[14] and from inscriptional references.

The frailty of the data permits little more than the present gross analysis according to the broad periods of about a century and the broad spatio-cultural units of the maṇḍalams. And even here a caution must be entered. That is, in only three of the four historical maṇḍalams is there anything like complete spatial coverage: Koṅgumaṇḍalam, Pāṇḍimaṇḍalam, and Naduvilnāḍu. Toṇḍaimaṇḍalam is incomplete because its ancient northern and western portions presently comprise parts of modern states of Karnāṭaka and Āndhra, from which states no comparable temple survey data are available. And, as has been noted, Chōḷamaṇḍalam is excluded altogether because of lack of comparable data from Thanjavur district which has made most of temple returns from most of Tiruchirapalli district as well as parts of South Arcot district useless for the analysis.

[13]K.V. Raman has drawn attention to the early religious significance of Mylapore: *The Early History of the Madras Region*, Madras, Amudha Nilayam Private Ltd., 1959, pp. 189-207.

[14]The *śatakams* are: *Pāṇḍimaṇḍala Śatakam* by Aiyan Perumal Asiriyar of Madurai, Sirkali, 1932; *Chōḷamaṇḍala Śatakam* by Atmanathar Desikar Velur (1650-1728), ed. by Somasundaradesikar, Maynar, 1916; *Toṇḍaimaṇḍala Śatakam* by Paddikkasuppulavar (1686-1773), Madras, 1913; *Koṅgumaṇḍala Śatakam* by Karmegkkavinar of Vijayamangalam, ed., T. A. Muthuswami Konar, Tiruchengodu, 1923; and *Karmaṇḍala Śatakam* by Araikilar of Avanasi, ed. by P.A. Muthuthandavaraya Madras, 1930 See the author's forthcoming essay entitled, "Circulation and the Historical Geography of Tamil Country," *Journal of Asian Studies*.

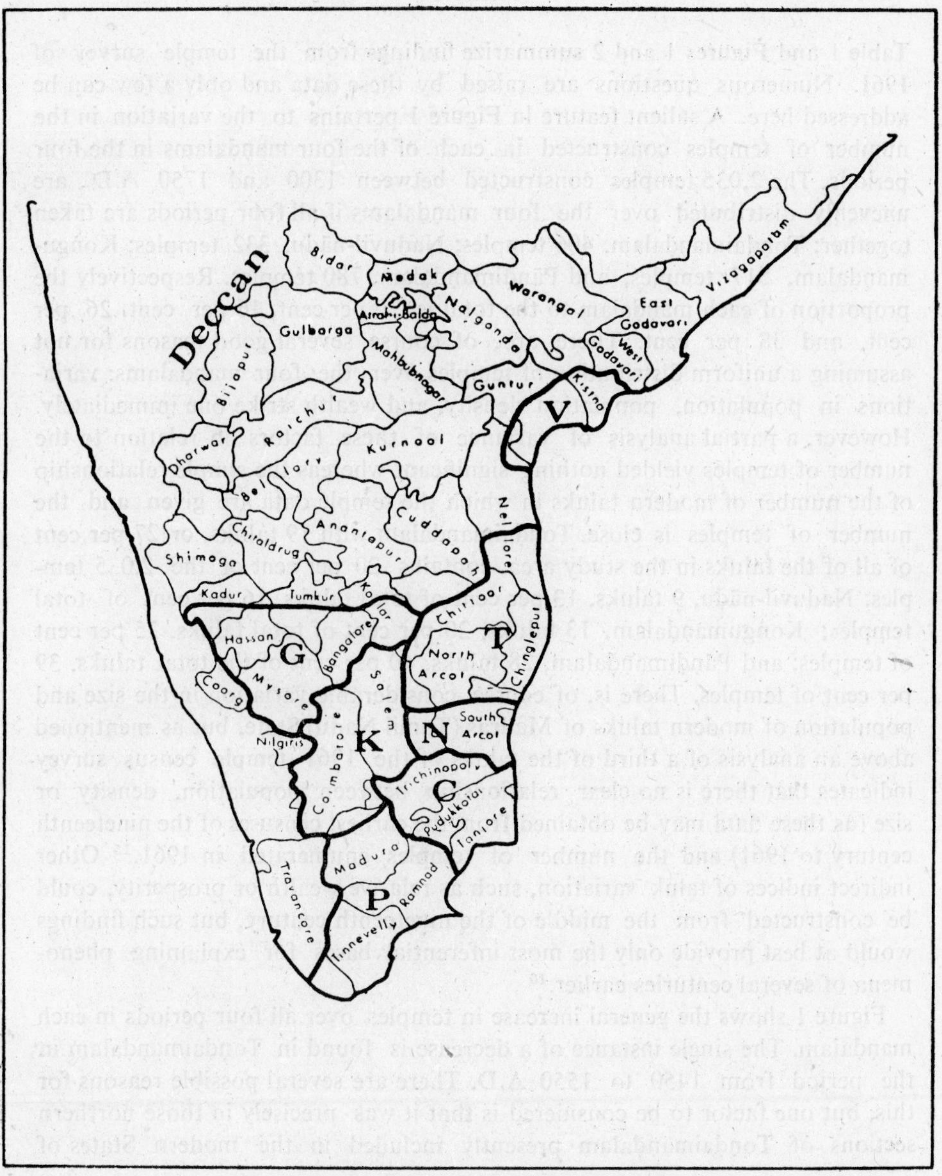

MAP 1: CHŌLA MACRO-REGION, c. 1300 A.D.
V: Vēṅgi; G: Gaṅgavāḍi; T: Toṇḍaimaṇḍalam;
K: Koṅgumaṇḍalam; N: Naduvil-nāḍu; C: Chōlamaṇḍalam; P: Pāṇḍimaṇḍalam

FINDINGS

Table 1 and Figures 1 and 2 summarize findings from the temple survey of 1961. Numerous questions are raised by these data and only a few can be addressed here. A salient feature in Figure 1 pertains to the variation in the number of temples constructed in each of the four maṇḍalams in the four periods. The 2,035 temples constructed between 1300 and 1750 A.D. are unevenly distributed over the four maṇḍalams if all four periods are taken together: Toṇḍaimaṇḍalam, 406 temples; Naduvil-nāḍu, 332 temples; Koṅgu-maṇḍalam, 517 temples; and Pāṇḍimaṇḍalam, 780 temples. Respectively the proportion of each maṇḍalam to the total is: 20 per cent, 16 per cent, 26 per cent, and 38 per cent. There are, of course, several good reasons for not assuming a uniform distribution of temples over the four maṇḍalams: variations in population, population density, and wealth strike one immediately. However, a partial analysis of variance of these factors in relation to the number of temples yielded nothing significant whereas the simple relationship of the number of modern taluks in which the temple data are given and the number of temples is close. Toṇḍaimaṇḍalam with 19 taluks, or 27 per cent of all of the taluks in the study area, contains 20 per cent of the 2,035 temples; Naduvil-nāḍu, 9 taluks, 13 per cent of total taluks, 16 per cent of total temples; Koṅgumaṇḍalam, 13 taluks, 20 per cent of total taluks, 25 per cent of temples; and Pāṇḍimaṇḍalam, 28 taluks, 40 per cent of the total taluks, 39 per cent of temples. There is, of course, considerable variation in the size and population of modern taluks of Madras (Tamil Nadu) State, but as mentioned above an analysis of a third of the taluks of the 1961 temple census survey indicates that there is no clear relationship between population, density or size (as these data may be obtained from the earliest censuses of the nineteenth century to 1961) and the number of temples enumerated in 1961.[15] Other indirect indices of taluk variation, such as relative wealth or prosperity, could be constructed from the middle of the nineteenth century, but such findings would at best provide only the most inferential bases for explaining phenomena of several centuries earlier.[16]

Figure 1 shows the general increase in temples over all four periods in each maṇḍalam. The single instance of a decrease is found in Toṇḍaimaṇḍalam in the period from 1450 to 1550 A.D. There are several possible reasons for this, but one factor to be considered is that it was precisely in those northern sections of Toṇḍaimaṇḍalam presently included in the modern States of

[15]Twenty-three taluks of the sixty-nine in the analysis changed in size by less than ten per cent between 1872 and 1961 thus permitting use of censuses from 1872 to 1961.

[16]For example, data are available on the proportion of wet and dry cropping, the proportion of double cropping, and the vulnerability of particular taluks to famine hazard between 1871 and 1891 from, among other sources, Charles Benson, *A Statistical Atlas of the Madras Presidency; Compiled from Existing Records*, Madras, 1895.

FIGURE 1: TEMPLES OF MADRAS STATE, 1300-1750 A.D., BY MAṆḌALAM, DEITY AND PERIOD

N=2035 Source: Data of Table 1

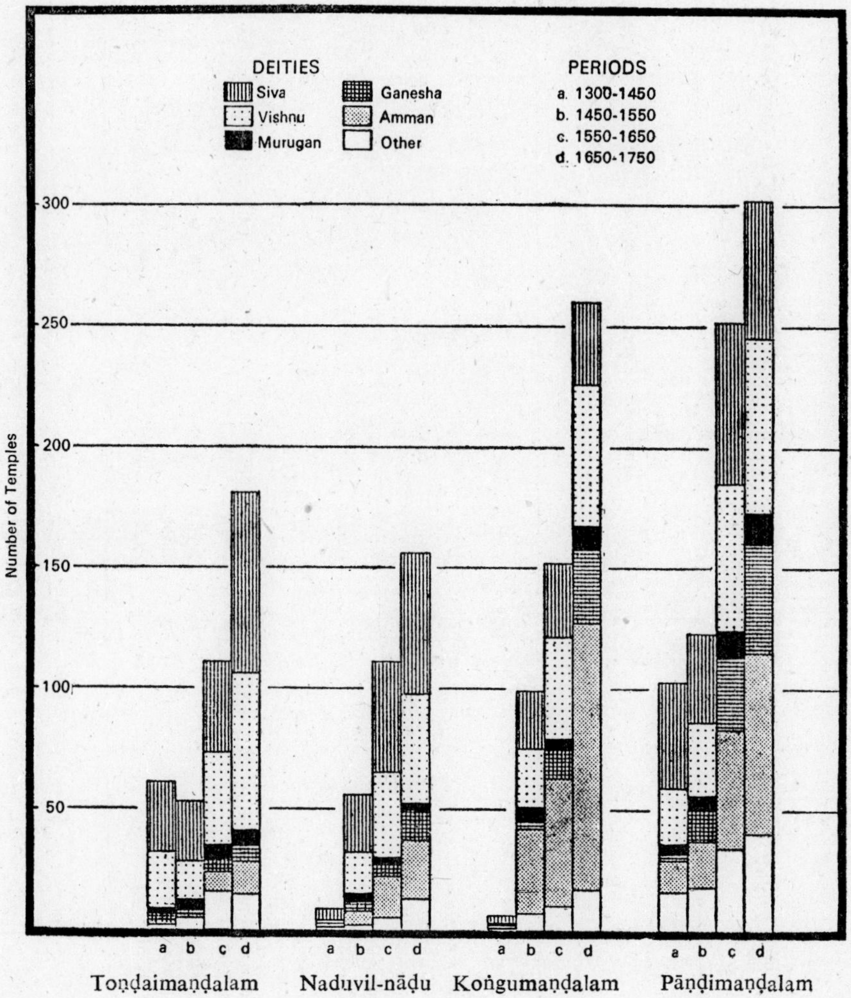

TABLE 1

TEMPLES OF MADRAS STATE, 1300-1750 A.D., BY DEITY, PERIOD, AND MAṆḌALAM

N=2035 Figures in parentheses are percentages of totals.

	Deity							
	Siva	*Vishnu*	*Murugan*	*Ganesha*	*Amman*	*Other*	*Total by Maṇḍalam*	*Total of Period*
a. 1300-1450 A.D.								
N_a=179 (9% of N)								
Toṇḍaimaṇḍalam	29(47)	23(38)	2(3)	3(5)	2(3)	2(3)	61(100)	(34)
Naduvil-nāḍu	5(55)	4(45)	0(0)	0(0)	0(0)	0(0)	9(100)	(5)
Koṅgumaṇḍalam	3(49)	1(17)	0(0)	1(17)	0(0)	1(17)	6(100)	(3)
Pāṇḍimaṇḍalam	44(43)	23(23)	4(4)	3(3)	13(13)	18(15)	103(100)	(58)
Total for Madras	81(45)	51(29)	6(3)	7(4)	15(8)	19(11)	179(100)	(100)
b. 1450-1550 A.D.								
N_b=331(16% of N)								
Toṇḍaimaṇḍalam	25(48)	16(30)	2(4)	5(9)	0(0)	5(9)	53(100)	(16)
Naduvil-nāḍu	24(43)	17(30)	3(5)	4(7)	6(11)	2(4)	56(100)	(17)
Koṅgumaṇḍalam	24(24)	24(24)	6(6)	3(3)	35(36)	7(7)	99(100)	(30)
Pāṇḍimaṇḍalam	37(30)	30(24)	6(5)	13(11)	19(15)	18(15)	123(100)	(37)
Total for Madras	110(33)	87(28)	17(5)	25(8)	60(18)	32(10)	331(100)	(100)

c. 1550-1650 A.D.								
N_c=628(31% of N)								
Toṇḍaimaṇḍalam	38(34)	38(34)	5(5)	6(5)	8(7)	16(15)	111(100)	(18)
Naduvil-nāḍu	46(41)	35(31)	3(3)	5(5)	17(15)	5(5)	111(100)	(18)
Koṅgumaṇḍalam	31(20)	42(27)	4(3)	12(8)	53(35)	10(7)	152(100)	(24)
Pāṇḍimaṇḍalam	67(27)	61(24)	11(4)	30(12)	49(19)	34(14)	252(100)	(40)
Total for Madras	182(29)	178(28)	23(4)	53(9)	127(20)	65(10)	626(100)	(100)
d. 1650-1750 A.D.								
N_d=339 (44% of N)								
Toṇḍaimaṇḍalam	75(42)	65(36)	6(3)	7(4)	13(7)	15(8)	131(100)	(20)
Naduvil-nāḍu	59(39)	45(29)	2(1)	13(8)	24(16)	13(8)	156(100)	(17)
Koṅgumaṇḍalam	34(13)	59(23)	9(3)	31(12)	110(43)	17(6)	260(100)	(29)
Pāṇḍimaṇḍalam	57(19)	72(24)	13(4)	45(15)	75(25)	40(13)	302(100)	(33)
Total for Madras	225(25)	241(27)	30(3)	96(11)	222(25)	85(9)	849(100)	(100)
TOTALS: 1300-1750 A.D.								
Toṇḍaimaṇḍalam	167(41)	142(35)	15(4)	21(5)	23(6)	38(9)	406(100)	(20)
Naduvil-nāḍu	134(40)	101(32)	8(2)	22(6)	47(14)	20(6)	332(100)	(16)
Koṅgumaṇḍalam	92(18)	126(24)	19(4)	47(9)	198(58)	35(7)	517(100)	(26)
Pāṇḍimaṇḍalam	205(26)	183(28)	34(4)	91(12)	156(25)	108(14)	780(100)	(38)
Total for Madras	593(29)	568(27)	76(4)	181(9)	424(21)	201(10)	2035(100)	(100)

FIGURE 2: PROPORTIONS OF TEMPLES OF MADRAS STATE, BY DEITY, FOR FOUR PERIODS, 1300-1750 A.D.

N=2035   Source: Data of Table 1

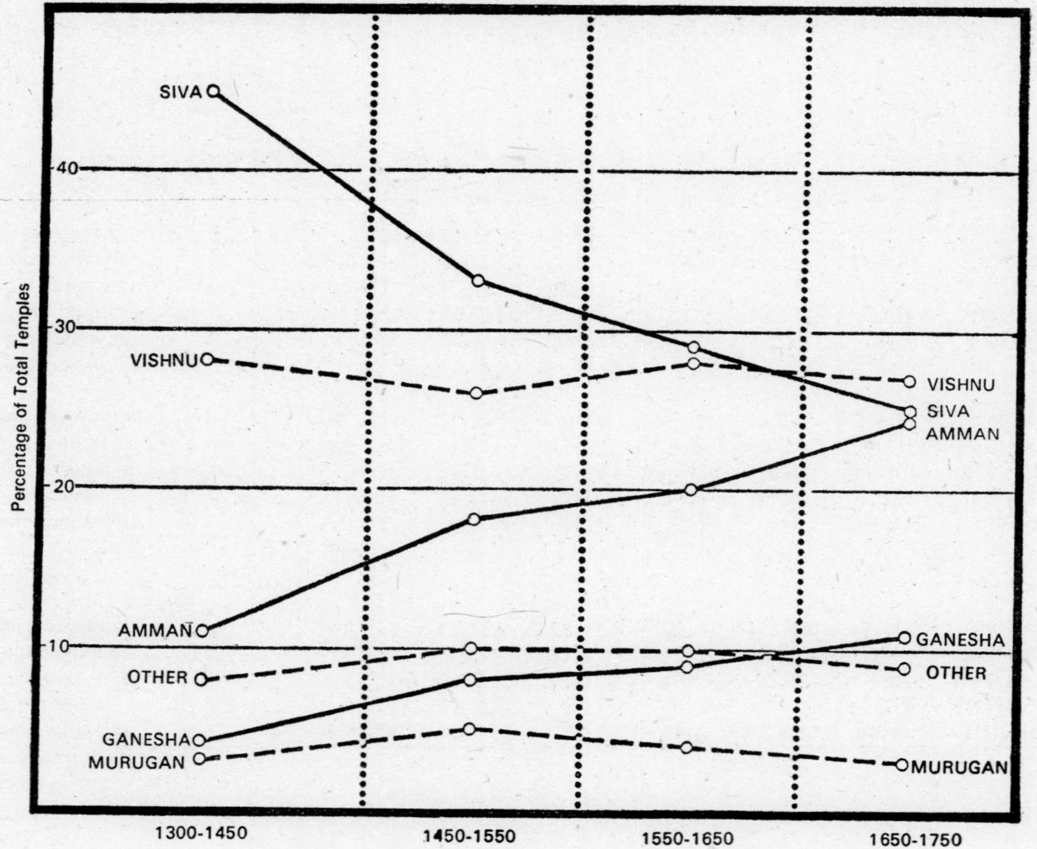

Andhra and Mysore that substantial temple development occurred in the period from 1450 to 1550 A.D. Like much of Koṅgumaṇḍalam, the northern section of Toṇḍaimaṇḍalam was a region which saw rapid development in the post-Chola period. In contrast, the present nineteen taluks of the southern part of Toṇḍaimaṇḍalam were areas of the much earlier settlement and development of the Chola period. During the period 1450-1550 A.D., the relatively short-lived Sāḷuva dynasty (1486-1505 A.D.) controlled the fortunes of the Vijayanagara State from its base in northern Toṇḍaimaṇḍalam. The dramatic growth of the Tirupati temple during this period may be taken as symptomatic of the general support for existing temples of this region as well as the construction of new temples by warriors of this region whose fortunes rose with those of Sāḷuva Narasimha and his successors.[17] Resources for the support of temples within the core territories of these warriors were drawn from a large region, including the southern parts of Toṇḍaimaṇḍalam.

Striking variation in the number of temples constructed between 1300 and 1750 A.D. is shown in Figure 1. Considering variation from one period to the next, in Toṇḍaimaṇḍalam and Pāṇḍimaṇḍalam the number of major temples doubled between 1550 and 1650 A.D.; in Naduvil-nāḍu, there was a sixfold increase between 1450 and 1550 A.D.; and in Koṅgumaṇḍalam there was an even more dramatic, sixteenfold, increase in temple construction between 1450 and 1550 A.D. These relatively short-term variations may be compared to the changes in the rates at which temples are recorded over all periods. The most impressive development is seen in Koṅgumaṇḍalam where temples increased by a factor of forty between 1300 and 1750 A.D. and in Naduvil-nāḍu where the increase was sixteenfold. In contrast, Pāṇḍimaṇḍalam, with the largest number of temples for the whole period, showed a threefold increase between the first and the last periods and that of Toṇḍaimaṇḍalam was even less.

Figure 2 moves the discussion to more pointed analysis. The most striking finding is the interaction of temples dedicated to Siva and to Amman deities. In the line graph, the relationship between the two temple types over the four periods and all maṇḍalams is one of reciprocal symmetry. That is, the proportion of temples dedicated to Amman deities increased over the four periods in the same proportion as those dedicated to Siva diminished. At the same time, the proportion of temples dedicated to Vishnu remained high and steady at around 30 per cent while those dedicated to the other deities display some of the same stability in the range of five to ten per cent of the total.

[17]Burton Stein, "The Tirupati Temple: An Economic Study of a Medieval South Indian Temple," unpublished Ph.D. thesis, Department of History, University of Chicago, December 1958, pp. 53 and 61-62, especially Table 3, p. 53 recording grants of land to the Tirupati temple between 830 and 1628 A.D. as 168 of which all but 21 grants came between 1456 and 1564 A.D. and grants of money as 397 of which all but 126 came in the same period.

The table and graphs expose certain clear differences in the proportions and numbers of temples presided over by the six types of deities. Taking all maṇḍalams for the entire period, the 2,035 temples analyzed here show Siva temples comprising 29 per cent, Vishnu temples 26 per cent, Murugan temples 4 per cent, Ganesha temples 9 per cent, Amman temples 21 per cent, and "Other Deities" 10 per cent. Each of the maṇḍalams contributes to the total array in quite different ways. Thus, in Toṇḍaimaṇḍalam, Siva temples comprised 41 per cent for all periods while in Koṅgumaṇḍalam, Siva temples comprised only 18 per cent of the temples of the period between 1300 and 1750 A.D. Or, considering the same two maṇḍalams, Amman temples in the former comprised only 6 per cent whereas in Koṅgumaṇḍalam, Amman temples accounted for 38 per cent of the total.

The six types of deities can be reduced to three classes in order to elicit certain differences. The gods Siva and Vishnu are universal deities of the highest order in Hinduism; Murugan and Ganesha may be regarded as secondary universal deities in medieval Hinduism;[18] while the Amman and "Other Deities" are essentially local, tutelary gods. Thus arranged, Siva and Vishnu together constitute the majority of temples—76 per cent—of all those constructed from 1300 to 1750 A.D in Toṇḍaimaṇḍalam These two deities together constitute 72 per cent of the presiding deities in temples of Naduvil-nāḍu. In both of these maṇḍalams, Siva temples predominate. By contrast, Siva and Vishnu temples together contribute only 42 per cent of the temples of Koṅgumaṇḍalam and those dedicated to Vishnu enjoy about the same predominance as Siva temples do in Toṇḍaimaṇḍalam and Naduvil-nāḍu (i.e., about 6 per cent). In Pāṇḍimaṇḍalam, Siva and Vishnu temples together and in almost equal proportions comprise half of the temples constructed during the period.

Murugan and Ganesha temples are unevenly distributed over the four maṇḍalams, ranging from 9 per cent of the total in Toṇḍaimaṇḍalam, where Ganesha temples are three times as numerous as Murugan temples. In Koṅgumaṇḍalam, temples dedicated to this pair of gods comprise 13 per cent, and in Naduvil nāḍu they comprise 8 per cent; in both of these maṇḍalams Ganesha temples were most numerous.

Most important for the present discussion is the range of variation among the four maṇḍalams with respect to Amman temples. Toṇḍaimaṇḍalam's 409 temples in this analysis include only 23 Amman temples, and remarkably, returns from the taluks of Chingleput district in 1961 included no Amman

[18]While Murugan is a god of the Tamils, his association with Skanda Subrahmanyam, and Kārttikeya iconographically and hagiographically gives him an equivalent status with Ganesha, the other son of Siva. See Fred W. Clothey, "The Many Faces of Murugan: the History and Meaning of a South Indian God," Ph.D. thesis, University of Chicago, Divinity School, March 1968; and Alice Getty, *Gaṇesa: A Monograph of the Elephant-Faced God*, Oxford, Clarendon Press, 1936.

temples within the fourteenth to eighteenth century period.[19] Koṅgumaṇḍalam, with 38 per cent of its temples of the period 1300 and 1750 A.D. dedicated to Amman deities, was the highest in this category of any maṇḍalam. When Amman and "Other Deities" are combined for these two maṇḍalams, Toṇḍaimaṇḍalam shows the lowest proportion, 15 per cent, and Koṅgumaṇḍalam shows the highest with 42 per cent of the temples of the maṇḍalam dedicated to these tutelary deities. In Naduvil-nāḍu, 20 per cent of the temples dating from 1300 to 1750 A.D. were presided over by Amman and "Other Deities," the former comprising 14 per cent of that region's total; in Pāṇḍimaṇḍalam, 34 per cent of the temples in the period under study were dedicated to tutelaries, Amman shrines providing 20 per cent of the high total of 760 temples.

Interpretations

The 2,035 temples enumerated in the present analysis, incomplete as the numbers may be, for reasons already discussed, pose difficult problems of explanation. Certain of the findings conform with our present understanding of the later medieval history of Tamil country. Thus, variations noted above which contrast the rapid and large increases in temple construction in the formerly peripheral areas of Chola times—Koṅgumaṇḍalam and Naduvil-nāḍu—with that of Toṇḍaimaṇḍalam and Pāṇḍimaṇḍalam, each with well established ancient core areas, conform well with the general historiography of the Vijayanagara period. And, the large numbers of temples involved in this study confirms the profound devotional faith of Tamilians to the gods of bhakti Hinduism.

Temples represent an impressive commitment of resources to that faith. It is to be remembered that the temples enumerated in this analysis are often structures of great size and often constructed on hills, which would have required large and sustained inputs of skilled and unskilled labor. Once completed and consecrated, temples also required the mobilization and maintenance of personnel ranging from various kinds of ritual specialists to menials. These temple centers also became the principal resort of Brahmans and other learned persons whose livelihoods were supported by laic clienteles and whose activities generated even more permanent construction in the form of *maṭhas* and similar institutions capable of sheltering and feeding long-termed residents. Nor must it be forgotten that, apart from regular ritual performances and periodic festivals which were required to maintain the consecrated condition of temples, other kinds of cultural performances regularly occurred there,

[19]Madras City reported sixteen Amman temples half of which date from 1550 to 1650 A.D. and the rest for the last period. Amman temples accounted for twenty-four per cent of the Madras City total for the 1300-1750 A.D. period.

including Sanskrit dramatic presentations.[20] Finally, temples were sect and cult centers to which a large and dispersed clientele—from kings to humble cultivators—regularly gathered to pay homage to the presiding deity and to sect gurus. Feeding houses for pilgrims had also to be constructed along with other facilities for their stay. The thousands of structural shrines constructed during the fourteenth to eighteenth centuries, and enumerated in the 1961 census temple survey, provide a foundation for the more comprehensive definition of sub-regional cultural profiles than scholars have thus far undertaken. These census data, while not complete, permit a level of analysis which might be called "macro" to augment and provide a context for the growing number of separate temple studies which have been undertaken.

Among the questions raised by this analysis of temple construction in Tamil country are the following. What accounts for the statistical interaction of Siva and Amman temples in the portion of Tamil country covered by the four maṇḍalams? Why did temples dedicated to Siva decline relatively while the construction of Vishnu temples remained proportionately stable? What differential religious, cultural and social objectives were satisfied by devotion to Murugan and Ganesha in comparison to that offered Amman and "Other Deities," on the one hand, and the universal gods Siva and Vishnu, on the other? Other questions raised by these data could certainly be posed (e.g., factors involved in the variation within taluks and maṇḍalams over time), but these require further analysis of the temple census data.

The relationship of reciprocal symmetry between temples constructed to shelter Siva and Amman deities from 1300 to 1750 A.D. is the most interesting finding in the analysis. It is unexpected and paradoxical in the sense that Siva is the most ancient and entrenched of the universal deities among Tamilians whereas Amman deities are folk deities; theirs was a relationship of long-standing coexistence The commitment of most Tamil Brahmans has generally been to Siva, and the most impressive religious development in the age—the Saiva Siddhanta movement—was a renewed and resurgent devotion to Siva by the highest non-Brahman groups among Tamilians. Thus, the diminishing proportion of structural shrines dedicated to the Siva deities may be viewed as a significant shift of sectarian affiliation of most Tamils, a turning away from Siva to other deities, most notably to goddesses Such a view may be considered consistent with those interpretations of religious developments of the later medieval period which stresss the impressive development of Vaishnavism, on the one hand, and the importance, on the other hand, of devi

[20]This matter was recently discussed by Dr V. Raghavan in a paper entitled: "Sanskrit Drama in Performance," presented to an international conference on Sanskrit drama in Honolulu, 19-23 March 1974. Papers of this conference are to be published under the editorship of Professor Rachel v. M. Baumer and James Brandon of the University of Hawaii.

shrines in Tamil country.[21] The former development is supported in the 1961 census survey data, especially in the showing of a steady and high (about 30 per cent) proportion of temples dedicated to Vishnu deities in comparison with the declining rate of new Siva temples.

But, the suggestion of competition and displacement may be quite incorrect. What little is known of sectarian affiliations among South Indians now and in the past does not support the notion that most people forsook older sectarian associations and formed new ones That this occurred among Brahmans is of course true; the history of medieval Vaishnavism and the growth of non-Vaikanāsa Brahmanism can only be explained by the shift of sectarian affiliation of Siva Brahmans. However, for most non-Brahmans, exclusive sectarianism appears to be rare if the sectarian information provided of the eighteenth century and later is credited.[22] These eighteenth century reports and later ethnographic evidence provided, especially by Dr Brenda E. F. Beck and Professor Louis Dumont, suggest that most non-Brahman Tamilians maintained multiplex sectarian affiliations, seldom shifting from one to another, but more often adding to their affiliational connections through time.

There is another reason for rejecting the proposition that the increase in Amman temples between 1300 and 1750 A D. represented a transference of sectarian affiliations from Siva deities to goddesses. That is, both of these types of gods may be considered to possess strong territorial characteristics and the relative growth of Amman temples was essentially complementary with, rather than at the expense of, older patterns of Siva devotion. It is to be recalled that temples dedicated to Siva deities continued to be built; only the proportion diminishes.

To pursue the complementarity argument, it is noted that in proposing a threefold classification of deity types above, Amman and "Other Deities" were called "tutelaries," guardians of particular places and peoples. Supporting that assertion are the reports in the *Bāramahal Records* on "sudra" castes

[21]B Stein "Devi Shrines and Folk Hinduism in Medieval Tamilnad," in *Studies in the Language and Culture of South Asia*, Edwin Gerow and Margery D. Lang (eds.), Seattle, University of Washington Press, 1973, pp. 75-91. This discussion is based on the earlier discussions of K. R. Srinivasan in, for example, his *Some Aspects of Religion as Revealed by Early Monuments and Literature of the South*, Sankara Parvati Endowment Lectures, University of Madras, 1959-60, Madras, University of Madras, 1960, pp. 32-35

[22]E.g.: Madras, Records of Fort St. George, the *Bāramahal Records*, III, "Inhabitants" (Madras: 1907) and Francis Hamilton, *A Journey from Madras Through the Countries of Mysore, Canara, and Malabar*, v. 1, pp. 236-61, v. 2, pp. 329-31, London, 1807. B.E.F. Beck, *Peasant Society in Konku: A Study of Right and Left Subcastes in South India*, Vancouver, University of British Columbia, 1972; Louis Dumont, *Une Sous-Caste de L'Inde du Sud: Organisation Sociale et Religion des Pramalai Kallar*, Paris, Mouton and Company, 1957, Pt. 3, "La Religion," pp. 315 ff. and his "A Structural Definition of a Folk Deity of Tamil Nad: Aiyanar the Lord," *Contributions to Indian Sociology*, 3 (1959), pp. 75-87, reprinted in his *Religion/politics and History in India; Collected Papers in Indian Sociology*, The Hague, Mouton Publishers, 1970.

of that region in the 1790s as well as sections of Buchanan's report of 1800 A.D. From these sources, it is clear that there existed three levels, tiers, or concentric zones of sectarian affiliations of the non-Brahman, agricultural and artisan populations. The first level of religious activity, beyond the often elaborately described domestic ritual in the *Bāramahal Records*, pertains to clan and place tutelaries. Most often these were goddesses, several of whom were worshipped by any single group. However, in most cases, there was one goddess, or less frequently a male tutelary, who was worshipped in a locally important and often impressive structural shrine to which all or most of a particular group extended ritual homage. Such a shrine might at times have had Brahman pujaris, at other times it might have been officiated over by a non-Brahman priest (generically: *paṇḍāram*). The second level of ritual affiliations involved temples of pilgrimage usually presided over by a Siva or Vishnu deity under an established order of Brahman priests following agamic practices. The third level was that maintained through guru networks culminating in one of the premier temple centers of South India. In the Bāramahal, for many of the landed castes that temple center was Tirupati; for most of the Kongu castes, however, the place would have been the Siva temple at Pērūr in modern Coimbatore taluk.

It is precisely from the regions described in the *Bāramahal Records* and in Buchanan's report of 1800 that the highest proportion of Amman temples are recorded in the 1961 census survey. This interior upland of Tamil country was also among the most variegated social regions in the macro region. Kongu country attracted immigrants from Andhra and Karnāṭaka as well as the lowland portions of Tamil country.[23] The resulting structure of cultivating and artisan castes is a mosaic in which boundaries among various ethnic elements seems to have included varied sectarian affiliations. Buchanan's discussion of Vellalas ("*Vaylaylar*, a tribe of Tamils")[24] in Coimbatore provides a good illustration of this. Seven Vellala groups are identified as comprising a large portion of the Tamil population of Coimbatore. Among these were the Sendalai ("Shayndalay") Vellalas.

> All *Vaylalars* can eat together; but these [seven] different kinds do not intermarry, nor can a man marry a woman of the same family with himself in the male line. The *Vaylalars* are farmers, day-labourers, and servants who cultivate the earth; many of them can keep accompts [sic] and read books written in their native language. At Canghium [Kangayam, Dharapuram

[23]The 1901 census of Madras reported the following linguistic variety for Coimbatore: Tamil speakers, 66 per cent; Kannada, 12 per cent; Telugu, 21 per cent. Compare with: Tanjore, Tamil speakers 94 per cent; North Arcot, Tamil speakers, 26 per cent and Telugu speakers, 39 per cent. *Census of India 1901*, vol XV-A. *Madras*, Pt. II, v. 1, p. 107, Subsidiary Table 5.

[24]Buchanan, *Journey*, v. 2, p. 329.

taluk] resides *Canghium Manadear*, hereditary chief of all *Shayndalay Vaylalars*.... They are all worshippers of *Siva*; but the proper *penates*, or family gods, are various *Saktis*, or female destructive spirits; such as *Kālī*, *Bhadra Kālī*, and the like .... The *Pūjāris* or priests in these temples are *Pāndarams* [sic], who are the *Sūdras* dedicated to the service of *Siva*'s temples ... Their *Gurus* are *Siva Brāhmanas*, or *Brāhmans*, who act as *Pūjāris* in the temples of *Siva*, and the great gods of his family. These are considered as greatly inferior to the *Smartal*, either *Vaidīka*, or *Lokika*. The *Guru* comes annually to each village, distributes consecrated leaves and holy water, and receives a *Fanam* from each person, with as much grain as they choose to give.[25]

Thanks to the detailed research of Dr Brenda Beck on Vellalas (Beck's "KavuNTar") of Kangayam, we have a model of modern territorial religious affiliations which conforms well with descriptions of 150 years ago and which may even be taken as operative during the late medieval period. That model, in relation to the 1961 Census data on temple distribution for Koṅgumaṇḍalam particularly, where the largest proportion of Amman temples are found, suggest a persuasive explanation for the sharply contrastive, reciprocal interaction of Siva and Amman temples.

In her discussion of religion, as in other aspects of the society of Kangayam nadu in Coimbatore, Dr Beck distinguishes a fundamental division of Kongu castes (approximately two-thirds of the population of the district)[26] into a right division (*valaṅkai*) and left division (*iḍaṅkai*). This division provides a major theoretical focus for her discussion and revives an ancient social division long thought defunct among Tamils.[27] Within the right division of castes, worship is concentrated upon "territorially based divinities who protect well-defined local areas" as well as particular subcastes and clans; contrastively, left division castes worship universal gods of the Hindu pantheon, those whose renown and whose sacred domains are universal, not narrowly territorial. Each division is further contrasted with respect to other ritual features: among right division castes hierarchy is emphasized during worship whereas among left castes there is equality of worshippers;[28] among right division castes sectarian allegiences are restricted to the Kongu region whereas left castes seek and maintain preceptorial and pilgrimage affiliations outside of the region.[29]

The right division of Kongu castes consist of agriculturists, particularly those of the Vellala or Gaunda (Beck: KavuNTar) community and their ser-

[25] *Ibid*, pp. 329-30.
[26] Beck, *op. cit.*, pp. 58-59, Tables 1-3.
[27] Here the divisions are analytical categories, not empirical ones as in the past
[28] *Ibid.*, p. 14.
[29] *Ibid.*, pp. 71 and 74-75.

vice dependents. Kangayam nadu consists of twelve major villages under the dominance of Gaundas, and in each village there is a Siva temple. The Siva temple of one of these villages, Sivaṉmalai, is the primary Siva temple of the locality, "spoken of as representing the [Kangayam] nāTu as a whole."[30] Moreover, each Kongu Gaunda subcaste has a chief temple for its constituent clans (*kulam*), and each clan in turn has a chief shrine for its constituent lineages (*pangāḷi*), and finally, each lineage maintains shrines for its constituent families (*Kudumbam*) units.[31] There is therefore a well-articulated territorial system of sacral associations which ties Kongu Gaundas of Kangayam together within their locality and with other Kongu subcastes elsewhere and, always, in opposition to other non-Gaunda groups. And the prime objects of caste temple devotion are goddesses who are often hagiographically connected with a particular Gaunda subcaste.[32]

Dr Beck judiciously proposes that the Kangayam system of religious affiliation is part of regional one of Kongu as a whole; she also proposes that the system is quite ancient. There is reason to accept both proposals.

Inscriptional evidence pertaining to these central Siva temples of Kangayam nadu date from the eleventh to the thirteenth centuries for the most part.[33] Of the twelve Siva temples referred to by Beck as the shrines of the major villages, inscriptions mention eleven.[34] These Tamil language inscriptions are no earlier than the twelfth century and for the most part refer to two local dynasties of the eleventh to thirteenth centuries: so-called "Kongu Cholas" or "Kongu Konāttār."[35] There are also several Vijayanagara inscriptions principally of the time of Mallikarjuna, whose regnal years were 1447-1465 A.D.

[30]*Ibid.*, p. 66, note 10.

[31]*Ibid.*, pp. 78-79.

[32]*Ibid.*, p. 31.

[33]Sivanmalai (Arasanpalayam village). Pālvannēsvarasvāmi temple, *A.R.E.* 256-72/1920; Kangayam, *Inscriptions of the Madras Presidency*, v. 1, p. 532, No. 123A; Kiranur, Adinathesvarasvami temple, 247-251/1920; Marudurai, Pattisvarasvami temple, 240/1920; Nattakkaraiyur, Jayangondanathasvami temple, 230-239/1920; Kannapuram, Vikrama Cholesvara temple, 218-224/1920; Parajervali, Madhayapurisvara temple, 558-560/1920; Muttur [Kadagattur], Cholesvara temple, 193-196/1910; Velliyarasal, Mandisvara temple, 619/1905; Pappani, Arda Kapilisvarasvami temple, 225-229/1920; and Vellakovil, Parakrama-Cholesvara temple, 216/1920

[34]Beck, *Peasant Society in Koṅku*. p. 67. The only village for which there appears to be no inscriptional material is Alampati. However, this village is mentioned in an early Vijayanagar inscription of another major village of Kangayam nadu, Pappani, 225/1920 without providing any information about a Siva temple.

[35]On these dynasties see: Robert Sewell, *Historical Inscriptions of Southern India*, p. 362 and *A.R.E.*, 1920, paragraph 24, pp. 108 ff; the most critical discussion of these dynasties, especially the Kongu Cholas, is by K.V. Subrahmanya Aiyer, *E.I.*, xxx (1953), No. 19, "Seven Vatteluttu Inscriptions from the Kongu Country," pp. 95-112 in which he argues that this designation be replaced with the more accurate, "Kongu Kōnāttār" chiefly lineage

Disappointingly little can be culled from these temple inscriptions about either the relationship among deities in Kangayam nadu during this early time or about the relationships of its dominant landed people to such deities. A set of Vijayanagara inscriptions of the sixteenth century from the Jayangondanāthasvāmin temple at the major Kangayam village of Nattakkaraiyūr (Beck: "NattakāTaiyūr") refer to local Kongu chiefs, with the title "Kongavēladaraiyar," as "Vellalāpayirar."[36] This confirms Beck's identification of one of the four Vellala "titled families" (*Paṭṭakkārar*) of Kongu as the "Payira clan." Beck also relates an account of this Kongu Vellala family in which an ancestor was rewarded for service to the Pandyan ruler Jatāvarman Sundara Pāṇḍya (regnal years: 1251-1268 A.D.) with land and the title "Nalla Sēnāpati Cakkarai Manrādiyar." This too is confirmed in a Nattakkaraiyur inscription dated 1622 A.D. in which among other things, the title "*gaundar*" is mentioned.[37] The several inscriptions from the Siva temple at the base of Sivanmalai hill, in the hamlet of Arasanpalayam, all date from the time of the so-called Kongu Cholas, and several are of the earliest of these local warriors, Vikrama Chōḷadēva of the early eleventh century.[38] This shrine to Siva as Pālvaṇṇēśvara appears to be among the oldest in Kangayam nadu which may account for the present recognition that this is the premier Siva temple of the nadu, as Beck reports.

There appear to be no suggestions in the inscriptions of the Pālvaṇṇēśvarasvāmin temple or the other Siva shrines of Kangayam that these territorial religious centers were linked together as Beck observes in present-day Kongu. Such an organization can by no means be excluded, however. According to Dr Beck, major Murugan and Siva temples of Kongu are linked hierarchically through affiliations of temple priests.

> Each of these groups of . . . temples is organized around a leading or primary shrine: a single great temple in which all the Konku linked manifestations of the deity converge. In the case of the Civā temples this shrine [Sri Pattesvarasvamin temple] is found at Pērūr [Coimbatore taluk], while in the case of Murukan an equivalent status is ascribed to the [Sri Dandayudhapani] temple at . . . Palani. Each of these religious centers represents

---

recognizing that the rulers of Kongu from the tenth century were warriors from Kōnādu, in modern Pudukkottai, abutting on southern Kongu, rather than scions of the Chola family. Also see K.V. Subrahmanya Aiyer, *Historical Sketches of Ancient Dekhan*, 2, Coimbatore, K.S. Vaidyanathan, 1967, pp. 64 ff.

[36] 235/1920, dated in the reign of Mallikārjuna of Vijayanagar.

[37] 239/1920. The title on this record is: "Nallatambi-Gaundar Visvanātha Chakkarai Uttamakkāmindamanradiyar, A Vellalapayirar of Karaiyur."

[38] Subrahmanya Aiyer, *E.I* XXX, No. 19, p. 105 points out that an inscription from the village of Piramiyan, Dharapuram taluk, of Vikrama Chōḷadēva begins with the words: "I am Vikrama Chōla of Kōnāḍu"; this is dated 1025 A.D.

the pinnacle of a local organization of priests who serve that deity in the Konku area. All priests who work in the local Civā temples look ultimately to Pērūr for direction and for decisions in ritual matters.[39]

Just as the Siva pujaris at Sivanmalai (Arasanpalayam) look to Pērūr, the priests of the Siva temples of the twelve major villages of Kangayam are linked to the Sivanmalai temple.[40] Whether this linkage is replicated in each of the twenty-four nadus of Kongu, Dr Beck is understandably tentative about, but she believes it to be the case.[41]

Another way in which temples might have been linked horizontally or vertically was by the caste ties of most temple priests in Coimbatore and elsewhere. According to the 1961 temple census survey and to commentators from the eighteenth century, the priests of lower level temples were non-Brahman, *Paṇḍārams.* Thurston's summary statement on *paṇḍārams* identifies them generically as non-Brahman priests who are recruited largely from Vellala and Palli castes, who are Saivites, vegetarians, and celibate. Many underwent formal priestly investiture *(dhikshai)*, and many were the manager/priests of richly endowed temples.[42] That the ritual custodianship of non-Brahman priests was significant can be seen from a further analysis of the 1961 temple survey. Considering several of the most important districts in the present study, Table 2 summarizes evidence on officiating priests as provided in the 1961 temple census volumes.

Several features in Table 2 are important. One is the considerable variability in the proportion of all temples under Brahman priests. In three of the districts, the majority of priests in substantial structural temples were non-Brahmans: Coimbatore, Salem, and Madurai. In these same districts were the highest counts of Amman shrines, and here the priestly custodians of Amman temples were non-Brahman to the extent of 90 per cent. A second noteworthy feature of this table is that in Chingleput, where the overwhelming number of priests were Brahmans, one quarter of the Amman temples of the district were under Brahman ministration, and in Ramanathapuram district, where about 70 per cent of all temples were under Brahman priests, over a third of the Amman temples were also under Brahmans. These varying proportions of Brahman temple priests are independent of the number of Brahmans in the various districts of Madras. According to the 1901 census, the Presidency average of Brahmans as a proportion of the total population was 3 per cent. In the eight districts shown in Table 2, the percentage of Brahmans varied between 1 per cent in Salem and South Arcot and 3 per cent

[39]Beck, *Peasant Society in Konku,* p. 26.
[40]*Ibid.*, p. 66.
[41]*Ibid.*
[42]Thurston, *op. cit.*, vi, pp. 45-46.

in Tiruchirapalli and Tirunelveli; the district with the highest proportion of Brahmans in 1901 was Tanjore, with 6 per cent.[43]

TABLE 2

MADRAS (TAMIL NADU) STATE TEMPLES BY OFFICIATING PRIESTS FOR SELECTED DISTRICTS*

*District*** (*Vol., p.*)	*1* Number of Temples	*2* Temples under Non-Brahmans		*3* Amman Temples		*4* Amman Temples under Non-Brahmans	
		No.	%	*No.*	%	*No.*	%
Salem (iii, 335)	1135	665	60	402	35	374	93
Madurai (vi, 5)	477	272	57	104	22	96	93
Coimbatore (iii, 3)	1201	677	55	424	37	403	95
Tiruchirapalli (ii, 2)	1226	411	33	284	23	227	80
Tirunelveli (v, 171)	864	270	31	162	19	136	84
South Arcot (ii, 92)	922	287	31	175	19	133	76
Ramanathapuram (vi, 188)	508	158	31	96	19	61	64
Chingleput (i, 3)	610	95	15	82	13	61	75
Total	6943	2833		1729		1491	

*Covers all of the temples enumerated, not only those from 1300-1750 A.D.

**SOURCE: India (Republic), Census Commissioner, *Census of India, 1961*, v. IX, Part XI-D, "Temples of Madras State", v. 7.

Coefficient of correlation between:

Columns 1 and 2: $r_{1,2} = .30$ N.S.

Columns 3 and 4: $r_{3,4} = .735$, $p \angle .025$

Columns 2 and 4: $r_{2,4} = .794$, $p \angle .01$

Columns 2 and 3: $r_{2,3} = .834$, $p \angle .005$

While several factors may be involved in the often wide disparities among districts with respect to the incidence of non-Brahman priests, one interpretation of the findings in Table 2 is that in many parts of the macro region, the fact that its priests are not Brahmans need not diminish the status of a particular temple. And even where temples are reported as being under the direc-

[43]*Census of India, 1901, Madras*, v. XV-A, Pt. II, Table XIII, "Caste, Tribe, Race. . . ."

tion of Brahmans, the role of non-Brahman officiants may be important. This is suggested by one of the early scholar-administrators of the Madras Presidency, F.W. Ellis, when he observed that in many, if not most, temples of the Bāramahal, the Arcots, Tanjore, Tiruchirapalli, Madurai, and Tirunelveli, the non-Brahman *paṇḍārams* managed and held important ritual offices of the temple while Brahman Gurukkals officiated over only a portion of the ritual.[44] The data in Table 2 also raise the further question of a probable close kinship relationship between the principal non-Brahman landed castes of a region and those *paṇḍārams* who officiate over its temples. This linkage, if demonstrable, would have the effect of strengthening the horizontal integration already extant where local temples dedicated to tutelary goddesses are sponsored by clans of the same subcaste (as in Kangayam according to the findings of Beck). It would also suggest the possibility that in many cases, the central Siva temple to which subcaste tutelary goddesses were vertically linked through the devotion of the major local subcaste representatives and their clients also drew its priests (or some of them at least) from the same locally dominant subcaste.

The kind of multilevel, hierarchical system of religious affiliations involving established Siva shrines and subcaste/clan temples dedicated to Amman deities described by Dr Beck receives some support from inscriptional records, but demographic evidence of the eighteenth century supports the historical persuasiveness of her position rather more fully. As already noticed, Buchanan in 1800 A.D. referred to seven "Vaylalar" groups of Coimbatore.[45] According to the 1881 census of Coimbatore, the core of Kongu country, Vellalas of various subcaste division numbered 629,540 persons, 83 per cent of the agricultural population of the district.[46] Other major agricultural caste groups in Coimbatore at the time included Vokkaligas, Kannada-speaking cultivators, comprising 6 per cent of the dominant agricultural population of the district and located almost entirely in the northwestern taluk of Kollegal, bordering on Mysore.[47] Telugu Kammas comprised 3 per cent of the agricultural population.[48]

In Salem district, a similarly high count of Amman temples is found (34 per cent of all of the temples constructed between 1300 and 1750 A.D.). Here, Tamil Vellalas and Telugu cultivating castes accounted for about thirty per cent of the total population in almost equal proportions and comprised a

[44]Thurston, *op. cit.*, v. 6, pp. 47-48.

[45]Buchanan, *Journey*, v. 2, p. 329; the groups enumerated are: "Caracatu [Karaikattu], Palay [Palai], Chōla, Codical, Cotay, Pandava, and Shayndalay." Also see Arokiaswami, *The Kongu Country*, Madras, 1956, pp. 267-71.

[46]Nicholson, *op. cit.*, p. 18.

[47]*Ibid.*, p. 18; Kollegal is now part of Mysore State, and its population comprised Kannada-speakers to the extent of 80 per cent, *ibid.*, p. 23.

[48]*Ibid.*, p. 18.

majority of the district's agricultural population, though the single largest agricultural caste here were Pallis (especially the subcaste of Arasa Vanniyur Pallis) who comprised 28 per cent of the district population.[49] The spatial distribution of Tamil- and Telugu-speaking cultivating castes in Salem lends support to the argument made for Kongu. Almost eighty-five per cent of the Vellalas are concentrated in the southern portion of Salem district, below the upland divide, or the Talaghat.[50] Here, they constitute dominant landed communities. Most are called "Kongu Vellalas" and are further divided into two sections: a northern section (*Vadatalai*) in Salem, Attur, and Uttankarai taluks and a southern section (*Tentalai*) in Tiruchengodu and some Coimbatore taluks.[51] Other Vellalas are similarly segmented territorially.[52] Telugu-speaking landed groups in Salem included Reddis, Kammas, Telagas, and Velamas of whom 80 per cent were concentrated in the Hosur taluk.[53]

In the *Bāramahal Records*, sectarian affiliations of important localized agricultural groups were centered upon shrines serving a circle of several villages. This is specified for the following groups: Morsu Vellalas worshipping the tutelary Timraisvāmi, Bandi Vellalas worshipping Chandēsvara, Malaiyandi Vellalas worshipping Kaliyamma, and Telugu Kammas worshipping Yellama.[54]

The Tamil agricultural caste of Paḷḷis, or Vanniyars as they increasingly insisted on being called, comprised the single largest agricultural community in the Madras Presidency. They exceeded Tamil Vellalas by 100,000, Telugu Kapus by 200,000, and untouchable Paraiyans by 400,000.[55] Paḷḷis too were concentrated in several districts in addition to Salem where they reportedly comprised 28 per cent of the population: in North Arcot they comprised 25 per cent of the population; in Chingleput, 21 per cent; and in South Arcot, 31 per cent.[56] Like other peasant castes, Paḷḷis worship a variety of dieties with a preference for Siva.[57] However, Paḷḷis are also reported to favor a

[49]Richards, *op. cit.*, pp. 92, 139, and 142. The Census of 1921 and 1931 return somewhat lower proportions of Pallis in Salem: 23 per cent and 25 per cent respectively.

[50]Richards (*op. cit.*, pp. 164-67) cites returns from the 1911 census showing the Vellala population of Salem as 268, 649 the bulk of whom were in Tiruchengodu taluk (96,000), Attur taluk (29,000), and Uttankarai taluk (31,000).

[51]*Ibid.*, pp. 140-41.

[52]*Ibid.*

[53]These are called "Kapus" or "Tottiyans," generic terms for Telugu-speaking Telugu groups in Tamil country, but many appear to have been Kannada-speakers; *Ibid.*, p. 167.

[54]Section III, "Inhabitants," in the chapter on "Sudras."

[55]India, Census Commissioner, *Census of India, 1921*, v. 13, *Madras*, Part I (Madras: Government Press, 1922), p. 155 and Part II, Table 13, p. 131.

[56]*Ibid.*, Provincial Table 1, pp. 328 ff.

[57]India, Census Commissioner, *Census of India, 1872, Madras, Report*, Madras Government Press, 1872, pp. 157-58.

caste deity variously identified as Draupadi or, in a male form, Kuttandevar.[58] This last affiliation appears to be supported by data from the 1961 Census survey, though a full demographic analysis of this has not been undertaken.[59]

The proposal in this paper that the relationship between the declining rate of construction of Siva temples and the rising rate of Amman temples was complementary in Kongu and in the Pāṇḍya country appears to be supported by Dr Beck's recent findings, by the historical, inscriptional evidence related to Kangayam, and by demographic evidence of the eighteenth and nineteenth centuries.

Where an agricultural group lacked sufficient number in any place to maintain its own territorial shrine, it often retained an affiliation with a shrine at some distant place where their kinsmen were numerically powerful. Toṇḍaimaṇḍalam Vellalas in the Bāramahal are said to worship their tutelary, Yellama in the distant Arni taluk of modern North Arcot district.[60] Certain clans of Kongu Vellalas living in Tiruchengodu taluk of Salem district, the Nattan Vellalas, are reported to have maintained affiliations with a clan center in Kangayam nadu, fifty miles from their villages in Salem, from which the Nattans probably originally migrated.[61]

In her study of Kangayam nadu, Dr Beck confirms this with her observation that clan temples are only found in those places where the particular clan of the Kongu Vellala subcaste are the dominant landed group of the locality. Thus, neither other clans of Kongu Vellala subcastes nor the non-Vellala subcastes bound in service relations to the locally dominant Kongu Vellalas maintained shrines of their own in settlements or in localities under the dominance of another Kongu Vellala clan. Instead, all Kongu groupings—whether they were Vellalas or service castes—worshipped at the shrines of the dominant landed Kongu patrons of the place:

> Not all clans and lineages belonging to the Konku KavuNTar subcastes. . . have their own separate set of temples. A full complement of levels with tiers [subcaste, clan, lineage, household] seems to develop only when a particular subcaste, clan, or lineage becomes numerically and economically dominant in a given place. . . .[62] [Other Kongu castes] instead of establi-

[58] H. Whitehead, *Village Gods of South India*, London, Oxford University Press, 1921, pp. 27-28; Thurston, *Castes and Tribes*, v. 6, p. 10; K.A.N. Sastri, *Development of Religion in South India*, Madras, Orient Longmans, 1963, p. 116; and Oppert, *op. cit.*, pp. 122 ff

[59] A total of 138 Amman shrines are enumerated of South Arcot district of which 38, or 28 per cent, were devoted to the goddess "Dhrowpathiamman": India (Republic), Census Commissioner, *Census of India, 1961*, v. 9, *Madras*, Part 11-D, "Temples of Madras State," v. ii.

[60] *Ibid.*

[61] F.J. Richards, *Madras District Gazeteers: Salem*, Madras, 1918, p. 144; F.A. Nicholson, *The Coimbatore District Manual*, Madras, 1898, p. 51.

[62] Beck, *Peasant Society in Konku*, p. 79.

shing independent sacred structures to express parallel divisions within their own community . . . tend simply to worship at the clan or subcaste temple of whatever landed family they have traditionally served.[63]

These findings of Dr Beck together with the fragmentary evidence of the eighteenth century sect networks reported in the *Bāramahal Records* and by Buchanan suggest that in those parts of the South Indian macro region where tutelary, especially Amman, deities were established in impressive structural shrines and where such temples constituted a large proportion of all temples, local peasant groups were completing a pattern of sectarian affiliation long based upon the worship of Siva as a territorial deity, i.e. as a nadu deity. This completion—a filling in—of the pattern of territorial worship at local levels was accomplished by raisin the sacral credentials of non-vedic, tutelary deities worshipped by the dominant cultivating groups of a locality and their dependents to a higher order while not divesting them of their local significance.

Indeed, it is precisely the enhancing of the independent, local importance of established local subcaste tutelaries by dominant landed groups that seems to explain the most interesting findings uncovered in this analysis. Continuing to focus upon Koṅgumaṇḍalam and Pāṇḍimaṇḍalam, where goddesses and to a lesser extent other tutelaries were installed in structural temples in proportionately large numbers, it is proposed that this is to be seen as a means by which locally dominant landed subcastes strengthened their local control. Subcaste goddess shrines, when linked to established Siva temples of a locality contributed both to the dominance of peasant subcastes in Kongu and Pāṇḍya countries and to the horizontal and vertical integration of an agrarian region. Horizontal integration among various peasant subcastes, already extant in shared ethnic titles (e.g. Kongu Vellalas), allegience to regional chiefs (e.g. Kongu *Pattakkārar*), and even kings (e.g. Kongu Cholas, or Kōnāṭṭār), was deepened by shared ritual affiliations to the locally dominant subcaste tutelary by all related subcastes of a place. Simultaneously, vertical, or spatial, integration was strengthened by the linkage of all such tutelaries to local Siva shrines and through these to great regional Siva centers. Secular dominance based upon subcaste segmentation of land control was thus joined to ritual affiliation to distinguish the core of peasant peoples of a territory from non-peasant, local groups on the one hand (Beck's left division of castes of mobile traders and artisans) and from outsiders (e.g. Telugu and Palli cultivating groups in Kongu) on the other hand. Established Siva temples under Brahman and agamic direction had long constituted one of the significant religious affiliations of peasant groups in every nadu. This assertion is supported by the temple inscriptions of Kangayam where, in ancient times as well as

[63]*Ibid.*, p. 87.

in the present time, major support and worship of local Siva shrines came from "gaunda" or "Vellala" subcastes.

Neither the early inscriptions of Kangayam nor those from other parts of the macro region refer to the nature of linkages between subcaste, tutelary shrines and locality Siva temples; tutelary shrines appear never to have had inscriptions, and the inscriptions of Siva temples, not surprisingly, say nothing about the relationships with minor, non Brahmanical shrines. How these two kinds of shrines are linked can only be guessed therefore. It would not be expected that the subcaste shrines were formally subordinated to local and supra local Siva temples, even in the loose manner of sacred centers of Brahmanical *sampradāyas* (e.g., Srivaishnava centers linked subordinately to Tirupati). In contrast to Brahmanical sacred networks, the linkage between lineage shrines and territorial Siva shrines as in Kongu involved no sharing of doctrinal or ritual traditions requiring instruction, initiation and guidance. Pujaris at the two kinds of shrines were custodians of very different sacred lore, preserved and transmitted within families.

Beck's observation is that linkages among shrines in Kongu were essentially those between priests, that is, priests serving in local Siva temples of Kangayam were oriented to the major Siva center at Pērūr. Whether it is, moreover, appropriate to interpret Beck's sparce description of this relationship between the two kinds of shrines as comprising a *hierarchy* of shrine affiliations is also unclear. Certainly, one view of Beck's findings on this relationship is to suppose a hierarchical structure of shrines at the base of which are the lineage shrines of the dominant subcaste of Kongu Vellalas of a locality. These lineage shrines, in turn, are linked to subcaste shrines and these to local Siva temples. The capstone of such a presumed hierarchy would then be a primary Siva shrine, such as the one at Pērūr. A structure of this sort certainly goes beyond, but is consistent with, the descriptions of sectarian affiliations in the *Bāramahal Records* and other contemporary evidence. In these late eighteenth century records, affiliations of a number of peasant groups ranged from varieties of domestic worship to occasional relations with learned preceptors of the primary sacred centers of South India; but there is no suggestion of local and supralocal hierarchies of religious affiliation.

Whether or not linkages between subcaste, tutelary shrines and nadu Siva temples are seen as hierarchical, there is another question which deserves attention. That is, why did the elaboration of structural shrines of goddesses occur when it did?

Once again, considering the question of timing in Kongu and Pāṇḍya countries, notice is taken of the high overall proportion of Amman shrines in these two Tamil regions: 38 and 20 per cent respectively. Note is also taken of the very rapid growth of Amman shrines after the first period in this analysis, 1300-1450 A.D. What accounted for this rapid increase between 1450 and 1750 A.D.?

Two different kinds of factors can be considered. The first may be thought of as internal to the religious system. Here, the salient fact would be that the Hinduism of Kongu and Pāṇḍya countries gave greater prominence to non-vedic gods than the variants of Hinduism in Toṇḍaimaṇḍalam, Naduvil-nāḍu, and Chōlamaṇḍalam. Though detailed comparative figures are not available for Chola country, summary information in the Thanjavur volume of the temple census (volume vii, part 1) for temples of all periods reveals that, as in Toṇḍaimaṇḍalam and Naduvil-nāḍu, temples dedicated to Siva and Vishnu comprised 75 per cent of all temples surveyed. One reason for the differences between Kongu and Pāṇḍya countries and these other places is that the former were more remote and thus later to fall under the influences of efflorescence of puranic Hinduism during the Pallava and Chola periods. One student of this early period, Suresh B. Pillai, has argued that under the Cholas a deliberate policy of "canonization" of temple deities resulted in the demise of non-canonical temples in Thanjavur, especially those devoted to independent goddesses.[64] Another possible reason for the prominence of Amman shrines in the interior portions of Tamil country is that there was a lower density of the foremost institution of South Indian puranic Hinduism prior to the fourteenth century, the great Brahman (*brahmadēya*) settlements of the Coromandel coast. These reasons can hardly be accepted as final ones; they obviously confound a variety of issues which are not exclusively religious (e.g., environmental and political factors). However, these factors may explain a part of the variance among the subregions of Tamil country.

Yet another explanation of this variance would stress exigent demographic factors. The principal of these would be the incursions into Koṅgumaṇḍalam and Pāṇḍimaṇḍalam of Vijayanagara warrior groups. Both of these territories became increasingly diverse in their ethnic composition from the middle of the fifteenth century as a result of the movement of Telugu- and, to a lesser extent, Kannada-speaking, Vijayanagara soldiers into the Tamil interior upland. Even before the fifteenth century, however, both of these interior subregions of Tamil country had received waves of Tamil-speaking migrants from the coastal plains whose descendants retained an identification with their place of origin. This process is outlined by Arokiaswami for Kongu.[65] Moreover, prior to the fifteenth century, people like the Maravars, Kaḷḷars were well marked off from others in Pāṇḍya country and in the border region between there and Chola country (e.g., Pudukkottai) and in other less hospitable parts of the macro region. To this ethnic mosaic were added new and quite different elements of population during and after the fifteenth century. Telugus serving

[64]"The Raajaraajeesvaram at Tancaavuur," *Proceedings of the First International Conference Seminar of Tamil Studies*, v. 1, Kuala Lumpur, International Association of Tamil Research, 1968, pp. 439-43.

[65]M. Arokiaswami, *The Kongu Country*, Madras, University of Madras, 1956, Ch. 10.

in Vijayanagara armies invaded Tamil country several times, and each time a residue of these warriors remained behind to establish themselves as dominant in some of the more sparsely settled zones along the foothills marking the edge of the Coromandel Plain. From these bases, before very long, these intruders extended their dominance elsewhere. The result of all of these developments were numerous, highly variegated local societies within the Tamil interior country, each with different patterns of cultic affiliations. These affiliations when orchestrated as locality religious systems resulted in very complex overall arrangements.

The Kongu territorial system of Dr Beck is centered upon the Kongu castes of the region, perhaps two-thirds of the population. There are Telugu-speaking and Kannada-speaking groups as well. Coimbatore thus shares with several other Tamil districts the kind of ethnic mosaic which prompts consideration of other findings in the 1961 census temple survey. One promising possibility pertains to the often remarked relationship between Telugu-speakers in Tamil country and Vishnu worship.

It has long been recognized that ancient Telugu settlement in Tamil country followed a distinctive spatial pattern. Thus, in the *Report* of the Madras volumes of the 1931 Census, M.W.M. Yeatts observes:

> A remarkable feature of Telugu is its persistence throughout the region between the Western and Eastern Ghats. With the exception of the southern taluks of South Arcot, the whole of Tanjore district, Pudukkottai State, the Ramnad and Sivaganga zamindaries and Tinnevelly south of the Tampraparni river, Telugu remains throughout an appreciable though never majority element. Its course is capricious but two points can be observed (*i*) a tendency to follow the higher ground and (*ii*) a preference for the black soils similar to those of the Ceded Districts. The deltaic or coastal belts are practically free of Telugu. The stretch of red soil that runs along the Eastern foot of the Ghats in Tinnevelly and Ramnad has a smaller Telugu element than the black cotton soil which thrusts down the centre of the region through Sattur, Srivilluputtur, Sankaranayanarkovil and Kovilpatti. Similarly Tirumangalam taluk in Madura which is largely black cotton soil has stronger Telugu element than Melur to the East which resembles Eastern Ramnad and Pudukkottai in its peculiar yellow soil. . . .[66]

It has also long been supposed that Telugu-speakers in Tamil country showed a marked preference for the worship of Vishnu deities. Charles S. Crole noted that in Chingleput district:

[66]Census of India, 1931, v. 14, *Madras*, Pt. 1, "Report," Madras, Government Press, 1932, p. 289, graphically supported by a map on a p. 286.

> While the religion of Siva seems to have taken hold of the original people of the district and became naturalized among them, so as to make it difficult to tell whether, in its principal form, it is not a local superstition with an Aryan name and surroundings, the Vishnuvite creed seems never to have got rid of its foreign and intrusive flavour. . . a very numerous class of brahmins, chettis or merchants, nāyudus, who are soldiers and so forth, together with many other northern and Telugu-speaking people. . . are all, without exception, Vishnuvites, and it might be said that to these foreigners, is the creed of Vishnu even yet confined.[67]

Nelson in Madurai makes a similar observation, and later census officials and compilers of the district gazetteers of the Madras Presidency also notice this relationship.[68]

Utilizing the 1961 Census temple survey, it would appear that there is little support for this presumed relationship between Telugus in Tamil country and Vishnu temples. There are 15 taluks among the 69 taluks analyzed here which consist of black soil tracts and in which the proportion of Telugu-speakers is relatively high, in excess of 15 per cent of the population of each taluk. Table 3 shows that in only 9 of the 15 taluks with substantial Telugu population in Tamil country (i.e., 15 per cent or more) do Vishnu temples exceed the proportion of Vishnu temples in the districts to which each taluk belongs and, calculated on a maṇḍalam basis, the proportion is smaller: 8 of 15. This would seem scant support for the observations noted above and suggest caution in attempting to attribute any clear sociological causation to the distribution of Vishnu temples for the period from 1300 to 1750 A.D. in terms similar to those adduced for the distribution of Amman temples. Further, if all of the 69 taluks of this study are examined for the relationship of the distribution of Telugu-speakers and Vishnu temples of the fourteenth to eighteenth centuries, this cautionary position is confirmed.

Considering all 69 taluks, the coefficient of correlation of Telugu-speakers as reported in the Tamil districts in 1961 and Vishnu temples of the same taluks which can be dated to the period of the fourteenth to eighteenth centuries is 0.13, not significantly different from zero. If the taluks are grouped by maṇḍalams, as in Table 4, the findings are not significantly different.

Conclusions

This paper has presented a unique view of temples in Tamil country during the later medieval period. It is a first attempt to enumerate ancient temples

[66] *Chingleput: A Manual*, Madras, 1879, p. 27.

[68] J.H. Nelson, *Madura Country*, Madras, 1868, p.81. Also, see *Madura Gazetteer*, p. 108; *North Arcot Gazetteer*, p. 185; Thurston, *op. cit.*, v. 6, p. 248.

TABLE 3
VISHNU TEMPLES (1300-1750 A.D.) IN TALUKS SELECTED FOR HIGH PROPORTION OF TELUGU-SPEAKERS

1 Maṇḍalam [% Vishnu Temples, 1300-1750] District (% Vishnu Temples 1300-1750)	*2* Taluk	*3* Telugu-speakers (% 1961)*	*4* Total Temples (1300-1750 A.D.)	*5* Vishnu Temples	*6* Col. 4/ Col. 5
Toṇḍaimaṇḍalam [35]					
Chingleput (34)	Ponneri	21	25	8	32
	Tiruvallur	21	23	7	30
	Tiruttani	31	11	4	37
	Arkonam	16	19	9	47
	Gudiyattam	23	30	7	23
Salem** (27)	Krishnagiri	18	72	23	32
	Hosur	37	40	11	28
Koṅgumaṇḍalam [24]					
Coimbatore (24)	Palladam	20	54	11	21
	Udumalpet	35	27	8	30
	Gobichettipalayam	20	45	12	26
Pāṇḍimaṇḍalam [24]					
Madurai (25)	Periyakulam	21	46	10	21
Ramnad (19)	Sattur	27	19	4	21
	Srivilliputtur	15	21	6	29
	Aruppukottai	20	21	3	15
Tirunelveli (30)	Kovilpatti	20	23	8	35

*India (Republic). Census Commissioner, Census of India, 1961, Vol. IX, Madras, Pt. X-IV, "District Census Handbook" for the above districts, Table C-V, "Language (Mother Tongue)."

**These Salem taluks are not included in any traditional maṇḍalam.

for a substantial part of the Tamil region and to probe some of the findings pertaining to the distribution of some of these temples. The evidence and the method of analysis raise obvious problems. Caution is mandated as a result of the, at times, casual and inexpert way that the age of temples was determined by census enumerators and to some extent by the way the major deity of particular shrines was assigned. And, some uneasiness must attend the necessary homogenization of great temples of all-India fame with very local shrines in order to make the counts required in this analysis. The results are therefore to be considered quite tentative. However tentative the findings and interpretations, the analysis has raised several interesting issues. Particular attention was given to the finding of a symmetrical and reciprocal relationship between the proportion of Siva shrines which attained importance from 1300 to 1750 A.D. and shrines devoted to independent goddesses (Ammans). Secondary attention was given to the presumed relationship between Vishnu temples of the time and the distribution of Telugu-speakers in Tamil country.

Often eloquent on the religious enthusiasm of Hindus in Tamil country and elsewhere in South India, the extant historiography gives deserved prominence to the importance of temples: to temples as a manifestation of the devotional faith of the time; to the variety of social, cultural, and even economic function which temples carried out; and to the significance of sectarian organizations and cleavages. A few major shrines have also received monographic attention. Until recently, however, it has not been possible to consider other questions, specifically, those raised by an aggregative analysis.

TABLE 4

CORRELATION OF TELUGU-SPEAKERS AND VISHNU TEMPLES*
(1300-1750 A.D.) IN ALL TALUKS AND BY MAṆḌALAMS

1 *Maṇḍalam*	2 *No. of Taluks*	3 *Average Proportion Telugu-speakers*	4 *Average Proportion Vishnu Temples*	5 *Correlation Col. 3:4*
Toṇḍai-	19	12.32	35.11	—.11
Pāṇḍi-	28	6.54	23.07	.27
Koṅgu-	13	18.46	26.92	—.36
Naduvil-nāḍu	9	6.78	29.78	.06
All Maṇḍalams	69	10.41	27.00	.13

*As in the tables above, i.e., 69 taluks excluding those of Chōlamaṇḍalam.

The volumes of the 1961 Census in Madras entitled "Temples of Madras State" do permit such an analysis. A set of findings emerges which in some ways was to have been expected and in other ways could not have been anticipated. Thus, it would be expected that there would be a considerably larger proportion of older structural shrines in Toṇḍaimaṇḍalam and in Pāṇḍimaṇḍalam than in Koṅgumaṇḍalam and Naduvil-nāḍu. The former were the more ancient settled territories, and each was the seat of a major ancient kingship. It might also have been anticipated that in Toṇḍaimaṇḍalam, the proportion of universal canonical deities—Siva and Vishnu—would be greater than in other territories owing to the density, and probable origin there, of the uniquely brahmanical institution, the *brahmadēya.* The last expectation would obviously apply to Chōḻamaṇḍalam for which comparable returns were not available. The data in Table 2 pertain to and support such expectations; these data also form the basis for an empirical hypothesis about Chōḻamaṇḍalam when comparable data in this region are finally prepared.

But contrary to reasonable expectations were other findings of this aggregative analysis. Among these are: the differential distribution in time and space of the deities for whom impressive structural shrines were constructed; the apparently simple correlation of the number of taluks and the proportion of temples on a maṇḍalam basis; the relatively stable proportion of Vishnu temples over time and to some extent across maṇḍalams in contrast to the general (and in some places, the sharp) decline in the proportion of Siva temples, and finally, the relationship between Siva and Amman temples to which the major attention of this discussion has been addressed.

With respect to the last finding, what has been proposed is an explanation based on conflict. The conflict was not between devotees of rival gods as might be suspected. This displacement thesis was rejected Rather, the explanation of the declining proportion of Siva temples and the almost symmetrical rise of Amman shrines is seen as complementary.

Religious affiliations of various locally dominant Tamil landed groups and particularly their temple building activities reflected an effort to buttress their landed dominance against others who might be somewhat like themselves (e.g., other Tamil-speaking Vellalas) or quite different (e.g., Telugu Reḍḍis). One way of accomplishing this was to solidify cultic cooperation by building temples to which only members of the same landed group of a locality, together with their dependents, offered worship. Often, in Kongu and Pāṇḍya countries these temples would be dedicated to ancient female tutelaries, and these tutelary shrines, now transformed architecturally and possibly transvalued in ritual practice, were linked to established Siva temples of the locality and region. Analytically, the choice of the diety to be sheltered in a new temple may be taken as a clue to the principle of segmentation operating among dominant landed groups in various parts of Tamil country. In those parts of Koṅgumaṇḍalam and Pāṇḍimaṇḍalam where Amman temples were complementarily linked to established locality and regional Siva shrines, the principle of segmentation of land controllers was that of subcaste membership.

Elsewhere in Tamil country, other orchestrations of religious affiliation are conceivable. Where Tamil Vellalas competed with other Tamil castes (e.g., Maravar, Kaḷḷar, Paḷḷi) or with non-Tamil agricultural groups, it is hypothesized that the latter did not support established Siva temples, but established shrines for other deities. These included male tutelaries (e.g., Karuppuswami) or deities with better sacral credentials, such as Murugan.

Whatever the weaknesses of the 1961 Census evidence on temples—and these are acknowledged to be considerable—the volumes offer a unique opportunity to extend our knowledge about religious affiliations of the recent and remote past. These volumes also present a challenge to our methods of analysis which this study has attempted to address.

Kings, Sects and Temples in South India, 1350-1700 A.D.*

ARJUN APPADURAI
University of Pennsylvania

Problem and Hypothesis

It is a commonplace of Indian social history that Indian society has lacked an overarching, hierarchical and authoritative religious organization. How then are we to account for the pervasiveness of shared religious beliefs, and the endurance of institutions predicated on such beliefs in India? Similarly, it has recently been argued that the pre-modern State, at least in South India, lacked the unitary, bureaucratized and centralized features of political systems in the medieval West and elsewhere.[1] How then are we to account for the durability, size and widespread legitimacy of political systems such as that of the Vijayanagara period in South India?

A solution to these two problems can be generated by following a single line of argument. The hypothesis of this essay is that, at least in South India in the three centuries preceding the arrival of the British, a *single* system of authoritative relations existed, which combined features that have elsewhere been divided between religious and political hierarchies. The historical components of this system can be summarized as follows: in the period between 1350 and 1700 A.D., Srī Vaiṣṇava temples in South India provided a nexus for ritual and economic transactions between warrior-kings from outside the Tamil country and Srī Vaiṣṇava sectarian leaders who belonged principally to the Tamil country. These transactions had two consequences: Telugu warrior-kings were able to establish the stable and legitimate links with core Tamil institutions required to consolidate their authority in South India, and Srī

*This essay is based on Chapter II of a doctoral dissertation on "Worship and Conflict in South India: The Case of the Srī Pārtasārati Svāmi Temple 1800-1973," University of Chicago, 1976. An earlier version of the essay was presented at the Annual Workshop of the Society for the Study of South Indian Religion, Bucknell University, June 1975. For their many helpful comments and criticisms, I am grateful to B. Stein, A.K. Ramanujan, K.K.A. Venkatachari and Carol A. Breckenridge.

[1]B. Stein, "The Segmentary State in South Indian History" in R.G. Fox (Ed.), *Realms and Regions in Pre-Modern India*, Duke University Press (forthcoming).

Vaiṣṇavism itself became divided into two sub-sects, which in the eighteenth and nineteenth centuries, became self-conscious and antagonistic competitors for temple-control. In the essay that follows, the hypothesis of a single system of authoritative relations is supported by the historical documentation of these transactions and their consequences.

The general framework which underpinned the relationship of kings, sects and temples during this period can be described in terms of four propositions:

1. Temples were fundamental for the maintenance of kingship.
2. Dynamic sectarian leaders provided the links between kings and temples.
3. While the day-to-day management of temples was left in the hands of local (generally sectarian) groups, the responsibility for solving temple conflicts which resisted local resolutions vested clearly in the sovereign.
4. In a specific ethnosociological sense, kingly action re: temple-conflict was not *legislative* but administrative.

TEMPLES AND KINGSHIP

In classical Indian thought, generosity to Brahmans, codified as the "law of the gift" (*dānadharma*), was an important element of the role of kings.[2] It has recently been carefully demonstrated that in South India, under Pallava rule, in the late seventh and early eighth centuries, a fundamental change occurred in the conception of what constitutes sovereignty: the giving of gifts, which was previously only one element of the basic definition of kings as *sacrificers*, now became the central constituent of sovereignty.[3] This shift during Pallava rule coincides with the beginnings of temple-building associated with Purānic deities, such as Viṣnū and Sivā. During the next period of South Indian history, when the Chōla house dominated the South (ca. 900 to 1200 A.D.), this model of kingly generosity was the basis for generous royal endowment of temples, as well as for the establishment and subsidy of *brahmadēyas* (settlements of learned Brahmans, with highly favorable tax-assessments). However, in the articulation and public display of sovereignty, even in the Chōla period, it appears that temple-construction had begun to play a peculiar and powerful role.[4]

[2]Marcel Mauss, *The Gift*, 1967, pp. 53-59; V.R.R. Dikshitar, *Hindu Administrative Institutions*, Madras, 1929, pp. 102-104.

[3]Nicholas B. Dirks, "Honor, Merit and Prosperity: From Ritual as Gift-Giving to Gift-Giving as Ritual in Early South Indian Kingship," June 1975 (unpublished Mss.), *passim*. but particularly p. 29.

[4]George W. Spencer, "Religious Networks and Royal Influence in Eleventh Century South India," *Journal of the Economic and Social History of the Orient*, XII, Pt. I, January 1969, pp. 42-56; *ibid.*, "Royal Initiative under Rajaraja I," *The Indian Economic and Social History Review*, Vol. 7, No. 4, December 1970, pp. 431-42.

Starting from about 1350 A.D., and during the next three centuries of Vijayanagara rule, there was a serious decline in the status of *brahmadēyas*, and a concomitant growth and expansion of temples in South India.[5] Royal endowments to temples became a major means for the redistributive activities of Vijayanagara sovereigns, which played an important role in agrarian development in this period.[6] At the same time, temple-endowment was a major technique for the extension of royal control into new areas, and transactions involving both material resources and temple "honors," permitted the absorption of new local constituencies into Vijayanagara rule. This latter process is documented in the body of this essay.

Sectarian Leaders as Mediators

Even before the commencement of the Vijayanagara period, the relationship of sovereigns to their predominantly agrarian localities was mediated by a host of powerful local personages and groups.[7] This continued to be so, although in rather different ways, in the Vijayanagara period. The relationship of kings to temples in the Vijayanagara period cannot be understood without taking into account the wide variety of local corporate groups and local leaders who were responsible for the management of temples.[8] But of all these groups and persons, increased prominence was gained by local sectarian assemblies and mobile sectarian leaders. The function of these sectarian leaders and the local sectarian constituencies which they represented, in facilitating the linkage of sovereigns to temples, is dealt with in detail later in this essay.

Local Management and Royal Intervention

Although royal figures conducted extensive and elaborate relationships with temples (by the building of new temples and the extension and enrichment of old ones), the day-to-day management of temples remained in the hands of local notables.[9] Nevertheless, it is clear that Vijayanagara kings and their

[5]Burton Stein, "Integration of the Agrarian System of South India" in R.E. Frykenberg (Ed.), *Land Control and Social Structure in Indian History*, Madison, 1969, pp. 191-194; *Ibid.*, "Goddess Temples in Tamil Country, 1300-1750 A.D.," presented to the CSRI Workshop, University of Chicago, May 24-26, 1974, *passim*. but especially Fig. 1; K. Sundaram, *Studies in Economic and Social Conditions in Medieval Andhra* (1000-1600 A.D.), Madras, 1968, *passim*, but especially Ch V; A. Krishnaswami, *The Tamil Country under Vijayanagara*, Annamalainagar, 1964, pp. 98-105.

[6]Burton Stein, "The Economic Function of a Medieval South Indian Temple," *Journal of Asian Studies*, XIX, 2 (1960), pp. 163-176.

[7]Dirks, *op. cit.*, p. 24; Burton Stein, "The Segmentary State in South Indian History," *op. cit.*

[8]T.V. Mahalingam, *South Indian Polity*, Madras, 1967, pp. 386-389.

[9]Mahalingam, *op. cit.*, pp. 386-389; see also B.A. Saletore, "The Sthānikas and Their

agents played an active role in the supervision of these increasingly complex religio-urban centers. This supervisory role, which is demonstrated in the increased participation of royal agents in all sorts of local decisions,[10] was activated primarily in contexts where the locality was unable to internally resolve temple-conflicts.

In analyzing these authoritative settlements of temple-disputes, it is important to notice that they are neither vertical administrative fiats nor pieces of royal legislation, but are rather administrative commands (*rāja-śāsana*) of an arbitrative sort. These publicly and communally arrived at decisions must be understood as *vyavasthās* (regulations) amongst members of local corporate groups, which were rendered authoritative by the participation of the king or his agents. In this context, the *rāja-śāsana* (royal command) was "the act by which the king sanctions a collective regulation."[11] Such *rāja-śāsanas*, which rendered local *vyavasthās* authoritative, were widespread in middle-period South India.[12]

KINGSHIP AS ADMINISTRATION, NOT LEGISLATION

This species of royal intervention presumes a model of the Hindu king as an *administrator* rather than a *legislator*, following the suggestive formulation of Robert Lingat.[13] This contrast is important in two senses. Firstly, it suggests that the commands of Hindu kings were administrative, in the sense that they were addressed to specific groups and individuals, were not of general applicability, and were subject to alteration or repeal according to the pragmatic needs of kingship.[14] On the other hand, legislative power would imply "a right attributed to a constitutionally competent authority to pronounce rules having a general application and possessing, in principle, a permanent character."[15] The most important consequence of this contrast is that royal judgements were only orders, which could not fix the law or even strictly serve as an illustration:

Although the intervention of the king in judicial matters may be decisive,

---

Historical Importance," *Journal of the University of Bombay*, Vol. VII, July 1938, Part I, pp. 29-93.

[10]For detailed examples of royal intervention, see: *Epigraphia Carnatica*, IV, Ch. 113, p. 15; *Ibid.*, V, P. 1, Bl. 5, p. 45; *Annual Reports on South Indian Epigraphy*, 1913, para 51; *Ibid.*, 1914, pp. 96-97; B.A. Saletore, *Social and Political Life in the Vijayanagara Empire* (2 Vols.), Vol. I, Madras, 1934, p. 371.

[11]Robert Lingat, *The Classical Law of India*, Delhi, 1973, p. 229, fn. 54.

[12]*Ibid.*, p. 227.

[13]Lingat, *The Classical Law of India*, *op. cit.*, p. 228.

[14]*Ibid.*, 224-32.

[15]*Ibid.*, p. 224.

it brings no new element to interpretation. In settling disputes between his subjects, the king merely does his duty, which is to secure order and peace in his realm. This is the office of an administrator and not a legislator.[16]

But the orders of Hindu kings in reference to temples were "administrative" only in a special ethnohistorical sense. The administrative actions of the king did not necessarily imply a centralized bureaucratic staff on the Weberian model of legal-bureaucratic authority.[17] As in the validity of royal commands, so also in the machinery of making and enforcing such decisions, context-sensitivity was the rule. In much of the inscriptional evidence describing cases of royal arbitration, the "staff" that makes and carries out the decision is a complex, and contextually variable, nesting of local individuals and corporate groups, forming a single, unique, interlocking system, linking the king, his agents, local assemblies, sectarian groups and leaders, temple functionaries, and, in some cases, local worshippers.[18] There was thus no single, centralized, permanent bureaucratic organization, but a temporary affiliation of local groups, authoritatively constituted by, or in the name of, the king, and empowered to make public decisions on specific matters.[19]

In classical Indian thought, the distinctive function of the king is expressed in the formula "*prajānām paripālanam*" (protection of his subjects)[20] or in some other variant formulaic expression of the same idea. In respect of temples in South India, the central aspect of this royal function was the responsibility of the king to maintain peace between his subjects and order in his

[16] *Ibid.*, p. 256; I am grateful to Prof. A.K. Ramanujan, University of Chicago, who in unpublished work as well as personal communications, first suggested to me the widespread importance of this kind of "context-sensitivity" in various aspects of Indian culture; these features of royal arbitration of conflicts, namely, their freedom from precedent and their particularity, explain much that is crucial in the impact of British legal institutions and ideas on the temple in the 19th and 20th centuries. This impact, which was fundamentally a product of the orientation to precedent as well as the partial legislative (i.e. generalizing) basis of British courts, is dealt with in Ch. V of my Ph.D. dissertation, *op. cit.*

[17] Max Weber, *The Theory of Social and Economic Organization* (T. Parsons, Ed.), New York, 1964, pp. 329-36

[18] See n. 10, for several examples; in one such case, we are told that: "The great minister Nāgaṇṇa and various important officials like *Pradāhni* Dēvarasa, along with other *arasus* or lords, and the Jaina Mallappa summoned the elders of the three cities and the Eighteen Kampanas, and held an equiry . . " (Saletore, *Social and Political Life . . ., op. cit.*, Vol. I, p. 371) Such examples could be multiplied.

[19] This is an extension of the argument in B. Stein, "The Segmentary State in South Indian History," in R.G. Fox (Ed.), *Realms and Regions in Pre-Modern India*, Duke University Press (forthcoming).

Here again, the British bureaucracy in the 19th century broke down this delicate relationship between local participation and royal authority, with important consequences for temple politics, a subject dealt with in Chs. 3 and 4 of my doctoral dissertation, *op. cit.*

[20] Lingat, *op. cit.* p. 222.

realm.[21] However, given the spatial and temporal variability in the set of "staffs" through which kings did actually arbitrate temple-disputes, they could only stimulate, ratify and render authoritative reasonable local agreements. The actual day-to-day maintenance of these royally sanctioned *vyavasthās* was necessarily the responsibility of authoritative local groups. Thus, we find in the bulk of the inscriptions from temples in middle period South India, a stylized conclusion to these inscriptions, whereby the protection (*raksai*) of these *vyavasthās* was entrusted to local sectarian groups: for example, in the inscriptions of the Tirupati temple, the stylized formula is: "Śrī Vaiṣṇava Rakṣai."[22] The second aspect of the kingly role, the lavish endowment or temples, did not by itself distinguish kings, since temple-donors, in the middle-period, came from a wide cross-section of society.[23] In relation to temples, the distinctive function of royalty was the combination of generous endowment with the task of "protection" (paradigmatically: dispute-arbitration). It was this second aspect of the kingly role that formally distinguished it from other social roles, and thus we have a record of a sixteenth-century dialogue between a Paṇḍya ruler and the learned Brahmans at his court, as to which was preferable: donation or protection They declared protection to be superior, saying: "Render thou protection which is purifying."[24]

Hindu kings in middle-period South India, thus, had two sorts of relationships to temple-deities: endowment and protection. The latter aspect of their role, however, did not connote a capacity to legislate in the modern Western sense, nor did it imply centralized bureaucratic management of temple affairs. The effective bearers of royal commands, and thus of the "protective" function were local, generally sectarian, groups and leaders. Without endowment, the king would cease to place himself in an active relationship with the redistributive powers of the deity, and thus would fail to acquire the honor constitutive of sovereignty. Without protection, i.e. the authoritative ratification of local *vyavasthās* by royal edicts (*rāja-śāsana*), the king would have abnegated his fundamental duty towards his subjects. In South India, between 1350 and 1700, this cultural model formed the basis for a dynamic set of relationships between warrior-kings, sectarian leaders and temples, which had important consequences for Vaiṣṇava sectarian development.

THE TRANSACTIONAL FRAMEWORK

Towards the middle of the fourteenth century, certain scholastic disputes

[21] *Ibid.*, p. 223.

[22] *Tirumalai-Tirupati Devastanam Epigraphical Series*, 6 Vols., Madras, 1931-1937, *passim.*

[23] See, for example, *ibid.*, Vol. VI, Part 2, *Epigraphical Glossary*, Section III, "List of Donors for the Temples at Tirumalai and Tirupati."

[24] *Travancore Archaeological Series*, Trivandrum, 1930, Vol. 1, Group 6, pp. 108-9 and 113.

within the Śrī-Vaiṣṇava community in South India had divided its leadership into two schools. By the end of the seventeenth century, this rift had become the intellectual expression of a complex social phenomenon, namely, the division of the community into two antagonistic sub-sects, which were beginning to compete, pan-regionally, for control of Vaiṣṇava temples. To account for this fundamental alteration in the structure of the sect, it is necessary to appreciate a certain set of relationships which lay at the core of sectarian activity in this period. The method of the following section is to schematically describe this set of relationships, then describe its empirical manifestations and transformations over the entire period, and thus account for the ultimate shape of South Indian Śrī Vaiṣṇavism at the beginning of the eighteenth century.

In analyzing sectarian activities (whether Vaiṣṇava or not) in this period, a three-way transactional system emerges from the evidence. This set of transactions links political rulers, sectarian leaders and temples, in a complex triangular set of exchanges. Although, in the South Indian temple, "honors" and material endowments represent two aspects of a single redistributive process,[25] it is analytically possible to separate them. So separated, it is possible to see two parallel but distinct levels of transaction that link kings, sectarian leaders and temples: one involving transfers of "honor" and the other involving transfers of endowed material resources. In the medium of "honors," it is possible to see four kinds of transaction during this period. Temples confer "honors" on political rulers; political rulers confer "honors" on sectarian leaders; temples confer "honors" on sectarian leaders; and sectarian leaders confer "honors" on political rulers. This level of transaction can be schematized as follows:

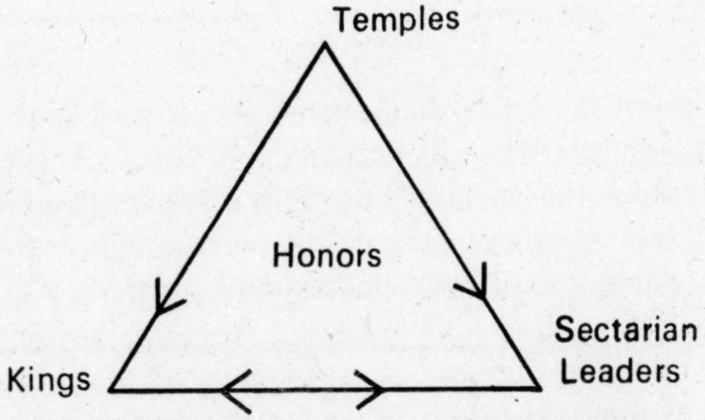

In the medium of endowed material resources, a different set of transactions obtains. Political rulers transfer material resources (most often shares in the

[25]For a detailed analysis of "honors" and the redistributive process of the temple, see Arjun Appadurai and Carol A. Breckenridge "The South Indian Temple: Authority, Honor and Redistribution," *Contributions to Indian Sociology: New Series*, December 1976.

agrarian produce of specified villages) to temples; political rulers also transfer such material resources to sectarian leaders; and sectarian leaders, in their own capacity, also endow temples. This transactional level can be schematized as follows:

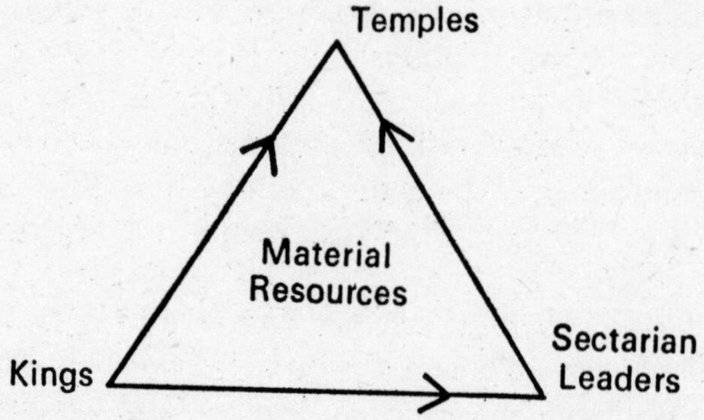

If these two transactional levels are visually juxtaposed, the complexity of the relationships between these three loci becomes obvious:

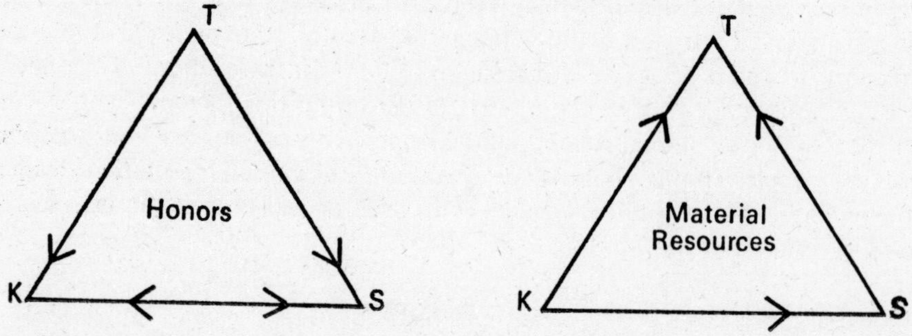

The juxtaposition of these two diagrams raises a problem. Except in one transactional case, the relationships between any two of these units is symmetrical, and involves the exchange of "honors" for material resources. The only problematic, and seemingly gratuitous, relationship is the conferral of "honors" by political rulers on sectarian leaders. That is to say, the relationship between political rulers and sectarian leaders, conceived in terms of "honors" and material resources, is asymmetrical. Political rulers confer "honors" as well as material resources on sectarian leaders, whereas sectarian leaders seem to repay this only in part, i.e. by the conferral of "honors" on political leaders. Is this asymmetry a real one? While this question can be posed in schematic terms, it can be answered only empirically and historically. What is proposed below is a hypothesis concerning the relationship between political rulers and sectarian leaders during this period, which will give empirical flesh to the above scheme, and suggest also that sectarian leaders did indeed repay the endowments given to them by political leaders, in a cognate medium. Specifically, it is argued below that in the socio-political context of the period from 1350 to 1700, sectarian leaders were crucial intermediaries for the introduction, extension and institutionalization of warrior-control over constituencies and regions that might otherwise have proved refractory. This intermediary role of sectarian leaders, which rendered control by conquest into appropriate (and thus stable) rule, was effected primarily in, and through, sectarian control of the redistributive capacities of temples. Thus, sectarian leaders permitted Telugu warriors to render their military expansion culturally appropriate by "gifting" activity, and its main product, temple honor. Put differently, it might be said that the ceremonial exchanges of honor between warrior-kings and sectarian leaders rendered public, stable and culturally appropriate, an exchange at the level of politics and economics. These warrior-kings bartered the control of agrarian resources gained by military prowess, for access to the redistributive processes of temples, which were controlled by sectarian leaders. Conversely, in their own struggles with each other, and their own local and regional efforts to consolidate their control over temples, sectarian leaders found the support of these warrior-kings timely and profitable. Empirically, and diachronically, this relationship between warrior-kings and sectarian leaders is neither simple nor transparent. It is a complex symbiosis in which mobile figures, of both types, augmented and sustained each other. How did this relationship come to apply to Śrī Vaiṣṇava institutions?

Śrī Vaiṣṇavism from 1137-1350 A.D.: Scholastic Fission

The activities and writings of Rāmānujā, the great synthesizer of South Indian Śrī Vaiṣṇavism, represented a complex institutional and ideological union of disparate traditions and groups: between the Sanskrit texts of the North and the Tamil devotional poetry of the Āḻvār poet-saints of South India, known as the *Prabandham*; between the largely domestic and anaconic ritual injunctions of the Vēdic tradition and the temple-centered and idol-oriented rituals of the Āgamic tradition; between the metaphysical severity of Advaita-Vēdānta and the personal, emotional intensity of popular devotionalism in South India; between the *varna* basis of the Vēdic tradition and the sectarian orientation of *bhakti* devotionalism in South India.[26] The two institutions that expressed these reconciliations were those of the *ācāryā* (sectarian leader/spiritual guide) and the organizationally complex sectarian temples, paradigmatically the great Vaiṣṇava temple at Srīrangam.[27] In Rāmānujā's own life

[26] J.B. Carman, *The Theology of Rāmānujā*, Yale, 1974, Ch.2; N. Jagadeesan, "History of Sri Vaisnavism in the Tamil Country (Post-Ramanuja)," Ph.D. Thesis, University of Madras, 1967, p. 60.

[27] V.N. Hari Rao (Ed.), *Koil-Olugu*, Madras, 1961, *passim*.

and work at Srīrangam, these two institutional emphases were directly connected. After Rāmānujā's death, traditionally dated in 1137 A.D., the weak institutionalization of this gigantic mosaic became apparent.

In the two centuries that followed the death of Rāmānujā, his followers became divided into two schools, whose main intellectual difference was their respective preference for the Sanskrit tradition, represented at its peak by Rāmānujā's *Srī Bhāsya*, and the Tamil *Prabandham* poetry of the Āḻvār poet-saints.[28] This linguistic and textual division had, as its most important doctrinal consequence, divergent interpretations by the two schools of the doctrine of *prapatti* (self-surrender), as a technique for salvation.[29] The Sanskrit (or Bhāsyic) school, which gradually shifted its base from Srīrangam to Kāncipuram, accepted a more conservative view of *prapatti*, expressed in later sectarian literature in the analogy of the "monkey" whose young make active efforts to attach themselves to their mothers. The Prabandhic school, which gradually grew dominant at Srīrangam, had a more radical view of *prapatti*, later described by the analogy of the "cat," whereby the devotee, like a kitten, makes no effort to help himself, and depends wholly on divine grace.[30]

Both schools linked their views on *prapatti* to another belief: submission to a human mediator, specifically an *ācāryā*, for salvation.[31] But the Tamil school laid much greater emphasis on the idea of submission to the *ācāryā*, and also laid more explicit emphasis on the link between these two ideas.[32] It has often been remarked that the Tamil school, because of its radical interpretation of *prapatti*, and because of its reliance on the Tamil *Prabandham* rather than the Sanskrit *Vēda*, was more flexible and open to the participation of Sūdras in sectarian life.[33] This is undoubtedly true, but what was probably of greater long-term significance is that, in relating individual helplessness to the need for an absolutely authoritarian sectarian leadership, the Tamil school made a much more imaginative intellectual leap, by granting doctrinal legitimacy to the link between wider recruitment and radical sub-

[28] V. Rangachari, "The Successors of Ramanuja and the Growth of Sectarianism among the Sri-Vaishnavas," *Journal of the Bombay Branch of the Royal Asiatic Society*, Vol. XXIV.

[29] A. Govindacharya, "The Astadasa-Bhedas ..," *Journal of the Royal Asiatic Society of Great Britain and Ireland*, 1910, pp 1103-12.

[30] A. Govindacharya and G. A. Grierson, "The Artha-Panchaka of Pillai Lokacarya," *ibid.*, p. 567.

[31] A. Govindacarya, "Tengalai and Vadagalai," *ibid.*, 1912, p. 716.

[32] T.K. Narayanaswami Naidu (Ed.), *Śrī Piḷḷai Lōkācāriyār Srīvacana Pūśanam: Manavāla Māmunikaḷ Tamil Ākkam*, Madras, 1970, *passim*, but particularly *sūtra* no. 450, p. 660; see also Govindacharya and Grierson, "The Artha.Panchaka...," *op. cit.*, p. 567; see also K. K. A. Venkatachari, "The Maṇipravāḷa Literature of the Srivaiṣṇava Acāryas, 12th to 15th Centuries A.D." Doctoral Dissertation, Utrecht University, 1975, pp. 139-149.

[33] See, for example, B. Stein, "Social Mobility and Medieval South Indian Hindu Sects," in J. Silverberg (Ed.), *Social Mobility in the Caste System in India: An Interdisciplinary Symposium*, Paris, 1968. See also K. K. A. Venkatachari, "The Maṇipravāḷa Literature...," *op. cit.*, pp. 36-49.

mission to sectarian leadership. Thus, while both schools, by 1350 A.D., had laid the groundwork for sectarian expansion through "discipleship" and initiation, it was the Tamil school which had placed the link between *prapatti* (self-surrender in the interests of salvation) and *ācāryābhimāna* (respect for the sectarian mediator) at the center of their teachings. It was this strategic leap in their view of the means of salvation combined with their natural advantage in the medium of religious communication, i.e. Tamil, which underlay the institutional expansion of Prabandhic Vaiṣṇavism, first at Srīrangam and later throughout the Tamil country. After 1350 A.D., the division between the two schools, which had so far been primarily scholastic, exploded out of textual and rhetorical arenas to the primary political arenas of temple and royal court.[34]

Telugu Control and Temple Politics, 1350-1500 A.D.

The growth of Śrī Vaiṣṇava sectarian activity, in the century and a half after 1350 A.D., has for its context a transitional political situation. It was during this period that the Telugu warrior-founders of the Vijayanagara Empire consolidated their control of South India. The first fifty years of this period, especially in the Tamil country, illuminate the process by which this Telugu penetration was achieved. Indigenous sources, both inscriptional and sectarian, describe this process in a remarkably unified stylistic code, of which the primary elements are: (1) the defeat of the Muslim invaders of the Tamil country by Telugu warriors; (2) the "restoration," by these warriors, of temple-worship (alleged to have been interrupted or destroyed by the Muslims); and (3) the establishment of new political order by these Telugu warriors. A typical example of this stylized description is an inscription from Tirukkalākuṭi in the Ramnad district, which states that "the times were Tulukkan (Muhammedan) times and that Kampana Odeyar came on his southerly campaign, destroyed the Muhammedans, established orderly government throughout the country and appointed many nāyakkaṉmār for inspection and supervision in order that the worship in all temples might be revived and conducted regularly as of old."[35]

The first 30 years of the Sangama dynasty (the first dynasty) of Vijayanagara are characterized by a number of inscriptions, which adhere to this

[34] This is not to imply that before the 14th century, the growth of Srī Vaiṣṇavism was a quiet textual affair. It was indeed characterized by conflict, sometimes violent, but these conflicts were rooted in somewhat different issues than the ones discussed here.

[35] A.R. 34 of 1916, in para 33, *Annual Reports for South Indian Epigraphy for 1916.* (In the rest of this chapter, this numbered series of inscriptions will be prefaced by the initials A.R. The text of these reports will be referred to as *Annual Reports . . .*). For an excellent sample of the indigenous sources that adhere to this code, see V.N. Hari Rao, *A History of Trichinopoly and Srirangam*, Ph.D. Thesis, Madras, 1948, pp. 299-307.

code. Several of these inscriptions involve Kōpaṇṇa, a Brahman minister-general of Kampana Udaiyar II, of the Sangama dynasty, who seems to have been the model for Telugu penetration of Tamil country through the "restoration" of temples. The inscriptional evidence shows that Kampana's conquest of the Tamil country, and his defeat of the Muhammedans, was followed by extensive involvement in temple-endowment, in South Arcot district,[36] Trichinopoly district,[37] Chingleput district,[38] and Madura district.[39] Kōpaṇṇa, his minister-general, seems to have been one of the main agents of Kampana Udaiyar II, in this institutional penetration of the Tamil country.[40] Three inscriptions from Kāncipuram,[41] in the Kailāsanātha temple, give us an idea of the nature of this Telugu involvement in Tamil temples. The first, dated 1364 A.D., comes from the Rājasiṃhavarmēsvaran shrine, and testifies to the restoration of temple lands and worship, by the order of Kōpaṇṇa.[42] The second inscription, also dated 1364 A.D., is from the same temple but is far more detailed and interesting.[43] It describes Kōpaṇṇa's order to the temple authorities, ratifying the sale of some temple property to a community of weavers and their leaders (*mutali*), with the right to mortgage and sell this property. Along with this property, however, they were to be free to mortgage and sell their "honors" as well: their precedence (*mutalmai*) in the receipt of the betel-nut honor (*aṭaippam*), their service of the deity (*tēvar aṭimai*), and their proper place in rank (*aṭaivu*). The third inscription, dated 1369 A.D., refers to the establishment of a *maṭha* (monastery) and the allotment of some property, in return for the job of sharing in the recitation of sacred hymns before the deity, to the religious preceptor of a chieftain in a town in South Arcot.[44] This last inscription indicates that one function of allocating such temple-privileges, by these Telugu warriors, was to ease their ties with Tamil rulers. In this case, Kōpaṇṇa appears to have done this by allocating a specialized ritual role in a temple in Chingleput district to the *ācārya* of a chieftain in South Arcot. Taken together, these three inscriptions from Kāncipuram suggest that the initial penetration of Tamil country by Telugu warrior-chiefs was not simply pillage. It involved inroads into some major Tamil temples, whose function was revived or extended, and whose resources were re-allocated to individuals or groups favored by these warriors. The

[36]A.R. 159 and 163 of 1904.

[37]A.R 282 of 1903.

[38]V. Rangachari, "The History of the Naik Kingdom of Madura," *Indian Antiquary*, Vol. 43, 1914, p. 7.

[39]A.R. 111 of 1903.

[40]E. Hultzsch, "Ranganātha Inscription of Goppanna; Saka-Samvat 1293," *Epigraphia Indica*, Vol. VI, pp. 322-330.

[41]A.R. 27, 28 and 29 of 1888.

[42]*See South Indian Inscriptions*, Vol. I, p. 120.

[43]*Ibid*., p. 122.

[44]*South Indian Inscriptions*, Vol. I, pp. 123-125.

result not only was to establish constituencies beholden to these warriors (such as the weavers), but also to establish links between these warriors and indigenous chiefs. In establishing such linkages, sectarian leaders were of considerable importance.[45] This linkage can most directly be observed in the case of Śrī Vaiṣṇava temples after 1350 A.D., particularly at Srīrangam. In this general atmosphere of intensification of royal involvement in temples, Vaiṣṇava sectarian leaders, particularly of the Prabandhic (Southern Tamil) school, made spectacular progress.

Telugu Warrior-Kings and Prabandhic Vaiṣṇavism, 1350-1500 A.D.

The first signs of institutionalization of the Southern school are expressed in the formation of the Śrīranganārāyaṇa Jīyar *Ātīna* (monastic organization) at Srīrangam. Although traditional hagiologies vary about the date of the establishment of this Prabandhic institution, it seems safe to assign it to the first quarter of the 14th century.[46] Kūranārāyaṇa Jīyar, the first occupant of this seat, appears to have been an outsider, but one who gained immense popularity at Srīrangam. As a response to his popular status, the temple-servants, lead by Periya Āyi,[47] installed him in this institution and also gave him several duties and privileges in the temple.[48] The honors and duties which were allocated to this *Jīyar*[49] indicate the growing power of the Prabandhic school. In the course of time, the honors allotted to the incumbent of this position increased and came to be on a par with the other prominent *ācārya-purusa* families at Srīrangam. Later incumbents of this position enhanced their power by offering discipleships to the Sūdra servants of the temple.[50] The primary index of the growing importance of this sub-sectarian institution was the nature of the honors given to its head: precedence in the receipt of *prasātam* (sacred remnants of the food consumed by the deity) in certain ritual contexts; exclusive receipt of the *prasātam* in certain physical areas of the temple; the periodical receipt of certain insignia from the temple-servants to indicate his fitness for this pontifical seat; the receipt of *tīrtam* (sacred water left over from the deity's meals or his bath), *parivaṭṭam* (a silk turban

[45]A R. 56 of 1900 in V. Rangacharya, *A Topographical List of the Inscriptions of the Madras Presidency* (3 Vols.), Vol. I, Madras, 1919, p. 57; see also T. Gopinatha Rao, "Soraikkavur Plates of Virupāksha; Saka Samvat 1308" *Egigraphia Indica*, Vol. VIII, pp 298-306.

[46]Hari Rao. "A History of Trichinopoly . . . ," *op cit.*, p. 295.

[47]The grandson of Mutali Aṇḍān, to whom Rāmānujā had assigned the *srīkāriyam* (management) of the temple.

[48]*Koil-Olugu*, pp. 121-122.

[49]This term indicates a sectarian leader who also has a fixed role in temple-management, and goes back, according to sectarian tradition, to Rāmānujā's organizational activities all over South India.

[50]*Koil-Olugu*, p. 124.

first worn by the deity), and a garland, also previously worn by the deity.[51] It appears, moreover, that the entry of this popular sectarian leaders into the redistributive process defined by temple-honors was not automatic. It was resisted by the members of the Kantāṭai family, who had been powerful in temple affairs since the time of Rāmānujā. They eventually accommodated the *Jīyar* and offered him an important share in these honors in deference to his popularity.[52] This monastic seat was subsequently to become one of the most important loci of Teṉkalai sectarianism.[53] To understand this process, however, it is necessary to take a lengthy detour, and to examine in detail the impact of Vijayanagara rule on Srīrangam in the period from 1350 to 1500 A.D.

The Srīrangam temple was a major example of the process by which Telugu warrior-chiefs "restored" Tamil temples after Muslim rule. Both Kōpaṇṇa and Sāḷuva Cuṇda, generals under Kampana II, were major benefactors of the temple, after 1371 A.D. But their endowments were not made directly: they were made through sectarian notables. Kōpaṇṇa, for example, is believed to have donated 52 villages to the temple through Periya Krishnarāya Uttamanambi.[54]

The rise to power of several sectarian leaders, and the involvement of Telugu warrior-kings in temple "honors" disputes is carefully recounted in the *Koil-Olugu.*[55] According to this narrative, Sāḷuva Cuṇda appointed a certain Uttamarkoil Srīrangarājan to be the fifth head of the Srīranganārāyaṇa Jīyar Ātīna, and established for him certain honors in the temple. The members of the Kantāṭai family took umbrage at this, seeing in it a reduction of their own status, and appealed to Kōpaṇṇa, the other Telugu general involved in the affairs of the temple But, we are told, "since that Durgātipati patronized the Jīyar, he overlooked it."[56] At this point, the Kantāṭai family appealed to Periya Krishna Uttamanambi, who was already rising in power as an agent for Vijayanagara interests in the temple. Uttamanambi is said to have proceeded to Vijayanagara in 1372 A D to lay these problems before the Rāya (king). Although the outcome of this dispute is not known, it certainly heralds the rise of the Srīranganārāyaṇa Jīyar Ātīna, as a base for Prabandhic Vaiṣṇavism, as well as the beginnings of a long and fruitful relationship between members of the Uttamanambi family and the Vijayanagara court.

The Uttamanambi family claim descent from Periya Āḻvār, who migrated to Srīrangam from Srīvilliputtūr.[57] Their rise to power began in the lifetime

[51]*Koil-Olugu*, pp. 122-25.

[52]*Ibid.*, pp. 121-22.

[53]V.N. Hari Rao, "Vaishnavism in South India in the Modern Period" in O.P. Bhatnagar (Ed.), *Studies in Social History* (*Modern India*) Allahabad, 1964, pp 129-30.

[54]*Koil-Olugu*, p. 135.

[55]*Ibid.*, pp 136-38.

[56]*Koil-Olugu*, p. 136.

[57]Hari Rao, "A History of Trichinopoly . . ," *op. cit.*, p. 307.

of Periya Krishna Uttamanambi. He appears to have received cash grants from Kampana II, as well as from Kōpaṇṇa and Virupaṇṇa Udaiyar, which he converted to land grants to the temple.[58] He apparently also used this cash to make various kinds of gifts to the temple such as ornaments, utensils, *maṇṭapas* (pillared halls adjoining shrines), *kōpuras* (towers on temple structures), and *vāhanas* (processional vehicles for the deity).[59] These endowments were sometimes explicitly in behalf of patron-kings,[60] but they were sometimes apparently wholly personal acts by this sectarian figure. This Uttamanambi made another trip to Vijayanagara in about 1375 A.D. and was commanded by Virupaṇṇa, one of the brothers of Kampana II, to build a special type of hall, and subsequently this chieftain came to Srīrangam and performed a special ceremony there: the *tulapurusa* ceremony.[61] According to the *Koil-Olugu*, Periya Krishnarāya Uttamanambi visited Vijayanagara several times, and obtained land-grants from a number of highly placed warriors in the Vijayanagara alliance, many of which he converted to specific ornamental and architectural additions to the temple, in the names of these warrior-chiefs.[62]

Between 1397 and 1419 A.D., fresh complications arose in the arena of temple-control and temple-honors, because of the rise to power of Vēdācārya Bhattar, a member of another *ācāryāpurusa* family, who is believed to have usurped some privileges belonging to the Kantāṭai family, which was temporarily in eclipse. This generated honors-disputes in the temple.[63] The disputes were settled by Mai-Nılai-Yiṭṭa Uttamanambi, who appears to have effected a compromise in 1418 A.D., whereby the powers of Bhattar were diminished and those of the Kantāṭai family revived. This settlement was made in the authoritative presence of an agent of the Vijayanagara ruler as well as agents of the Srīranganārāyaṇa Jīyar.[64]

During the reigns of Dēvarāya I and Dēvarāya II, (1406-1449 A.D.) two brothers of the Uttamanambi family became all powerful in the Srīrangam temple.[65] Their link with these rulers was expressed through the endowment of various lands to the temple by these rulers, whose supervision and application to specific purposes was entrusted to these sectarian leaders.[66] These land-grants permitted the Uttamanambis to associate themselves prominently

58*Ibid.*, pp. 307-308.

59*Ibid.*, pp. 307-10; *Koil-Olugu*, pp. 142-43; T.N. Subramaniam (Ed.), *South Indian Temple Inscriptions*, Vol. III, Pt. 2, Madras, 1957, p. 1300.

60*Koil-Olugu*, p. 143.

61*Ibid.*, p. 138; on the role of the *tulapurusa* ceremony in the fulfilment of the sovereign function, see Mahalingam, *South Indian Policy*, *op. cit*, pp. 26-27.

62*Koil-Olugu*, pp. 142-43.

63*Ibid.*, p. 144.

64*Ibid.*, p. 145.

65Hari Rao, "A History of Trichinopoly . . . ," *op. cit.* pp. 310-315.

66*Ibid.*, see also *Annual Reports* . . . (1937-38), para 63; *Epigraphia Indica*, Vol. XVI, pp. 222-23 and Vol. XVIII, p. 138 ff.

with the construction of new shrines, the installation of new deities, the building of *maṇṭapas*, and the gifting of ornaments to the deity, all activities bound to increase their share in the redistributive process of the temple.[67] For the Vijayanagara rulers, this relationship ensured the application of these resources to the proper ends, and ensured as well that they would be recognized as the benefactors of the temple. Indeed the relationship must have been a profitable one for the Vijayanagara rulers, since an inscription of Dēvarāya II states that Uttamanambi was the recipient of several royal honors such as a pearl-umbrella, a pair of *kāhalas* (musical instruments), two lamps, a golden vessel, and an ivory shield from Dēvarāya II, along with other royal emblems.[68] In this intricate set of transactions between Vijayanagara warrior-kings and the Uttamanambi family of sectarian leaders, we see the working out of a complex process: one in which the Telugu warriors linked themselves to the temple as a source of honor, through the patronage of sectarian leaders and the re-allocation of land and cash to these sectarian figures. At the same time, they associated these sectarian leaders with their own kingship by investing them with royal honors. This increased the local authority of these sect leaders at the same time as it made Vijayanagara rule locally honorable.

This fruitful and symbiotic relationship between Vijayanagara rulers and the descendants of Periya Krishna Uttamanambi continued throughout the fifteenth century: Tirumalainātha Uttamanambi had a similar relationship with Mallikarjunā (1449-1465 A.D.).[69] Similarly, Krishnarāya Uttamanambi, in 1487 A.D., mediated the endowments of Eṛṛamanji Timmappā Nāyakar to the temple.[70]

The last decades of the fourteenth century witnessed the breakdown of the First Dynasty of Vijayanagara and the concomitant rise of the Sāḷuva dynasty. This turbulent political shift had its effects on temple-politics at Srīrangam. The Uttamanambi family appears to have retained much of its power in this transitional period.[71] But they did have to make one major accommodation to the new rulers of Vijayanagara, by conceding considerable status to a foreign (*dēsāṇtiri*) sectarian leader called Kantāṭai Rāmānujadāsar. This particular individual is a model of the social and geographical mobility of sectarian leaders during this period, and of their close links with kings. Kantāṭai Rāmānujadāsar is best known for his activities at Tirupati, as the agent of Sāḷuva Narasiṃha, a subject which is dealt with later in this

[67] *Koil-Olugu*, pp. 146-58; *Annual Reports . . .* (1937-38), *op. cit.*

[68] A.R. 84 of 1937-38; see *South Indian Temple Inscriptions*, Vol. III, Pt. 2, pp. 1298-99; this inscription partly verifies the indigenous account in the *Koil-Olugu*, pp. 146-47 which describes the quasi-royal status of these brothers in Srīrangam.

[69] *Koil-Olugu*, pp. 158-61.

[70] *Ibid.*, pp. 161-63; Hari Rao, "A History of Trichinopoly . . . ," *op. cit.*, p. 331.

[71] Hari Rao, *ibid.*

essay. The available evidence makes it difficult to identify this person.[72] But it seems fairly certain that he rose from obscurity to prominence by the appropriate manipulation of his "discipleship" to prominent sectarian leaders, and his trading of this credential for political currency under the Sāḷuvas at Tirupati. He arrived at Srīrangam after having established his credentials as the agent of Sāḷuva Narasimha at Tirupati between 1456 and 1489 A.D. He seems to have entered the highest levels of the sectarian hierarchy at Srīrangam by becoming the disciple (*sishya*) of Kantāṭai Aṇṇan. He then gained the privilege of the "*dēsāṇtiri mutra*" (seal which gives certain rights to the prominent visiting sectarian figure), which seems to have been his sumptuary instrument for gaining a wedge into temple-affairs, and for appropriating certain honors, in precedence over a member of the powerful Uttamanambi family.[73] Kantāṭai Rāmānujadāsar also seems to have expanded his powers in the temple by associating himself with Narasa Nāyaka, a general of Sāḷuva Narasiṃha. Narasa Nāyaka's defeat of the provincial chief Kōnēri Rājā, the semi-independent representative of the previous dynasty in this region, signalled the establishment of Araviṭu rule in this region.[74] The *Koil-Olugu*, in fact, ascribes Narasa Nāyaka's defeat of Kōnēri Rājā, to the repeated requests of Kantāṭai Rāmānujadāsar for relief from the depredations of the latter.[75] The role of sectarian intermediary for Narasa Nāyaka at Srīrangam seems to have been as fruitful for Rāmānujadāsar as his relationship to Sāḷuva Narasiṃha had been at Tirupati. He managed Narasa Nāyaka's endowments, made some endowments himself, and as a consequence gained a significant share in temple-honors.[76] He also seems to have had a cordial relationship with the Srīranganārāyaṇa Jīyar Ātīna.[77] Kantāṭai Rāmānujadāsar's activities at Srīrangam testify to the close connection of sectarian intermediaries to warrior-rulers during this period, a connection which was pivotal to the rise of these leaders as also to the penetration by these warriors of the institutional structures of the Tamil country.

It was in this environment that Prabandhic Vaiṣṇavism at Srīrangam received its institutional form under the leadership of Maṇavāḷa Māmuni (1370-1445 A.D.). During the lifetime of Maṇavāḷa Māmuni, Prabandhic Vaiṣṇavism became the dominant sect of the Southern parts of the Tamil country, and made inroads as well into its Northern parts, and marginally into the Telugu and Kannaḍa countries. Maṇavāḷa Māmuni's activities involved a judicious combination of five kinds of strategies: (1) the enhancement

[72] *Ibid.*, p. 336; T.K.T. Viraraghavacharya, *History of Tirupati*, 2 Vols, Tirupati, 1953, Vol. II, pp. 582-83.

[73] *Koil-Olugu*, pp. 165-66.

[74] Hari Rao, "A History of Trichinopoly . . . ," *op. cit.*, pp. 338-43.

[75] *Koil-Olugu*, pp. 166-67.

[76] A.R. 13 of 1939 and *Koil-Olugu*, pp. 169-70.

[77] Hari Rao, "A History of Trichinopoly. . . ," p. 342.

of the *Prabandham* as an authoritative doctrinal source, (2) the elaboration of the importance of radical submission to the *ācārya*, (3) the creation of sub-sectarian networks organized around "discipleship," which spanned most of Tamil country, (4) the use of royal patronage, on a disaggregated, local basis, to provide both material resources and royal honors for sectarian leaders, in specific localities, and (5) the specific linkage of sub-sectarian affiliations to temple-control. Thc interdependent and synthetic use of this fivefold strategy by Maṇavāḷa Māmuni ensured specifically Teṉkalai control over a number of temples in South India. How was this strategy historically realized?

Maṇavāḷa Māmuni was a native of Āḻvār Tirunagari (in the Tinnevelly district) which had become, by the time of his birth in 1370 A.D., the stronghold of Prabandhic Vaiṣṇavism. After becoming the major Vaiṣṇava figure in Āḻvār Tirunagari, he proceeded to Srīrangam, the heart of Vaiṣṇava sectarian activities. In Srīrangam, early in the 15th century, he appears to have gained control of a *maṭha* (monastery) in Srīrangam and some share in temple honors through the Kantāṭai family.[78] He then went to Kāncipuram where he pursued Bhāsyic studies for some time, but returned to Srīrangam in 1425 A.D.[79] It was betweeen 1425 and 1432 A.D. that he seems to have become a decisive power at Srīrangam and acquired the title of "Periya Jīyar."

Maṇavāḷa Māmuni's major achievement was the conversion to discipleship of the powerful Kōyil Kantāṭai family. He also converted to discipleship the current head of the Uttamanambi family,[80] Prativāti Bhayaṇkaram Aṇṇān (a native of Kāncipuram and previously a strong adherent of the Sanskrit school), as well as Erumbi Appa, Emperumānar Jīyar, Bhaṭṭar Pirān, Appiḷḷai, Appiḷḷān. These seven individuals, along with Rāmānuja Jīyar (who had been his disciple and lieutenant originally at Āḻvār Tirunagari), came to be known as the *ashṭa-diggajās* (eight pillars of the faith). These eight individuals after the death of Māmuni carried on and consolidated the Prabandhic enterprise all over South India:[81]

> He authorized Aṇṇa and Aṇṇan to carry on his lectures in the Bhasya and Bhagavadvishaya. He sent Tōḷappa to Tirunarayanapuram to carry on his work there. He appointed Ramanuja Jiyar the guardian of his creed in the South, and Bhattar Piran Jiyar at Srirangam. He dispatched Erumbi Appa to his native place. . . . He appointed Appillai, Appillan on similar missions. All these who formed the *Ashta-diggajas* popularized the creed of their teacher, thanks to the support of stray kings and chiefs, and thus introduced

[78]V. Rangachari, "The History of Sri Vaishnavism," *Quarterly Journal of the Mythic Society*, Vols. 7-8, 1916-18, pp. 197-98.

[79]*Ibid.*, p. 118.

[80]*Koil-Olugu*, pp. 150-51.

[81]V. Rangachari, "The History of Sri Vaishnavism," *op. cit.*, p. 206.

a socio-religious change which was of a revolutionary nature.

These individuals provided the institutional basis of Teṉkalai Śrī Vaiṣṇavism in South India in the centuries that followed Māmuni's death. During Maṇavāḷa Māmuni's own proselytizing period at Srīrangam, and in his travels all over South India, he seems to have benefited from the patronage of local princes to assist his own activities. He converted a local chief called Sathagōpa-dāsa and was his intermediary for the construction of various *maṇtapas* in the Srīrangam temple.[82] He also appointed a *Jīyar* in Tirupati and converted a Tuḷuva prince under the name of Rāmānujadasar.[83] Similarly, in the Madurai/Ramnad region, he gained the discipleship of a king called Mahābalivāṇada Rāya, "who not only received the *panchasamskara* from the teacher but gave him all royal paraphernalia, lifted his palanquin and endowed the village of 'Muttarasan' or Aḷagia Maṇavāḷanallūr."[84] Finally, he managed to establish his second-in-command at the Vānamāmalai Maṭha in Tinnevelli, which is today the single most important base for Teṉkalai sectarian activity in South India.[85] After his last triumphal tour of the South, when Māmuni returned to Srīrangam, his decisive role in relating royal figures to his sect is noted in a traditional biography called the *Yatīndrapravaṇaprabhāva*, which points out that "the *Jīyar* brought with him costly jewels, umbrellas of silk, *chāmaras*, flags and colours, carpets, cushions and quilts of silk, and presented these to the deity, and how the temple authorities honoured him by escorting him in pomp to his *maṭha*."[86]

But it was not simply to the politics of conversion that Maṇavāḷa Māmuni devoted himself. He wrote a number of works, but most of these were of the nature of commentaries on the works of his predecessors.[87] The most important of these was his commentary on the *Śrīvacana-Bhūsana* of Piḷḷai Lōkācārya, which gave Māmuni further opportunity to clarify and elaborate the related Teṉkalai doctrines of *prapatti* and absolute dependence on an *ācārya*. But his most important intellectual and rhetorical act was the year-long lectures on the sacred *Prabandham* which he gave at Srīrangam between 1432 and 1444 A.D.[88] These lectures, which have a very special place in Teṉkalai historiography, were given at the peak of Maṇavāḷa Māmuni's powers, and symbolized the centrality of the *Prabandham* to all future Teṉkalai activity and affiliation.

[82]Rangachari, "The History of Sri Vaishnavism," *op. cit.*, p. 201.
[83]*Ibid.*, p. 206.
[84]*Ibid.*
[85]For a detailed description of this process and its consequences, see D. Ramaswamy Tatachar, *The Vanamamalai Temple and Mutt*, Tinnevelly, 1937.
[86]Rangachari, "The History of Sri Vaishnavism," *op. cit.*, p. 204.
[87]*Ibid.*, p. 203.
[88]*Ibid.*, p. 205.

Thus, by the time of the death of Maṇavāḷa Māmuni in 1445 A.D., Prabandhic Vaiṣṇavism, through its sub-sectarian proponents, achieved considerable success, measured by royal patronage and temple-control, in Tamil country, principally at Srīrangam, but also in numerous other temple centers. It also had made some minor headway at Kāncipuram, but this was negligible. In Tirupati, representatives of the Prabandhic school had achieved some success, but by no means controlled the temple. This consolidation of much of the Tamil country by this Vaiṣṇava sub-sect was doctrinally associated with the emphasis on the Tamil *Prabandham,* and with the skilled intermediary functions of sectarian leaders who, by linking royal patronage and temple-honor, managed to become powerful religious chiefs themselves, by 1500 A.D. It is after 1500 A.D., that members of the Sanskrit school began to consolidate their own institutional bases, along similar lines and by similar strategies. But to understand this transition, it is necessary to consider the nature of sectarian politics at Tirupati, the great "Northern" (in Tamil country) center of Śrī-Vaiṣṇavism.

The temple-complex at Tirupati, during the Vijayanagara period, evolved in three major ways that distinguished it from its structure in earlier periods: (1) the embellishment of the ritual calendar with a vast number of new festivals, supported by many architectural/iconic additions[89]; (2) the shift in the nature of endowments from an emphasis on things like the burning of perpetual lamps to an emphasis on food offerings: these food offerings and their redistribution as *prasātam* formed the core of temple economics in the Vijayanagara period[90]; and (3) the increased importance of the recitation of the *Vēdas* and the *Prabandham* by Brahman and non-Brahman devotees.[91] These three interlinked developments in the period from 1350 to 1650 A.D. transformed this temple-complex from a small set of shrines, dominated by the simple rituals of the Vaikhānasa priesthood,[92] to a vast socio-religious center, attracting rich endowments from rulers and merchants. This process was also reflected in the creation of numerous sectarian establishments, and the organization of numerous institutional structures, managed by sectarian leaders, for the housing and feeding of Śrī-Vaiṣṇava pilgrims from all over South India. This transformation was effected by the penetration of the temple by Tamil Śrī-Vaiṣṇava leaders and their disciples, and their fruitful mediation of royal (and non-royal) endowments to the temple.[93]

It was in the fifteenth and sixteenth centuries that Vaiṣṇava, primarily Tamil, sectarian leaders helped in the growth of popular and royal support

[89]S. Subrahmanya Sastry, *Report on the Inscriptions of the Devasthanam Collection with Illustrations,* Madras, 1930, *passim.*

[90]Burton Stein, "The Economic Function of a Medieval South Indian Temple," *op. cit., passim.*

[91]Viraraghavacharya, *History of Tirupati, op. cit.,* Vol. II, p. vi.

[92]*Ibid.,* Vol. I, pp. 517-19.

[93]Viraraghavacharya, *History of Tirupati, op. cit.,* Vol. I, pp. 519-41.

for the Tirupati complex, and used this growth to extend Vaiṣṇava sectarian activity into Telugu and Kannaḍa country. The model for the symbiotic relationship between rulers and sectarian leaders is the relationship between kantāṭai Rāmānuja Aiyengār (whose activities at Srīrangam have already been noticed) and the king Sāḷuva Narasiṃha of Vijayanagara.[94] It is worth investigating this relationship in some detail, since it casts light on matters that are pertinent to all such relationships.

Kantātai Rāmānuja Aiyengār was the agent through whom, starting in 1456 A.D.,[95] Sāḷuva Narasiṃha linked himself to the redistributive cycle of the Tirupati temple and publicly established his patronage of non-Brahman worshippers there. He did this by allocating taxes from some villages for some food offerings to the deity. He allocated the "donor's share"[96] of the *prasātam* to the *Rāmānujakūṭam*[97] established by him at Tirupati, to be managed by Rāmānuja Aiyengār. In this case, the *Rāmānujakūṭam* managed by Rāmānuja Aiyengār was for the benefit of non-Brahman Śrī-Vaiṣṇavas, a group of whom were his disciples.[98] It was this non-Brahman constituency that benefited from the "donor's share" of the *prasātam,* created by Sāḷuva Narasiṃha's endowment. Between 1456 and 1473 A.D., Rāmānuja Aiyengār was the intermediary between this non-Brahman constituency and the sanctified products of royal endowments,[99] as well as endowments by other land-controllers.[100]

Kantāṭai Rāmānuja Aiyengār was originally commissioned to simply oversee his royal patron's endowments and their proper redistribution to his non-Brahman disciples of the *Rāmānujakūṭam.* But he appears to have used his status to give these non-Brahmans some important roles in temple-worship and thus in temple-honors.[101] In the period between 1467 and 1476 A.D., he apparently used his influence with the Sāḷuva emperor to make crucial alterations in the redistributive cycle of the temple. He made an agreement with some Paḷḷis who had rights over some temple lands to pay them a fixed rent, and to give to his *Rāmānujakūṭam* the benefits of extra productivity created by building channels on the land.[102] On 25.4.1467, he made an agreement with the *Stānattār* (temple-managers) to create an offering to the deity, the "donor's share" of the *prasātam* being allocated to his non-Brahman constituency, by the investment of his own capital in the agrarian development of

[94]Stein, "Social Mobility . . . ," *op. cit.*, and Viraraghavacharya, *ibid.*, II, pp. 557-60.
[95]*Tirumalai-Tirupati Devastanam Epigraphical Series, op. cit.,* Vol. II: 4.
[96]Stein, "The Economic Function . . . ," discusses this term.
[97]This term designates a free feeding house for Śrī-Vaiṣṇavas, often non-Brahman pilgrims and devotees, at a sacred center.
[98]Viraraghavacharya, *History of Tirupati, op. cit* , Vol. II, p. 591.
[99]*T.T.D.E S., op. cit.*, II: 23, 31, 50.
[100]*Ibid.*, II: 64, 67, 68.
[101]*Ibid.*, II: 22, 81, 135, 31, 38, 50, 68.
[102]*Ibid.*, II: 24.

some temple land.[103] In November 1468, he persuaded the temple-managers to allot some temple-land for worship to an image of Kulasēkhara Āḻvār which he had installed in Tirupati.[104] Between 1469 and 1470 A.D., Rāmānuja Aiyengār made six arrangements with the temple-managers to develop temple land, endow additional temple ritual by the additional agrarian product so generated, and allocate the "donor's share" of the resulting *prasātam* to his non-Brahman constituency.[105] In one of these cases, he explicitly recognized his dependence on his royal patron, by describing the offering as being for "the merit of Narasiṃharāja-Uḍaiyar."[106]

The most interesting example of Rāmānuja Aiyengār's influence and his use of it to generate additional honor (in the form of *prasātam*) for his own non-Brahman following, is seen in an inscription dated 23.11.1476.[107] In this case, Rāmānuja Aiyengār seems to have been the intermediary for the endowment of a large sum of cash to the temple, by a local Śrī-Vaiṣṇava devotee. This sum was to be invested in agrarian development by the temple-managers, and from the resulting agrarian surplus, a number of ritual events was to be subsidized. But amongst these ritual events were two important innovations: the celebration of the natal stars (*tirunakṣattiram*) of all twelve *Āḻvārs* in front of the shrine of Rāmānuja, and the singing of the *Prabandham* by Brahman and non-Brahman devotees *together* in the same shrine.[108] The achievement of these innovations was made possible by embedding them in a complex scheme of allocation of resources for various items of worship, and an equally disaggregated allocation of *prasātam* honors for various temple functionaries as an inseparable part of this overall package.

Kantāṭai Rāmānuja Aiyengār served a crucial intermediary function linking outside endowers, temple officials, and local Śrī-Vaiṣṇava constituencies eager for shares in the honors represented in the leavings of the deity (*prasātam*). Such intermediaries were numerous at Tirupati, and it is precisely their large number that is an index of the wide range and large quantity of endowments (particularly land) that were gifted to the deity, transformed into *prasātam* and distributed according to the constituencies/ideas favored by the donor.

Although attempts were made by Śrī-Vaiṣṇavas of the Tamil school to give the recitation of the *Prabandham* a regular role in the ritual of Tirupati even as early as 1253 A.D.,[109] it was not until 1468 A.D., under the aegis of Rāmānuja Aiyengār, that this was achieved. From this time onwards, the recital of the

[103] *Ibid.*, II: 26.

[104] *T.T.D.E.S.*, *op. cit.*, II: 36.

[105] *Ibid.*, II: 38, 40, 44, 45, 47.

[106] *Ibid.*, II: 45.

[107] *Ibid.*, II: 68.

[108] Viraraghavacharya, *History of Tirupati, op. cit.*, discusses the potential resistance on the part of the Vaikhānasa priests in Vol. I, pp. 241-45 and Vol. II, pp. 590-91.

[109] Viraraghavacharya, *History of Tirupati, op. cit.*, Vol. II, p. 1016.

Prabandham hymns began increasingly to attract donors, who allocated a share of their *prasātam* to the reciters of the *Prabandham*.[110] In the first quarter of the fifteenth century, the increasing popularity of *Prabandham* recital among donors led to rivalry among the various sectarian leaders of the two schools at Tirupati, for the management and control of this aspect of temple-ritual.[111] Starting in 1516 A.D.,[112] one of the major leaders of Sanskrit persuasion, the *jīyar* of the Van Saṭakōpan Maṭha, made endowments in which there was a conspicuous absence of any part in the "donor's share" of the *prasātam* for the *Prabandham* reciters. Between 1520 and 1528 A.D., some inscriptions reveal a change in the relationship between this *jīyar* and the Kōyil Kēḷvi *jīyar*s, who were of the Prabandhic school.[113] During this decade, the individuals to whom these sectarian leaders allotted their shares in the *prasātam* were increasingly united by their common sub-sectarian preferences.[114] By 1530 A.D., therefore, it is possible to infer that the increasing prestige of Prabandhic Vaiṣṇavism at Tirupati had hardened the divisions between sectarian leaders of the two schools, and provided the motive for at least one set of leaders of the Sanskrit school, the *jīyars* of the Ahōbila Maṭha, to seek opportunities for their own sub-sectarian beliefs elsewhere (see below).

On the whole, by the early part of the fifteenth century, the activities of sectarian leaders of the Prabandhic school, given an organizational and ideological basis by Maṇavāḷa Māmuni and his network of disciples, had ensured that most of the Vaiṣṇava temples in the Tamil country, with the exception of some in the Chingleput district, were controlled by sectarian leaders of the Tamil school.

Warrior-Kings and the Sanskrit School, 1500-1700 A.D.

Sectarian leaders of the Sanskrit school were involved in temple-related activities before 1500 A.D. But it was only after A.D. 1500 that they created a counter-structure of an institutional sort, by linking themselves to Vijayanagara kings. Given the establishment, by this time, of Prabandhic Vaiṣṇavism in most of the Tamil country, it is not surprising that these leaders looked for new areas in which to promulgate and institutionalize their beliefs. They succeeded in setting up bases in Kannaḍa and Telugu areas, and in some temple-centers in the northernmost parts of the Tamil country. Three sets of sectarian leaders were responsible for the major part of this activity: the *jīyars* of the Ahōbila Maṭha in the Kurnool district; members of the Tātācārya family

[110] *Ibid.*, pp. 1031-46.
[111] *Ibid.*, pp. 1046-55.
[112] *T.T.D.E.S.*, *op. cit.*, III: 110, 114.
[113] *Ibid.* III: 143, 173, 178; Viraraghavacharya, *op. cit.*, Vol. II, pp. 1055-57.
[114] Viraraghavacharya, *History of Tirupati*, *op. cit.*, Vol. II, pp. 1055-57.

of *ācāryāpurusas*, who spread through the Telugu districts in the sixteenth century; and the *matādipatis* (monastic heads) of the Brahmatantra Parakāla Tantra Svāmi Maṭha in Mysore. Let us consider briefly these three institutional bases of Sanskrit school activity.

The heads of the Ahōbila Maṭha in Kurnool district were the successors of the *jīyars* of the Van Saṭakōpan Maṭha at Tirupati, where they conducted intermediary functions for some Telugu chiefs, even after the headquarters of the *maṭha* had shifted to Kurnool.[115] As we have already noticed, there is some evidence that the shift of this set of Sanskrit school sectarian leaders to Kurnool from Tirupati was probably linked to the increasing prestige of Prabandhic Vaiṣṇavism at Tirupati. In the period between 1554 and 1584 A.D., the heads of this *maṭha* established in Kurnool a complex set of temple-centered relationships with Vijayanagara chiefs.[116] By this time, these sectarian leaders must have gained sufficient control of the local Narasiṃhasvāmi temple, for their transactions with representatives of the Vijayanagara kingdom show them to have been at the center of various land transactions involving these chiefs, linked directly to temple-ritual as well as to agrarian development.[117] For example, in 1544-55 A.D., an inscription reports that "the Vaishnava teacher Parāṇkusa-Van-Sathagōpa Jiyamgāru, the trustee of the Ahobala temple and the agent of Aḷiya Rāmapayyadēva-Mahārāja, granted a *dasavanda-mānya* to Avubalarāja, son of Kōnēṭi Rājayya and grandson of Rāmarāja-Peda-Kondayadēva-Maharājā of Atrēya gōtra and the lunar race, for having built at Alamuru, which was a village of the temple (*tiruvaḷayāṭu*), the tank Kōnasamudram, otherwise called Nārāyaṇasamudram."[118] Also, these sectarian leaders re-allocated land originally granted to them by Telugu warrior-chiefs, to specific ritual purposes in the local temple: an inscription of 1563 A.D. reveals that "a gift of land in the village China-Komerḷa in the Ghaṇḍikōṭaṣīma, by Vaṇ Saṭhagōpa-Jiyyamgāru, to Ahōbalēsvara for providing offerings of rice-cakes on specified festivals in the maṇṭapa in front of the *maṭha* which he had constructed. . . . The village China-Komerḷa was a gift made to the Jīyyamgāru by the chief Krishṇamarāja, son of Nadēla China-Obaṇṇamgāru."[119] At the same time, these sectarian leaders cooperated with warrior-chiefs in the management of royal endowments.[120] In the period 1578-1584 A.D., these sectarian leaders appear to have invited Vijayanagara aid in ousting hostile Muslim forces from the locality and, subsequently, they granted temple-honors to the warriors responsible for this victory.[121] Thus,

[115] *T.T.D.E.S.*, *op. cit.*, II: 101.

[116] V. Rangacharya, *A Topographical List. . .*, *op. cit.*, Vol. II, pp. 970-74.

[117] A.R. Nos. 65, 69 and 79 of 1915 in *ibid.*

[118] A.R. 65 of 1916, in Rangacharya, *A Topographical List. . .*, *op. cit.*, II, p. 971.

[119] A.R. 82 of 1915, in *ibid.*, p. 975.

[120] A.R. 76 of 1915, in *ibid.*, p. 974.

[121] A.R. 70 of 1915, in *ibid.*, pp. 972-73; see also, "Ahobalam Inscription of Sri Rangarāya," in V. R. R. Dikshitar (Ed.), *Selected South Indian Inscriptions*, Madras, 1952, pp. 327-31.

by the end of the sixteenth century, the Ahōbila Maṭha became a major base for the sectarian activities of the Sanskrit school in Telugu country.

The second set of leaders of the Sanskrit school was provided by the Tātācārya family of *ācāryāpurusas* who, in the second half of the fourteenth century, settled in Eṭṭūr (Kistna District) and appear to have spread their activities through large parts of the Telugu country, as well as in the northern most parts of the Tamil country.[122] Sectarian tradition links them with the Vijayanagara court, and its increasing preference for Śrī-Vaiṣṇavism, starting during the reign of Vīrupākṣa I (1354-1378 A.D.).[123] Pancamatabhanjanam Tātācārya was the *rājaguru* (royal preceptor) of Sadāsiva Rāya and his minister Aḷiya Rāmarāya.[124] It is also interesting that this Tātācārya was the nephew of Parāṉkusa Vaṉ Saṭagōpa Jīyar, the sixth head of the Ahōbila Maṭha, thus indicating kin-based connections within the leadership of the Sanskrit school.[125] But it was during the rule of the Araviṭu dynasty of Vijayanagara in the sixteenth century that the royal patronage of the Tātācāryas reached its zenith, and was displayed in the massive control of temples by them. Lakshmikumāra Tātācārya, the adopted son of Pancamatabhanjanam Tātācārya, achieved great influence over his patron, Venkata I of the Araviṭu dynasty: both sectarian sources as well as inscriptions lay great emphasis on the coronation of Venkata I by a Tātācārya, although there is some question as to which of these two individuals was the sectarian leader in question.[126] Although inscriptions suggest that Lakshmikumāra Tātācārya was in charge of all the temples in the kingdom, he seems to have concentrated his activities in the Chingleput district, to some extent in the Srīperumbudūr and Tiruppukuḷi temples, but primarily in the Varadarāja Svāmi temple in Kāncīpuram.[127] In this last temple, it is clear that the power of Lakshmikumāra Tātācārya was great over land, ritual and the functionaries involved in the transformation of the one into the other.[128] In the 1660s, reflecting the decline of the Vijayanagara empire, and the growth of independent kingships all over South India, Venkata Varadācārya, Lakshmikumāra Tātācārya's son, migrated to Mysore and associated himself with the growing sovereignty of the Woḍeyār kings of Mysore.[129]

[122]S. Vijayaraghavachari, "A Few Inscriptions of Laksmikumara Tatacharya" in *Journal of Indian History*, Vol. XXV, Pt. 1, April 1947, pp. 121-31; see also Viraraghavacharya, *History of Tirupati, op. cit.*, Vol. II, pp. 760-61 for a genealogy of this family.

[123]Vijayaraghavachari, "A Few Inscriptions. . .," *op. cit.*, p. 124; see also T.A. Gopinatha Rao, "Dalavāy-Agrahāram Plates of Venkatāpatidēva Mahārāya I: Saka-Samvat 1508," *Epigraphia Indica,* Vol. XII, pp. 162-63.

[124]H. Heras, *The Aravidu Dynasty of Vijayanagara*, Madras, 1927, pp. 301-6.

[125]Rangacharya, *A Topographical List. . ., op. cit.*, Vol. II, p. 971.

[126]Heras, *op. cit.*, p. 302 and Vijayaraghavachari, *op. cit.*, pp. 126-27.

[127]Heras, *op. cit.*, p. 305; Vijayaraghavachari, *op. cit.*, pp. 130-31; *Annual Reports. . ., op. cit.*, 1920, pp. 115-16.

[128]A.R. 383 of 1919; *Annual Reports. . . , op. cit.*, p. 115.

[129]C. Hayavadana Rao, *History of Mysore*, Bangalore, 1943, Vol. I, p. 247.

It was probably at this very time in Mysore, during the reign of Dēvarāja Woḍeyār (1659-1673 A.D.) that the nucleus of the third base of Sanskrit school leadership, the Brahmatantra Parakāla Tantra Svāmi Maṭha, was laid.[130] This *maṭha* was founded in Kāncipuram in the fourteenth century, by a disciple of Vēdānta Dēsika, the revered figure of the Vaṭakalai tradition, through the support of an unknown royal patron.[131] The *maṭha* subsequently shifted to Tirupati, where its heads appear to have been intermediaries for the benefactions of the Mysore chiefs.[132] During the reign of Dēvarāja Woḍeyār, the then head of the *maṭha* shifted its headquarters to Mysore.[133] This was not unnatural, since the rulers of Mysore, from early in the seventeenth century, publicly displayed their commitment to Śrī-Vaiṣṇavism: by taking the rites of initiation from the *Svāmis* of the Parakāla Maṭha, by using the *varāha-mudre* (boar-seal) in their documents,[134] and by the building and endowment of Vaiṣṇava temples.[135] The foundation of this relationship of mutual benefaction between this *maṭha* and the Mysore royal court was probably laid during the headship of Periya Parakāla Svāmi (1677-1738 A.D.).[136] This enterprising leader, probably responsible for the beginnings of the pan-regional Vaṭakalai movement for temple-control, seems to have had the support of his royal patrons for his scheme.

A Kannaḍa *nirūpa* (order), probably dated in 1709 A.D., during the reign of Kāntirāva Narasarāja Woḍeyār, King of Mysore, contains a royal edict to the effect that "the practice of using *tanian* [invocatory verse] Rāmānuja Dayāpātra in sacred places like the Tirunārāyaṇasvāmi temple at Mēlukōte on the occasion of reciting Prabandhas which was in vogue from the time of Rāja Woḍeyār, King of Mysore, up to the reign of Kāntirava Narasarāja Vodeyar, shall continue in the future also in the same manner."[137]

This royal order represents the beginnings of self-conscious pan-regional conflict for temple-control between the two schools of South Indian Śrī-Vaiṣṇavism. Throughout the eighteenth and nineteenth centuries, and to some extent in the twentieth century, attempts were made by individuals and groups of the Sanskrit school to penetrate temples controlled by the Tamil school or to extend their rights in temples where they shared control with members of the Prabandhic school. In every such case, the introduction of the "Rāmānuja

[130] *Ibid.*

[131] A.R. 574 of 1919; see also N Desikacarya, *The Origin and Growth of Brahmatantra Parakala Mutt*, Bangalore, 1949, pp xii-xv.

[132] Desikacarya, *ibid.*, p. 8.

[133] *Ibid.*, p. 13.

[134] Hayavadana Rao, *History of Mysore*, *op. cit.*, Vol. I, pp. 169, 170-71, 224, 232.

[135] *Ibid.*, pp. 363-65, 166-68, 375-77.

[136] Desikacarya, *The Origin and Growth. . .*, *op. cit.*, p. 12.

[137] *Archaeological Survey of Mysore: Annual Report 1938;* also see Desikacarya, *op. cit.*, Appendix VI.

Dayāpātra. . ." invocatory verse[138] was the first stage in these battles for temple-control, wherein the Sanskrit school was united and inspired by the three sets of sectarian leaders previously described.[139] The examination of these post-medieval conflicts, however, lies beyond the scope of this analysis.

Conclusion

The hypothesis which this paper began can be reviewed as follows: in South India, in the three centuries that preceded British rule, a *single* system of authoritative relations united religious and political interests, and wedded them into a flexible and dynamic pan-regional network. The key components of this system were: (1) the growing number of temples which served as redistributive centers, where gifts to deities enabled the continuous transformation of material resources into status and authority;[140] (2) the shared orientation of political and religious figures to these myriad economic/religious centers; (3) the resulting willingness of religious and political leaders to transact with each other and share authority in a symbiotic, rather than in a mutually exclusive, fashion. If this hypothesis is taken as valid, or even as suggestive, the following questions need further investigation: (1) How did the role of Saivite, Mādhvā or other religious institutions complicate or coexist with this system? (2) What were the economic/technological changes at the end of the Chōla period that made possible the growth of this system? (3) Were there structural weaknesses in this system that hastened its breakdown in the late sixteenth and seventeenth centuries?

138For a discussion of the place of this verse in Śrī Vaiṣṇava temple-ritual, and for a Teṉkalai account of the circumstances of its origin, see P.B Annangarachariar, *Rāmānujā Dayāpātrā*, Kancipuram, 1954.

139V.N. Hari Rao, "Vaishnavism in South India in the Modern Period," *op. cit.*, pp. 120-25; N. Jagadeesan, "History of Sri Vaishnavism. . . ," *op. cit.*, pp. 252-58; K.S. Rangaswami Aiyengar, *A Second Collection of Papers Relating to Sri Ranganadhasvami Temple, Its Management etc.*, Trichinopoly, 1894.

140For a nineteenth century view of the immense complexity of the relationship between endowed material resources and ritual, at a single temple, see Carol A. Breckenridge, "The Śrī Mīnākṣi Sundarēsvarar Temple: Worship and Endowments in South India, 1833 to 1925," Unpublished doctoral dissertation, University of Wisconsin, 1976.

The Indian Economic and Social History Review, Vol. XIV, No. 1

From Protector to Litigant—Changing Relations Between Hindu Temples and the Rājā of Ramnad

CAROL APPADURAI BRECKENRIDGE
Cornell University

> . . . the wrathful and furious Maravars, whose curled beards resemble the twisted horns of the stag, the loud twang of whose powerful bow-strings, and the stirring sound of whose double-headed drums, compel even kings at the head of large armies to turn their backs and fly.[1]

Described in the nineteenth century as a fierce, capricious and cunning community skilled with arrows and boomerangs, the Maravars dominated the agriculturally dry strip of coastal land called Rāmanātapuram Samastāṉam (in present-day Tamiḻnāṭu).[2] Throughout the nineteenth century, the royal family of this proud and elegant people was referred to as litigious, bankrupt, and decadent. The royal court became known for its orgiastic *nautch* parties at which cock-fighting and other indulgences were thought to have squandered away the energy and resources of the people. According to the prescriptions of Manu as understood and interpreted by or for British officials, Maravars were ranked low for they were eaters of animal-flesh Similarly, their marriage alliance patterns, eating-habits and "martial" disposition did not correspond with the rules and practices of "clean" castes as understood by the institutions and officials of Government.

*This paper was originally presented under the title "Trifling Trinkets: Temple Honors, the Rājā of Ramnad and Anglo-Indian Courts, 1864-1908," at the Conference on the Study of South Indian Religion, Bucknell University, 1975.

[1]Edgar Thurston, *Caste and Tribes of Southern India*, Johnson Reprint Corporation, U.S.A., 1965, Vol V, p. 27.

[2]A samastāṉam is a kingdom, state, place of residence for a royal personage, capital *Madras University Tamil Lexicon*, p. 1296. Rāmanātapuram Samastāṉam has been variously referred to in the literature as: Maravar *Dēsam* (country), Maravar *Simai*, and Rāmanātapuram *Zamindari*(from 1803 to 1908).With the passage of the Estates Abolition Act, in 1908 the Zamindari became a district in the then Madras Presidency. The newly drawn district boundaries, however, include Rāmanātapuram (hereafter Ramnad) and Sivaganga Zamindaries, and Srivilliputtur and Sattur Taluks, previously situated in Tinnevelli District.

Yet, historically, the royal head of the Maravar community, entitled "Sētupati," had played a prominent role among Tamil kings.[3] Since at least 1600, Sētupatis had borne royal titles,[4] had carried royal paraphernalia, and had commanded contexts in which both to grant and to receive honors. Other markers also attest to his royal stature. He was successful in conquest, often returning from warfare with booty. His royal generosity was to be witnessed in his gifting activity to temples, feeding houses, and monastic institutions. And finally, such donations were protected by him. He was invoked when necessary to resolve disputes, and to determine who was, and who was not, appropriate for various roles and ranks pertaining to endowments in his domain.

In the mid-eighteenth century the independence of the Sētupati was challenged by the Nawāb of Arcot in collaboration with the Government of the British East India Company.[5] The Nawāb sought to extract revenue from the Sētupati, while the British sought to mobilize such commercial products found in Ramnad as cotton, textiles and saltpetre. Although their superior troops were periodically capable of overrunning Maravar battalions, they were not able to maintain systematic control in the Samastāṉam. Nearly fifty years of almost continual warfare resulted. Not until 1801 did this warfare, costly to all involved, cease. Subs quently, in an effort to consolidate their growing political interests in Madras Presidency, the Government of Madras introduced the zamindari system which conferred administrative responsibilities upon local elites. Among the newly titled zamindars of the Presidency, the Sētupati commanded one of the largest "estates."

In converting local royal figures into zamindars, however, the Madras

[3]The title Sētupati literally means the protector of the causeway (*sētu*) between the Indian subcontinent and the island of Śrī Lanka. For a review of the geneological tree of the Sētupati or Tēvar lineage see: Robert Sewell, *Lists of Inscriptions, and Sketches of the Dynasties of Southern India*, 2 Vols., Madras, Government Press, 1884, Vol. 2, pp 228-32; T. Raja Rama Rao, *Ramnad Manual* (no title page: *circa* 1892), pp. 211-72; and N. Vanamamalai Pillai, *The Setu and Rameswaram*, Madras, 1929, pp. 108-28.

[4]See, for example, "Copper-plate record of a Ramnad Setupati: Kollam 945," A.S. Ramanatha Ayyar, *Travancore Archaeological Series*, Vol. V, Part I, Trivandrum, Government Press, 1924, pp. 7-18.

[5]Considerable in erest has been displayed recently in the history of relations between eighteenth and nineteenth century overlords and local rulers (known variously as *poliyakars*, *collaries*, or *zamindars*) in Madras Presidency. See, for example, Burton Stein, "Integration of the Agrarian System of South India" in R.E. Frykenberg (ed.), *Land Contro and Social Structure in Indian History*, University of Wisconsin Press, Madison, 1969, pp. 175-216; Carol A. Breckenridge, "RamnathapuramZa mindari, 1801-1860," unpublished M.A. thesis, 1971; K. Rajayyan, *South Indian Rebellion: First War of Independence, 1800-1801*, Rao and Raghavan, Mysore, 1971; and *Rise and Fall of the Poligars of Tamilnatu*, University of Madras, Madras, 1974: and Pamela G. Price, "Nineteenth Century Ramnad and Shivaganga Zamindaries: Royalty in the Anglo-Indian Courts," presented at the Annual Meeting of the Association of Asian Studies, Toronto, 1976.

Government undermined the kingship of such people as the Maravar Sētupati. Kings were deprived of many activities which were illustrative of their kingship. Most conspicuously, the Sētupati could not engage in warfare, nor could he arbitrate either civil or criminal disputes.[6] Denied access to military and judicial powers, the Sētupati was to become a semi-autonomous agent of the Government of Madras who was responsible for insuring a continuous flow of revenue to the Government. His or her position was to be held at the suffrance of the Company's Government. Hence, when the newly installed Rāni reported that she could not enforce her injunctions, she was reminded by the Collector that her authority should be greater than it had previously been.[7]

From the perspective of the locality, however, in what did the authority of the Sētupati consist? The answer posed in this essay lies in the relationship between the Sētupati and temple-deities. Each depended on the other: temple-deities conferred royal honors on the Sētupat; and the Sētupati granted privileges to temple-deities. This symbiotic relationship may be observed in a variety of ritual contexts reported in the late nineteenth century. But, in this historical context, the generation of ritual events in which the source of the Sētupati's authority, namely his special relationship with temple-deities, was repeatedly invoked, seemingly presents a paradox. His claim to be, and to act as, a king would seem to have been inconsistent with the interests of an expanding imperial system under the Government of India. Moreover, the legitimacy of the Sētupati's claims was derived from a source other than the *raj*. This paradox is the focus of this essay.

The essay is divided into three parts, and three widely different sources have been used in it. Part One is a detailed examination of a prominent celebration known as Navarātri Naivēttiyam in which the Sētupati was celebrated as a king. An 1892 eye-witness account provides the text for this examination. Part Two relies on the Sētupati inscriptions for a reconstruction of the Sētupati's transactions, in the pre-nineteenth century period, as both donor and pretector in the temple. And Part Three considers the systematic attempt by the Government to deprive the Sētupati of the exercise of various aspects of his kingship in the late nineteenth century. Two precedent-setting court cases are used in this discussion. Throughout, reference is made to three different temples in Ramnad Samastāṉam. They are: the all-India pilgrimage center at

[6]The Madras Government allowed the local Ramnad battalion to continue to function between 1801 and 1810 as a tribute to Colonel Martinz, a European adventurer. Martinz had been faithful to the British in leading the Maravar corps during the "poligar wars" from 1782 to 1801. On Martinz' death in 1810, those who so desired were allowed to join the regular battalion with accumulated rights and titles. W.J. Wilson, *History of the Madras Army*, 4 Vols., Madras Government Press, 1883, Vol. 3, p. 348.

[7]*Guide to the Records of Madura District, 1790-1835*, 3 Vols., Madras Government Press, 1931, Vol. 1, p. 275.

Rāmēsvaram, the Śrī Rāmanātasvāmi Temple; in the town of Rāmanātapuram, the temple abode of the tutelary deity of the Sētupati's family, Śrī Rājarājisvari Ammaṉ; and a Śaivite temple in the neighboring town of Kamuthi in which the divine couple of Śrī Mīṉākṣi and Sundarēsvarar presided.

Navarātri Naivēttiyam: Long Live Our King

Hung over the outer gateway of the Sētupati's palace was a *bas relief* bearing a representation of Mahālakshmi. Below that was draped a banner bearing the slogan "Long Live Our King." The occasion was the celebration of Navarātri at Ramnad in the year 1892. During this fourteen-day event, the enduring relationship between the Sētupati and the royal family's tutelary deity, Śrī Rājarājisvari, was renewed. Likewise, the Sētupati's generosity was displayed. A pamphlet devoted to this celebration described the generosity of the then reigning Sētupati, known popularly as the Rājā of Ramnad, as follows:

> The religious zeal and public spirit that characterizes this ancient dynasty [was] amply testified to by the innumerable religious and charitable endowments for Devasthana Pujas [temple worships], Zenna Chatrams [choultries for the free distribution of food, both cooked and raw to poor Brahmins and religious mendicants of all castes], and for Tanni Pandals [water sheds for giving water, buttermilk, etc., to all castes and creeds], and for encouraging Vedic and Sanskrit Patasalas [schools and colleges] and Vidwat Sambhavanas [presents to eminent men of learning and piety], and for various other useful purposes tending to public good.[8]

Historically, to be a king, in South India at least, was to display symptoms of kingship. Such symptomatic behavior might have included conquest in the form of predatory plunder,[9] the subsequent redistribution of one's surplus (or booty), the arbitration or conciliation of disputes which interrupted this process, and the repeated and continual celebration of rites generated by it. In a list of royal activities, numerous rites could be performed: *rājasuya* (royal consecration), *apiṣēkam* (installation),[10] and the annual Navarātri festivities.

[8]"Celebration of the Navaratri Festival at Ramnad in 1892," *The Miniature Hindi Excelsior Series*, Vol. IV. Adyar Theosophical Society Library, Madras. Originally serialized in various issues of the October 1892 *Madras Times*, this eye-witness account was published with the blessings of the Sētupati in pamphlet form. Unless otherwise indicated, this pamphlet serves as the text for the remainder of this section.

[9]See G.W. Spencer, "The Politics of Plunder: The Cholas in Eleventh Century Ceylon" in *Journal of Asian Studies*, Vol. XXXV, 3, May 1976, pp. 405-19.

[10]See Ronald Inden, "Ritual Authority and Cyclic Time in Hindu Kingship," unpublished mss., 1976.

Under consideration here because of its prominence in Maravar country in the nineteenth century is the Navarātri celebration, a celebration of conquest. Traditionally, two conquests were celebrated: conquest by the goddess over demonic forces, and conquest by the king.

In the year 1892, the Rājā of Ramnad, H.H. Raja Bhaskarasamy Avargal, spent nearly one lakh rupees on the fourteen-day Navarātri Naivēttiyam. Under the supervision of the Marawart Department of the Samastāṉam, thousands of Brahmans and poor people were reported to have been fed daily. And we are told that during the dazzling event "many vedic scholars, pandits, musicians, artists, artisans, and other deserving persons were liberally presented with shawls, Benares clothes, jewels, money gifts and so forth." The event, which began on the morning of 22 September and was concluded thirteen days later on the evening of 5 October, is worthy of further detailed consideration. Although little was reported with respect to the numerous transactions which occurred during the festivities, many of the details pertaining to the halls, corridors, processionals, and ceremonies are available.

Halls and Processional Corridors. Basically four halls, all connected by canopied passageways, housed the elaborate festivities of Navarātri. They were the Sētupati's palace, the Rāmalinga Vilas (alias the Durbar Hall), the newly constructed Baskara Vilas, and the Navarātri Maṇṭapam. Of the four, details describing three of them follow.

Resembling the eighteenth century Banqueting Hall at Madras, the rectangular Rāmalinga Vilas contained numerous tall and largely unsculpted Grecian pillars. These were draped with heraldic art including life-size portraits of English and Maravar dignitaries. At the end of the central pillared-aisle was a slightly elevated platform on which the Sētupati, resting on a richly embroidered velvet pillow (*gaddi*), would sit in state. Facing this, suspended high above the dais, was a "painting of the ostrich feathers of His Royal Highness, the Prince of Wales, and a life-size Portrait of Her Most Gracious Majesty, the Queen Empress of India." It was reported that these were designed to "indicate the deeply felt loyalty and grateful attachment of the Setupatis to the venerable British throne." Even more prominently displayed was the mythic coronation of the first Maravar Sētupati by Rāma.[11] A dazzling painting of this coronation, known as *Rāmpattāpiṣēkam*, hung just behind the state chairs. This description of the Durbar Hall is concluded with a description of the passageways which connected it with other halls:

> In front of the Durbar Hall were put up two large. . .shamianas, the decoration of which passes description. By the side. . .was a canopied

[11]The place of Rāma and the *Ramāyana* in the mythic history of Ramnad requires further exploration. Rāma is said to have installed the first Sētupati who as guardian of the causeway assisted him in his defeat of Rāvana in the forests of Śrī Lanka.

passage which led to the Kaliyana Mahal, where marriages in the royal family were usually celebrated. On the front of this mahal was. . .a very big, well painted, life-size portrait of Rajah Muttu Ramalinga Setupati, the father of the present Sētupati. A beautiful garland graced this portrait as a mark of the present Sētupati's filial attachment.[12]

While the decorations and architecture of the Rāmalinga Vilas linked the Sētupati to the expanding imperial system under the dominance of the British the Bhaskara Vilas was a baroque mixture of Hindu and British influences. Constructed by its namesake for the 1892 celebration, this hall was elevated and octagonal in shape. Hung on the pillar supports were a wide range of gods and goddesses. And in the center was an iron band-stand with rows of globes and glowing chandeliers suspended above it.

Guests at the Navarātri celebration moved from the Bhaskara Vilas, which seems to have stood between the Rāmalinga Vilas and the Navarātri Maṇṭapam, via a passageway festooned with Tanjore tinsel work, flags and banners. This processional corridor itself was intersected by five right angled crossways with hollow spherical ceilings. Each crossway was "tastefully decorated with arches of Tanjore workmanship, chandeliers, globes and lustres of different colours, well-shaded, and glass portraits of the various manifestations of God and of distinguished personages." And the sides of the ceilings of these hallways were adorned with various marionettes and with figures representing various Hindu professions and crafts. Of the fourth crossway, it was noted that:

> Entering [it] the eyes of the spectators [were] dazzled with the sight of excellent portraits of Somaskandamurti and Minakshi Devi, with Piryavadai, Somasundareswarar and Minakshi on both sides, all ascended on Vrishaba Vahanas. Close by on both sides, [were] found portraits, one of Minakshi in the attitude of being crowned by her father, and the other representing the marriage scene of Minakshi and Sundaresvarar with Mahavishnu pouring out consecrated water in a stream on the palm of Siva. . . .[13]

And of the fifth crossway, the entrance to the Navarātri Hall, we are told:

> There [was] put up a well-decorated cupola with a splendid lustre suspended in the centre. Passing this cupola were seen on both sides of the crossway arranged in several rows, bands of young devotees dressed in pure orthodox style, and chanting select hymns from the *Tevaram* and *Tiruvasakam* accom-

[12] "Navaratri Celebration," n. 8.
[13] *Ibid.*

panied with music, which could not but excite the piety and admiration of every passer-by to the highest pitch of enthusiasm. On the gate-way of the mantapam [was] seen a painting of Maha Lakshmi with the figures of Siva and Vishnu on each side. . . .This outer hall [was] most beautifully decorated with excellent tinsel work in the shape of temple towers with two turrets on each side facing the mantapam.[14]

All guests focused their attention on the Navarātri Maṇṭapam where the central events of the celebration took place. This spacious hall in which the Amman̲, in her processional form (*utsavar*), sat in state, was divided into elevated and terraced verandas:

In the middle of this Mantapam, close to the wall, was placed Sri Raja Rajeswari Devi in a silver *vimana* with a beautiful canopy at the top, and with the painting of Mahishasura Mardani just behind the goddess and the Navaratri *kalassa* stapanams. . .in front. Portraits of Mahalakshmi, Maha-Saraswati, Hanuman, and Sugriva [were] also seen on the wall. . .behind the vimana. The golden image was placed on a small vehicle representing a lion, the favorite vahanam of *Mahakali*. The *Marakatapitam* was placed facing the goddess on a specially constructed and purified pedestal. . .surrounded by a canopy of flowers.

Seats. Although they were seldom occupied, two seats or *pītams* held particular ceremonial importance. They were the traditional seat of the Sētupati known as the *Sētu-pītam*, and the seat of the goddess known as *marakata-pītam*. Rivetted with silver plaques each bearing insignia of the Sētupati, the rectangular black granite seat of the Sētupati rested on the central dais at the end of a pillared corridor in the Rāmalinga Vilas. According to local tradition as reported in the *stalamakatmyas*, the *marakata-pītam* had been acquired by the Sētupati around the year 1600 when he is reported to have provided a Pandian king situated in neighboring Madurai with assistance in warfare. Triumphing over Mysorian forces, the Sētupati brought the *pītam*, as part of his booty, back to Madurai. There, he is supposed to have presented it to the Pandian king who returned it to the Sētupati "in recognition of his invaluable aid." Ordinarily housed in the Amman̲ temple inside the palace, it was carried to the Navarātri Maṇṭapam for the duration of the festival.

Insignias and Titles. Borne by the Sētupati were numerous titles and various objects of heraldry. His titles were proclaimed by a herald who, during the Navarātri Naivēttiyam, read out a statement of them known as *virutavalli*.[15] Included among his titles were: "Establisher of the Pandya Throne," "He

[14] *Ibid.*
[15] Rama Rao, *Ramnad Manual*, p. 207.

who conquers countries seen and never lets go countries conquered," and "Protector of the Queen's Tali." The Sētupati's royal honors included: flying flags bearing Hanuman and Garuda, riding in select palanquins, being accompanied by yellow-grey silk umbrellas, and wielding the royal staff, sceptre, and sword.

Schedule of Events. Any celebration of Navarātri was both complex and cosmopolitan. Its complexity could be seen in the series of rituals performed over the nine to fourteen day event. These rituals reflected such concerns as those of kinship and virginity, kingship and authority, and honor and sacrifice. The celebration's cosmopolitan nature could be observed in the wide variety of groups who celebrated Navarātri. Since it was not the exclusive preserve of either Brahmans or kings, anyone aspiring to replicate royal stature celebrated it, in their fields, in their homes, and in their shops.

Literally, Navarātri means nine (*nava*) nights (*rātri*). On each of nine nights, the offerer of worship honored a specified Ammaṉ.[16] The Sētupati honored Goddess Rājārājisvari.[17] In Tamiḻnāṭu at least, this celebration came to be coupled with another event known as *āyuta pūjā*, or the honoring of one's arms, tools, or instruments of trade.[18] For the king, this meant honoring his weapons, and for the clerk his stationery. Hence, a tenth day was added to the calendar for this ceremony. And for the sake of additional feasting, gymnastic races and fireworks, the 1892 celebration at Ramnad was extended for an additional four days.

For most worship celebrations in which gods, men or both were honored, the events of a given festival day could be broken into two elementary processionals: one in the morning and one in the evening. If, as we are led to believe by the text used here, the first day of the 1892 Navarātri celebration provided a model for subsequent days, then there were three daily processionals: one in the morning to the Navarātri Maṇṭapam; one in the mid-afternoon to the Rāmalinga (or Durbar) Vilas; and one in the night again to the Navarātri Maṇṭapam.

Commencement of the morning processional to the Navarātri Hall was preceded by elaborate preparations. In the initial preparatory rites, attention was concentrated on the Sētupati, the offerer of worship. He underwent shaving (*vapana*) and anointment (*abhayangana*). Then he himself honored the revered seat of his ancestrol line, the *Sētu-pītam* in a puja ceremony. A second set of preliminary rites began with a focus on the Sētupati and culminated

[16]Outside Tamilnāṭu, particularly in Bengal and Bihar, Navarātri is known as Durgotsava, and may coincide with Tivāli. For a review of both Durgotsava and Vijayadasami, see P.V. Kane, *History of Dharmasāstra* (*Ancient and Medieval Religious and Civil Law in India*), Bhandarkar Oriental Research Institute, Poona, 1930-62, Vol. V, Part I, pp. 154-94.

[17]According to local tradition, Rājarājisvari, a deity bearing a Cōla name, known in the *Markandēya Purānam* as Mahishasura Mardani.

[18]"Navaratri Celebration," n. 8.

with gifting activity and the honoring of the family's tutelary deity, Śrī Rājārājisvari. In an ablution rite known as *apiṣēka makōtsavam*, the Sētupati was bathed in water. While seated on the *sētu-pītam* under a silk canopy in the Rāmalinga Vilas, water was poured over his head in five stages: (1) water consecrated according to the Śaiva agamas from five vessels; (2) water consecrated in accordance with select *mantras* and poured from eleven vessels; (3) water brought from the sacred *tīrta* of nearby Dhanuṣkōṭi poured by Rāmēsvaram temple priests from one large vessel; (4) water collected from a variety of sacred springs in the districts of Tinnevelli, Madurai and Kanya Kumari; and (5) water brought from Allahabad by a Samastāṉam priest. And of course, at each stage the pouring was accompanied by "deafening cheers, various kinds of music and vedic hymns." His energy having been renewed through preparatory rites, the Sētupati then distributed general and special gifts known as *nitya* and *viśēca tāna*.

The preparation of the offerer of worship completed, attention turned to the preparation and honoring of the Ammaṉ, Śrī Rājārājisvari who was processed to the Navarātri Maṇṭapam. Worship of the Ammaṉ began by placing the royal sword and sceptre of the Sētupati at her feet. Then, in a rite known as *kalaca stāpaṉam*, new vessels containing water were consecrated. Accompanied by variegated flags, festoons, vedic hymns, a flourish of trumpets, and gurukkal priests, the golden processional form of the Ammaṉ was processed from her temple abode in the palace to the Navarātri hall. Arriving on a silver processional vehicle accompanied by the *marakata-pītam* she was greeted by the Sētupati, his son, and other relatives and guests. On a temporarily constructed square pyramid of brick-work a few yards in front of the dais on which the Ammaṉ was placed, her royal seat was installed. Between this *pītam* and the Ammaṉ, the Sētupati took a seat and honored nine earthen-filled vessels which had been placed before him. Then, to invite prosperity, five married women (*cumaṅkalis*) planted two seeds of different lentils in each of the vessels with the hope that they might sprout before the nine-day festivities were concluded.[19] Luxurious textiles were then presented to the women. This consecration of vessels was brought to a close with the performance of puja to "nine big and narrow-necked metal. . .vessels filled with water and arranged in a close square [and] having tender leaves at their mouths. . . ."

Before the worship of the Ammaṉ was brought to its conclusion, a tying and binding ceremony, known as *kāppukkaṭṭu* or *kankaṇapantaṉam*, was performed. As a marker of his determination to complete and to protect the ensuing nine days of festivities, a saffron-smeared thread was tied around the right wrist of the Sētupati by the officiating priests. After the Sētupati and his

[19]Interestingly, another puja historically associated with Navarātri celebrations in which a young female child was worshipped (*kumāri pūjā*) is not mentioned in the 1892 account of Navarātri at Ramnad.

purōhitaṉs completed several circumambulations of the *marakata-pītam*, the Sētupati engaged in another transaction with the priests who acted on behalf of the Ammaṉ. The priests brought the royal sword and sceptre from the feet of Śrī Rājārājisvari where these had been placed in the opening ceremony, and presented them to the Sētupati. He accepted them. In conclusion, the Sētupati processed with full regal paraphernalia back to his private quarters where once again he worshipped Śrī Rājārājisvari. Puja for her continued until about 2:30 in the afternoon.

At 3:00 p.m., the second processional began. This time the Sētupati was paraded to his Durbar Hall, the Rāmalinga Vilas. Guns were fired. Trumpets sounded. The grand processional which included dancers, musicians, and military battalions was described at length:

> First came the *Deva Dasis* of the different shrines of the Samastanam, accompanied by their train of musicians; then came groups of *Nagasaram* musicians, who had come for the occasion from different parts of the Presidency; next followed the palace band, playing both English and Karnatic music. The lancers, sepoys and liveried retinue then marched gracefully under the able direction of the palace Subedar. . . . These were followed by the state officials, the special guests, and the royal relatives. . . .[20]

Then, flanked by palace body guards (*ātaipukkars*), the Sētupati appeared, robed in full regal paraphernalia and canopied by silk umbrellas. The processional continued:

> On both sides of the Rajah were. . . rows of . . . torches, and silver and golden staff-bearers proclaiming the ancient glory of the Setupathis. Pandits, Bajanai parties, singing parties, and bands of devotees chanting select Tamil prayers from *Tevaram* and *Tiruvasakam*, closed up the rear. The Rajah was greeted all the way by thousands of spectators . . . and the salutations were readily responded to by the Setupati. Just when the Rajah passed through the Bhaskara Vilas, both the Samastanam and the Devastanam elephants, which stood at the gate. . .saluted the Rajah in a dignified and picturesque manner, waving their ponderous heads and lifting their trunks so as to touch their foreheads.[21]

Upon reaching the Durbar Hall, the Sētupati paraded through the central aisle where lancers and sepoys who lined the passageway presented arms and saluted him. The crowds cheered loudly and vociferously.

Seated on his velvet pillow under an elaborate patchwork canopy supported

[20]"Navaratri Celebration," n. 8.
[21]*Ibid.*

by silver posts, the Sētupati prepared to hold levee. His son and nephew sat by his side while his other relatives sat around him. Other guests, pandits, and officials were also seated nearby. Respect and honor were paid to the Sētupati respectively by temple stanikars and officiating priests of various Samastāṉam shrines, representatives of various monasteries, pandits, jesters and poets, guests and officials. Subsequently, the heir apparent, and other kinsmen prostrated themselves at the Sētupati's feet. Thrown out in front of them was a cloth known as *tittucīlai*, which indicated their "fealty to their paramount chieftain, the Raja Setupati." In stately procession, the Sētupati then marched to the family *zenāna* to pay obeisance to his venerable mother.

About 5:30 p.m. preparations for the third processional of the day began. Śrī Rājārājisvari was worshipped. Amidst jubilation, the Sētupati reached the Navarātri Maṇṭapam around 7:30. Under the tutelage of the officiating priests, he circumambulated the *marakata-pītam*, accompanied by his kinsmen and attendants, and chanted several devotional Sanskrit slokas. Rites of adoration (*upacāram*) were then offered to the Ammaṉ by the priests. The Sētupati, having retired to his private quarters, returned to the Maṇṭapam in dazzling royal robes and worshipped again. Subsequently, sitting on a velvet pillow near the *pitam*, he held a durbar which was attended by his kinsmen, officials, guests and Brahman reciters of the Vedas. Each was received by the Sētupati. Particularly conspicuous were temple priests and representatives of various monastic institutions (Brahman and non-Brahman) who presented the Sētupati with *prasātam*.

Entertainment, provided by vocal and instrumental musicians of the royal court, included songs in praise of the goddess which had been composed by an ancestor of the Sētupati.

In the meantime, worship of the Ammaṉ continued. A consecrated arrow was brought from the feet of the goddess to the Sētupati. He received it. He returned it. Subsequent to the presentation of gifts to the musicians and entertainers, the durbar was concluded with much ado. The hall, having been cleared of all Brahmans, became the scene of special, though unspecified in the text, sacrifices offered to propitiate the goddess. Whether or not these were blood sacrifices remains unclear. Having viewed these, the Sētupati retired to his quarters.

Some combinations of the events described above were repeated on the following six days (23-28 September).

On days eight and nine (29-30 September), weapons (*āyutam*), tools or instruments as the case might be, were honored in a ceremony now known as Sarasvati puja. The goddess was invoked by the worshipper who sought to conquer ignorance, and, hence, to acquire mastery over his or her occupation. For the Sētupati, this meant honoring various instruments of state and war:

The Rajah in the usual procession went to the Durbar Hall, and there

> offered puja to a beautiful vehicle representing a lingam and to the ancient setupitam. He next came to . . . Bhaskara vilas, and made similar pujas to the state elephants, horses, and camels which were all conducted before [him] one after another in richly embroidered kincob robes and costly caprisons set with precious stones . . . [they] were then made to race majestic[ally] with their foreheads facing the Setupati. The state palanquin which had the representation of a lion in front was next honoured. . . .Then the characteristic insignias of the Setupatis. . .were similarly respected and worshipped.[22]

Day ten (1 October), known as the victorious tenth or *Vijayadasami*, consisted of two processionals. In the forenoon, the Setupati paraded to a clearing outside the town for the arrow-shooting ceremony. Among the throngs in attendance at this ceremony were gods and goddesses from various temples in the Samastāṉam, priests, and other honored guests. The celebration was described:

> . . .the Rajah mounted on a beautiful Howdah placed on the back of the state elephant, with two side elephants bearing his characteristic umbrella and flags, [emerged from] the palace amidst constant firing of guns, flourish of trumpets, and the deafening cheers of the multitude that greeted him . . [He] forced his way through the dense crowd to the arrow shooting plain where the gods of the different local shrines had been carried in advance On reaching this plain, the Setupati made pradakshanam a number of times around the gods and goddesses, and under the guidance of the officiating priests, darted consecrated arrows in different directions amidst the loud applause of the vast crowd of spectators. The gods and goddesses were then carried back to their respective shrines and the Setupati returned to his palace in the same grand procession.[23]

In the evening, a grand durbar was celebrated in the Rāmalinga Vilas. Now seated on an English chair, the Sētupati held durbar. Prestations from various temple priests, monastic representatives, Vedic Brahmans, pandits and other learned men were received by him in the form of blessings (*anugrakams* and *akshatas*). Subsequently, members of the royal family, with their usual *tittucīlai* (cloth ceremony), prostrated before their king. Other officials and attendants followed suit.

Days eleven through thirteen (2-4 October) were designated for gymnastic competition, gymkhanas, fireworks, magical feats and jesting events.

Day fourteen (5 October), the final day of the celebration, was concluded

[22] *Ibid.*
[23] *Ibid.*

with a dinner party for European residents of the locality, followed by a *nautch* party in the Durbar Hall to which all the leading men of the town were invited.

The above description of the 1892 Navarātri Naivēttiyam held at Ramnad has been lengthy, though not exhaustive. In his concluding remarks, the author of this eye-witness account translated the traditional gifting-activities witnessed in this celebration in what were then "modern" terms. He noted, for example, that a major portion of the expenditure for the dazzling celebration had been "for the encouragement of science and learning and for various acts of piety and devotion." In an age dominated by imperial concerns with respect to moral and material progress, the interpretation of Navarātri as having been celebrated, however partially, for the "encouragement of science and learning" was particularly compelling. But, from the perspective of the imperial center in Delhi, how was the celebration of Navarātri in the year 1892 to be interpreted?

Throughout, the imperial presence was apparent. Englishmen, their practices, heraldry, music, military honors and photographs were there to be seen. But they were present as guests, however special, who transacted with the Sētupati. At no point in the ritual does it appear that the authority of the Sētupati, which was being renewed in this celebration, was derived from the imperial system itself. On the contrary, if the ritual is to be taken seriously, the source of the Sētupati's authority lay in his relationship with the deity. It was to that relationship that reference was made in the ritual.

Of all the transactions embedded in the multiple renewal ceremonies celebrated in this lavish Navarātri event at Ramnad, two were particularly revealing with respect to the relationship between the deity and the Sētupati. One occurred in the morning worship of the Amma<u>n</u>; and the other in the evening worship of her. Together, these two periods of worship bracketed the afternoon period when the Sētupati sat-in-state, in much the same way as the Amma<u>n</u> did, in his Durbar Hall. During the morning worship of Śrī Rājā-rājisvari, the Sētupati permitted himself to be tied and bound with the ceremonial *kāppu* or thread. In so doing, he committed himself to the protection of his relationship with the deity. The deity, reciprocating through the agency of her priests, presented the Sētupati with his royal sword and sceptre, markers of his kingship. Likewise, in the evening the Sētupati offered the Amma<u>n</u> rites of adoration (*upacāram*). The deity offered the Sētupati consecrated arrows which were eventually used in the performance of the tenth day "victory" celebrations in which the Sētupati's royal prowess was displayed.

In addition to the Sētupati's display of his prowess, on this tenth, and technically final, day of the celebration, the Sētupati and the Amma<u>n</u> each revealed the relationship which had been established between them to their respective audiences. Gathered together for the majestic arrow-shooting event on the plain outside the town were two potentially separate, if not competing, audiences: of the same generic order as the deity were gods and goddesses from other temples in Ramnad; of the same generic order as the Sētupati were various, unfortunately unnamed in the text, honored guests. These two audiences were united in the relationship of the Sētupati and the deity as this relationship had to be replicated by anyone aspiring to royal stature. It, and the reciprocal transactions which underlaid it, take on greater meaning in the context of pre-nineteenth century inscriptional data.

SĒTUPATI AS DONOR/PROTECTER, 1600 TO 1764

The historical context in which Navarātri took on particular meaning in South India was the Vijayanagara era. In the late Vijayanagara era beginning around 1t00, regional royal families surfaced as primary, rather than as secondary, units in which sovereignty was exercised.[24] In the shift of focus from Vijayanagara to regional centers, the celebration of Navarātri by local royal persons was important. It had been the celebration par excellence in the Vijayanagara period, and hence, its adoption by regional sovereigns suggests their desire to replicate the rituals of their predecessors, namely, Vijayanagara sovereigns

Known then in Telugu-speaking country as Mahanavami, and in Kannada country as Dassara, Navarātri was celebrated in the pre-winter season (*vamatamsatra kāla*) of September-October (the Tamil month of Purattāci). The harvest had been undertaken, and had been redistributed. Now, just as Rāma had vanquished Rāvana, the king was entreated to augment prosperity through conquest and victory. This was to be accomplished by infusing the *pītam* and weapons with cosmic energies, by warding off danger in the form of illness in the forthcoming cold season, and by providing a forum in which exchange and prestation was exercised.

The date attributed to the establishment of the first Sētupati in Maravar country is the year 1604. In 1608, while consolidating his position as sovereign, the Sētupati journeyed to the nearby island of Rāmēsvaram for a sacred bath. There, he ordered "the following grant of lands be enjoyed by the respectable Aryan people of the five countries[25] who perform mediation (*stāṉikam*), worship, and service (*paricārakam*), the respectable people who have

[24]In Kannada country, the Wodēyar lineage was placed on the throne around 1610, and instituted the royal festival of Navarātri in 1647; Ikkeri, Gingee, and Madurai were consolidated under their respective Nāyakas in the early seventeenth century; Tanjore, originally under a Nāyaka, subsequently became a Maratha principality. Likewise, in Travancore and Maravar country, powerful royal lineages emerged, and in the year 1659 Navarātri was introduced in Ramnad.

[25]In the literature pertaining to temples in Tamilnāṭu, "five countries" appears to be a stylized way to indicate that newcomers have been incorporated into the local system Myths of origin, for example, usually suggest that temple priests came from "five countries."

given us the sceptre (*seṅkol*). . . ."[26] The phrase "who have given us the sceptre" elegantly captures the relationship between the Sētupati and the priestly retinue of the presiding deity, Śrī Rāmanātasvāmi.

Receiving the sceptre from the priests indebted the Sētupati to the deity on whose behalf the priests had acted. The Sētupati became indebted for honor (*mariyātai*), since the deity, through the instrumentality of the priests, conferred the critical markers of kingship.[27] Upon receipt of the sceptre, the Sētupati had entered into what might appear to have been an asymmetrical relationship with the deity. But this apparent asymmetry was not real. The power in the relationship between the Sētupati and the deity lay in their being linked in a scheme of reciprocal exchanges which in turn generated a redistributive process. This yoking rendered the retinue of the deity (*paricanaṅkal*) and that of the Sētupati complementary rather than competitive.

This reciprocal relationship between the deity and the Sētupati was further complicated by the concluding injunction upon the Sētupati. He was enjoined to protect that which he had given to the priests, an injunction placed on every donor in the temple. Having taken the sceptre, and having reciprocated with a grant to the deity's priestly retainers, the inscription was concluded with:

> The protection [*paripālan*] of a donation [*kaṭṭaḷai*], is equal to twice the meritoriousness of the endowment [*kaṭṭaḷai*] made by oneself. Of donation and protection, protection is more praiseworthy than donation. By donation, man obtains a place in Svarga; by protection, the place of Achyuta himself.[28]

His generosity to the priests had made the Sētupati a donor in the Śrī Rāmanātasvāmi Temple, at Rāmēsvaram. And in so doing he fulfilled one of the two injunctions on those aspiring to royal status, namely an injunction to be

[26]Sētupati Inscription No. 2, James Burgess and Natesa Sastri (eds.), *Tamil and Sanskrit Inscriptions*, Archaeological Survey of Southern India, Vol. IV, Madras, 1899, p. 65. In this volume, twenty-six Sētupati inscriptions are recorded. Unless otherwise indicated, the translations from the Tamil texts used here are my own. I remain grateful to James Lindholm who provided useful comments on my translations.

[27]For an analysis of honors in the context of the temple see Arjun Appadurai and Carol Appadurai Breckenridge, "The South Indian Hindu Temple: Authority, Honour and Redistribution," in *Contributions to Indian Sociology: New Series*, December 1976.

[28]Sētupati Inscription No. 2, Burgess and Sastri, *op. cit.*, p. 65. Natesa Sastri's translation. This injunction seems to have first emerged as a result of a sixteenth century dialogue between Abhirama Pandya and learned pandits in his court as to which was preferable: donation or protection. The pandits declared protection to be superior saying, "Render thou protection which is purifying." Srivilliputur Plates, *Travancore Archaeological Series*, *op. cit.*, Vol. I, pp. 108-9.

generous. But what constituted fulfillment of the second injunction, namely to protect one's own generosity?

Protection seems to have pertained to the Sētupati's constitutive capacity: that is, his capacity to constitute persons appropriate for the privileges which they exercised. Even the deity itself was potentially the subject of this capacity of the Sētupati. The clearest such instance was recorded in a 1715 Rāmēsvaram Temple inscription. The presiding deity was granted the privilege of distributing honors to various courtiers associated with the ritual activities generated by the Sētupati's donation.

> We give to the god. . .as properly his own [*svatāntiram*] the giving of the honor *parivaṭṭam* on the sacred day in the month of Āti to those earning salary [*campulam*]; meals [*cātam*], and income in the temple endowment which bears our seal [*muttirai*]; and also, the giving of parivaṭṭam honors in the festivities of our own maṇṭapam.[29]

The giving of a highly valued honor, namely the tying of a sacred vestment (*parivaṭṭam*) around the head of the recipient, was specified as the special prerogative of the deity himself in the above grant. Just as the royal sword and sceptre given by the deity were critical markers of the Sētupati's sovereignty, so also the privilege of conferring honors might be considered a critical marker of the deity's sovereignty. In their transactions with each other, however, both the deity and the Sētupati were subjected to the peculiar prerogatives of the other's sovereignty: the deity conferred honor on the Sētupati, and the Sētupati granted privileges to the deity.

Moreover, there is evidence to suggest that the Sētupati caused priestly retainers of the deity to become appropriate for their services, privileges, and honors. Their fitness was contingent on the invocation of the Sētupati who generated the ritual contexts in which they performed their services. The Tamil verbal form *ērppaṭutti*, which occurs in the inscriptions, usually as a causative, reveals the constitutive capacity of the Sētupati.[30] It powerfully suggests that the inherent fitness (*urimai*) of priests who serviced the Sētupati was achieved through an order of the Sētupati which altered their substance. More empirical evidence is necessary in order to understand the conditions under which the Sētupati exercised his constitutive sovereignty. From the data which follows one guideline does emerge. He did so whenever new entrants were incorporated into the ranks of the deity's priestly retainers, particularly with respect to priestly entrants who were specifically endowed as the celebrants of the Sētupati's royal rituals.

Three inscriptions pertaining to a Rāmēsvaram priestly family reveal the

[29] Sētupati Inscription No. 10, Burgess and Sastri, *op. cit*, p. 84.

[30] The root of *ērppaṭu* is *ēl*, to be suitable for; becoming; change.

role of the Sētupati as the grantor of privileges, particularly to groups which were in the process of being incorporated as part of the Sētupati's domain.[31] All three inscriptions represent grants by the Sētupati to the family and descendants of Śrī Sankara Gurukkal, a Maratha priestly family. Originally, this family served the Maratha community which frequented Rāmēsvaram in the seventeenth century. The period spanned by the three inscriptions is 1659 to 1764. During that time, this family was incorporated into the temple priesthood with privileges which permitted them to serve as the celebrants of royal rites and ceremonies. Subsequently, they were elevated to the position of mediator (*stāṉikar*) between the king and the deity, and as priests in the Ammaṉ Temple situated in the Sētupati's palace.

The first two of the three grants were ordered in the year 1659. Raghunāta Sētupati alias Tirumala Sētupati (c. 1645-1670) was in the process of consolidating his rule. He reunited Ramnad with neighboring Sivaganga; moved the capital to the town of Rāmanātapuram (ten miles from the former capital); added structurally to Rāmēsvaram's Śrī Rangunata Rāmasvāmi Temple; built *cāvatis* (feeding houses), introduced Telugu into his royal court;[32] defeated Mysore, protecting the dignity of Madurai; and assumed new titles, such as "Protector of the Queen's Tali." Notwithstanding his presumed relationship to the Madurai Nāyakas, the introduction of the *Hiraṇyagarbha* sacrifice, in the year 1659,[33] followed by the celebration of Navarātri Naivēttiyam, clearly established this Sētupati as a king in his own right.[34] It was in this historical context that the Sētupati's concern for his expanding, yet precarious, authority must be viewed.

In the first of the two 1659 inscriptions, the Sētupati ordered that:

> Since former kings have not allocated either village or land for your share of worship (*arcanāpākam*), we command you, the assembly of Marāṭṭa gurukkals who perform worship, service and cooking for Rāmanātasvāmi and Paruvatavartti Ammaṉ, to enjoy the following:
>
> 1. you alone shall act as water-*purōhita*;
> 2. you alone shall enjoy the income [thereof];

[31] For a rich description of ritual see J. Burgess, "Ramesvaram Temple Ritual," *Indian Antiquary*, 1883.

[32] "Copper-plate Record," *op. cit.*, p. 7.

[33] Sētupati Plate No. 5, *Catalogue of Copper-Plate Grants in The Government Museum, Madras*, Government Press, 1918, p. 38.

[34] For quelling the invasion of Muslims from Mysore, the Sētupati is reported to have "received the title 'he who propped up the kingdom,' and was granted permission to celebrate 'the nine nights festival' in his own capital, with the same pomp and magnificence with which it was celebrated at Madura." J. Nelson, *Madura Country*, Madras Government Press, 1868, Book II, Part III, p. 138. Nelson does not provide his reader with his source for this information. To date, I have been unable to satisfy myself that the Madurai Nāyaka had anything to do with the Sētupati's celebration of Navarātri.

3. you alone shall perform svāmi pucai [pūjā], service and cooking for Maharāstrians and all caste members[35] who come for a glimpse of the deity. . . .[36]

Through this order, the Sētupati incorporated Maratha priests into the temple priesthood. Formerly mediators of offerings for a single donative group, namely the Maharashtrian community, these priests were to become mediators for a wider audience of worshippers. They became linked to the offering of "public" worship (*pūjā*) in addition to "private" worship (*arccanai*). Moreover, in this grant, their performance of puja linked them to the Sētupati as his *purōhitaṉs*.

The second inscription recorded in the year 1659 further refined the role of these Maratha *purōhitaṉs* who served the Sētupati. They were granted privileges, namely the privilege of wearing the "protective" sacred thread (*kāppu*), which entitled them to act as the agents of the Sētupati for the performance of royal ceremonies and vows, including the Navarātri naivēttiyam, initiated in Ramnad at this time. The inscription read:

As we have given as a gift for your own hereditary prerogative (*kāṇiyātci*): your wearing of the *kāppu*,[37] while we wear our *kāppu* for the Rājarāsisvari Ammaṉ Navarāttirai festival, may you enjoy performing the Navarāttirai ten day festival, and the festival *pucai* for the Ammaṉ, including the income deriving therefrom. . . .[38]

The initiation of Navarātri in 1659 placed the Sētupati directly in the Vijayanagara tradition. To celebrate Navarātri on a grand scale was to summon one's equals, namely those with whom one had an alliance, to exchange gifts for *prasātam* from one's own hand, as well as one's subordinates, namely those from whom one commanded services and tribute.

One final inscription, dated 1680, dramatically captures the force of the Sētupati's constitutive capacity. The Sētupati ordered:

We leave in your possession all. . . which previous tēvars have endowed for

[35]The inscription is unclear at this point. It could also read "for all Maharashtrian caste citizens." I am unfamiliar with the hieroglyph at the end of the word for Maharashtra, and have, therefore, been consistent with Natesa Sastri's translation: Maharashtrian *and* all.

[36]Sētupati Inscription No. 5, Burgess and Sastri, *op. cit.*, p. 70.

[37]This crucial portion of the inscription is not intelligible according to our present understanding of Tamil grammar. It could also possibly mean: your wearing of the kāppu which is the kāppu we wear for the Ammaṉ Navarātri festival. The inscription reads: *namakku kāppu tarica* (here it changes to the second side of the plate) *tāmmū kāppu tarissukkoṇṭu*. Spelling and grammar mistakes are common in these inscriptions, so it is difficult to know exactly what is meant here.

[38]Burgess and Sastri, *op. cit.*, p. 73.

> the morning and noon sacred bath, *pūcai* and meals (*naivēttiyam*) of Rāmanātasvāmi. . . .Having made you fit (*ērpattutti*) to be the first gurukkal in the Rāmanātasvāmi Temple, we allow you all the first honors· priority in the betel distribution (*akkiratāmpūlam*); double cāmaras; double torches; silk umbrella; village palanquin hung from silk chords. In light of this, we allow you this *tānacācanam* for your enjoyment: the *kaṭṭaḷai vicāraṇai mirāci*[39] and the *mirāci* of the Tēvar seal bearing our name, and the Rakṣāpanda for the marriage festivals which occur in the months of Māci, Āni, Āṭi and Āvani. . . .[40]

Careful attention to the sequence of events in this inscription reveals the causal relationship between the Sētupati's constitutive capacity and the receipt of honors from the deity. In the opening clause, all grants made by his predecessors to the priestly family were honored by the Sētupati. The stages followed in the specifications of the inscription. The first stage involved the appropriateness of the priests. The inscription read: "Having made you fit to be the first gurukkal in the Rāmanātasvāmi Temple, we allow you all the first honors: priority in the betel distribution; double flywiskes; double torches; silk umbrella; village palanquin hung from silk chords." Stage two specified what the priests were entitled to as a result of their newly acquired appropriateness. The inscription continued: "In light of [your appropriateness and the honors granted to you], we allow you this gift for your enjoyment." The gift included a series of privileged roles in relation to temple services, rituals and donors.

The role of honors in the above grant is particularly intriguing. According to this inscription, in light of the honors which the Sētupati bestowed on the priest, the priest was entitled to perform certain functions and roles. The order in which these two things occurred is also worthy of note. Entitlement to perform specified functions did not then entitle the priest to receive certain honors. Rather, the receipt of honors entitled him to perform certain sacred services both in the temple and in relation to the offerer of worship, the Sētupati. These services appear to have been of a mediational nature between the deity and the king.[41]

The Sētupati inscriptions selected for examination here reveal the Sētupati to have been both a donor in and a protector over the temple. He was a donor insofar as he generously redistributed his resources whether in the form of land, produce, or honors. He was a protector insofar as he constituted

[39]The hereditary honor of supervising worship, greeting honored guests, and resolving disputes.

[40]Sētupati Inscription No. 8, Burgess and Sastri, *op. cit.*, p. 79.

[41]For an analysis of temple *stānikars* as mediators between the court of the king and that of the deity, see Carol A. Breckenridge, "Madurai Stanikars: Mediators of Royal Culture" in A.V. Jeyachandran (ed.), *The Madurai Temple Complex*, Madurai, 1974, pp. 205-11.

members of the deity's royal court appropriate for their tasks such that they were unambiguously incorporated into the redistributive process of the temple. Thus, it might be suggested that whenever new entrants were incorporated into the temple, the Sētupati was invoked, either to preempt or to resolve conflict.

It might be asked, to what extent was the Sētupati's constitutive capacity exercised with respect to other donors who were new entrants in the temple? The answer to this question would require evidence which is not presently available in these Sētupati inscriptions.[42] Nevertheless, some observations with respect to other donors in the temple may be briefly made.

The evidence presented above pertained to the transactional relationship between the deity and the Sētupati. But this is not meant to suggest that this relationship with the deity was the monopoly of the Sētupati. On the contrary, every donor who participated in temple worship was an aspirant to royal stature. As such, he sought to replicate the reciprocal relationship of the Sētupati and the deity. This was so because inevitably a donor was, or attempted to be, the head of a donative group, such as extended families, sectarian followers, monastic disciples, or fellow caste members. The source of his appropriateness as "headman" of a group was his receipt of honors from the deity. To receive sacred honors, it was necessary to place oneself in a direct transactional relationship with the deity. Such placement was achieved through donation. Put another way, the donor was the product of a constitutive process, in which he and his constituency were incorporated into the temple through their transactions with the deity. This replication of the relationship between the deity and the Sētupati by numerous other donors in the temple had the effect of rendering the temple a system in which authority was dispersed. In relation to this system, the Sētupati was the ideal-typic donor, and in the final analysis the arbitrator of disputes, the grantor of privileges.

SĒTUPATI AS DONOR, 1800 TO 1912

In the course of the nineteenth century, the Sētupati's protective role with respect to deities, other donors and temple servants, was eroded by decisions of the Government. The revenue bureaucracy of the Madras Government, and subsequently courts of law assumed elements of his "protective" function. As a result, the Sētupati was rendered a mere donor in the temple, and the honors therein distributed were rendered, in the eyes of the law, trifling trinkets.

Decisions in two celebrated court cases in which the Sētupati was a litigant may be adduced as evidence for pursuing this argument. The first decision

[42]For an analysis of donors and their Incorporation into the temple, see Carol Appadurai Breckenridge, "The Śrī Mīṉākṣi Sundarēsvarar Temple: Worship and Endowments in South India, 1833 to 1925," Ph d. dissertation, University of Wisconsin, 1976.

was rendered in 1874, in a case popularly known as the "Ramesvaram Temple Case." The second decision came in the "Kamuthi Temple Case of 1908." These decisions had significant ramifications. They applied not only to the relationship between the Sētupati and the particular temple involved in each case, but also to numerous other temples in Ramnad Samastāṉam. Before discussing the pertinence of the two cases cited above, a brief overview of the religious and "charitable" institutions with which the Sētupati maintained various transactions is in order.

In 1892 at least, Samastāṉam revenue was administered through four funds, three of which were either religious or charitable in nature. They were: Ayan (referred to as the Samastāṉam) Funds, Dēvastāṉam (or temple) Funds, Chattram (or choultry) Funds, and Dharma Makamai Funds. Of the 2,167 villages which comprised the Samastāṉam in 1803, more than half or 1,340 villages were administered as *ayan* lands.[43] Another 827 villages (or about per cent of the total) had been "alienated" for "charitable and religious" purposes. Of these, 366 villages were attached to temples, 67 to chattrams, 345 to private persons, and 46 to other. Between 1803 and 1892 another 330 grants were made, bringing the total number of villages "alienated" for religious and charitable purposes to 1,157 villages or nearly half of the villages in the Samastāṉam.

Of the 379 temples associated with the Dēvastānam Fund of the Samastāṉam, seventy important temples as well as numerous smaller ones were under the direct management of the Sētupati.[44] Of these, eleven were designated as Vaiṣṇavite, forty-nine as Śaivite, seven as goddess, and three as other. Various Sētupatis were cited as having been the founders or original donors of nine of these seventy temples. Other pre-nineteenth century founders of the seventy temples under Sētupati management in 1892 included: 3 royal officers, 18 Pandian kings, 9 sages, 4 Chakravartis, 1 Ceṭṭiyar, 2 Mahajanams, 1 Piḷḷai, 3 paṇṭārams, and 17 other. Other than the seventy temples referred to above, there were numerous temples under what came to be known as "private" management. Between 1873 and 1887, when Ramnad was under the administrative control of the Court of Wards, the annual income collected from Samastāṉam temples ranged from Rs 76,021 to 151,279.[45] And in the year 1887-88, a surplus of Rs 267,141 remained in the Dēvastānam Fund of the Samastāṉam.

Throughout Madras Presidency in the nineteenth century, temple management came to be a hotly disputed issue. In the course of repeated litigation, for example, a paṇṭāram[46] rather than the Sētupati, came to be the "manager"

[43]Rama Rao, *Ramnad Manual*, p. 10.

[44]*Ibid.*, p. 79.

[45]*Ibid.*, p 80.

[46]A non-Brahman priest. In the case of the Rāmēsvaram Temple, it is likely that the pantarams performed the services of *stānikars*.

of the renowned, all-India pilgrimage center at Rāmēsvaram, the Śrī Rāmanātasvāmi Temple, and its fifty-seven villages which yielded an estimated 40,000 rupees annually. Tension between the Sētupati and the pantaram resulted in the famous and precedent-setting, Ramesvaram Temple Case, the first of the two cases under consideration here.

In 1864, simultaneous with the reorganization of the Madras court system which resulted in the formation of the Madras High Court of Judicature, the Sētupati took the case known as *Rajah Muttu Ramalinga Setupati v. Perianayagum Pillai*, to court.[47] Ten years and three court decisions later, the Judicial Committee of the Privy Council rendered their decision in the appeal case. The Sētupati was deprived of any role in the "appointment" or the "confirmation" of the *dharmakarta* who managed the Rāmēsvaram Temple. This decision confirmed in the courts what had, since 1801, been established in the revenue bureaucracy: kings possessed no sovereign "rights." These rights, albeit usually unspecified, were in turn claimed by the Governments of Madras, Bengal and Bombay, and subsequent to 1858, by the Government of India. The decision read:

> The powers they enjoyed as sovereigns, whatever they may have been, have now passed to the British government, and the present zemindar [Sētupati] can have *no* rights with respect to the pagoda [temple] other than those of a private and proprietary nature, which they can establish by evidence to belong to them.[48]

Effectively, in the eyes of the law, the Sētupati ceased being the "protector" of temple donations, and was rendered one among many donors.

Encroachments on the Sētupati's relationship to Hindu temples was not new. In general, the revenue bureaucracy had long before assumed the right of supervision over temple lands. Authority with respect to temples in Madras Presidency had been formalized in the preamble of Regulation VII of 1817. It declared that "the duty of the Government [was] to provide that all. . .endowments be applied to the real intent and will of the grantor." This supervisory role of the Government was designed to prevent or to punish misappropriation of temple lands, produce, and income, while providing for the continuation of those ceremonies necessary to insure the contentment of the people. Up until 1874, misappropriation of funds or mismanagement of land was, therefore, the general reason for interference by the government, usually through the Board of Revenue, in temple affairs. The Privy Council decision in the Ramesvaram Temple Case, however, altered the legal authority of the

[47]Reported in (1874) Moore's *Indian Appeals* 209 (233); and in *The Revenue Register*, 15 June 1874, 6, Vol. 8, pp. 171-78.

[48]*Ibid.*, p. 175.

revenue bureaucracy. Now, revenue authorities could exercise control over temple servants and personnel as well as temple lands and villages. Unwittingly perhaps, revenue and judicial authorities, therefore, came to determine who qualified for what in the temple, the historical function of the Sētupati. Emphasis had shifted from the Sētupati's constitutive role to his donative one.

The protracted litigation which preceded this case is sobering. It suggests the inability of local institutions under the Madras Government to bring disputing parties to a position of conciliation. Moreover, attempted resolutions to the dispute reveal that each time a problem was posed, the Collector created, and then enforced, new rules with respect to temple management, as well as with respect to the Sētupati's relationship to the temple. Between 1815 and 1864, when the case finally went to court, both the Sētupati and the temple pantaram (Venkatachellam), a non-Brahman Śaivite "priest," claimed to be the *dharmakarta* of the temple.[49] Similarly, the Sētupati claimed a role in the installation of any new pantaram in the temple. In an 1815 pantaram-Sētupati succession dispute, the Rāni requested the Collector to "prevent. . .Venkatachellum being invested with the parivattam cloth and other emblems of the pandaram office."[50] A recital of petitions followed, with the result that the Rāni claimed the role of temple *dharmakarta*, thereby denying the claim of the pantaram. A Collector's decision in 1816 disregarded the Rāni's claim by ordering the Tahsildar to permit Venkatachellam to be installed in the office "with the appropriate honors and offerings." In supporting the claims of the pantaram, however, the Collector introduced one major innovation: the supervision of temple endowments was to be shared between the pantaram *and* a servant from the Collector's office. Here, misappropriation was an excuse for gaining a share of control over temple finances, which had not been considered in the original settlement of the Samastāṉam in 1803.

Again in 1832 the dispute surfaced. Arguing that custom ought to be followed so as to avoid disturbances, the Acting Collector of Madura ordered the government appointed guardian of the Ramnad Sētupati, then a minor, to restore to the pantaram's management the villages of the temple, and to do so without delay. A compromise reached in 1837 determined how the Sētupati and the pantaram would address one another. The petition from Setu Ramanada Pandaram, *vicaraṇai-karta* of the Rāmanātasvami Dēvastāṉam, to the Collector of Madura, read:

> I shall abide by the directions of said zemindar in regard to the aforesaid devastanam pagoda villages, sibbundies and other affairs, dispose of all the receipts and disbursements in conjunction with the *samprathi* appointed by

[49] A rough translation of the term *dharmakarta* is temple manager.

[50] *The Revenue Register, op. cit.*, p. 174.

> the said zemindar, and send to the zemindar accounts of receipts and disbursements, with my signature therein. That in addressing arzis [petitions] to the zemindar, I shall state "addressed by Setu Ramanada, Pandaram of Ramesvaram Devastanam, to the presence of Setupati Rajah Avergal," and that the zemindar will, in his communications to my address, state, "addressed to Setu Ramanada, Pandaram of Ramesvaram Devastanam." As the zemindar has forwarded an arzi to your presence, praying for making over to me the said devastanam etc., from attachment, I beg you will be pleased to make over the said devastanam etc. to me as per mamool.[51]

The pantaram was reinstated in the temple where he remained as manager until 1854 when he died. Again, the succession dispute arose, and resulted in a case before the newly formed Madras High Court in 1864.

After protracted litigation in the lower courts, it was decided that the proper framing of the issues in the case was:

> Is the zemindar the real trustee [*dharmakarta*] of the pagoda, and the defendent pandaram, the wrongdoer, or is the zemindar seeking, without legal title, to possess himself of a valuable property to which, as the defendents allege, he has not title?[52]

The Court found that "during the whole period of the existence of British rule, these opposing parties have been in litigation upon the matter, and that the titles now claimed have been constantly disallowed by tribunals having power to pass a provisional decision." With that, the case was dismissed on the grounds that the Sētupati could not prove he had historically played a role in the pantaram's installation.

On appeal to the Judicial Committee of the Privy Council, agents of the Sētupati argued that when a new pantaram succeeded to the *dharmakarta* position, a ritual transaction with the Sētupati was necessary:

> The evidence of usage through a long series of years proves that the pandaram ought to be nominated by the zemindar, but if not. . .he ought at least, to be presented to him for confirmation, and the lack of confirmation makes his appointment void. The zemindar is the *dharmakarta* of this pagoda, and it is to be inferred from the very title that this confirmation of the pandaram is necessary.[53]

Considering the disputed title of *dharmakarta* inconsequential, the Judge

[51]Moore's *Indian Appeals, op. cit.*
[52]*Ibid.*
[53]*Ibid.*

ordered "Their Lordships. . . to abstain from using this appellation. . . ." Thereupon, he argued that he would "proceed to consider the substantial issue" of the case, namely "whether the zemindar [had] established the right, under whatever name, to make or confirm the appointment of pandarams." He astutely concluded that probably:

> pandarams, on their elections, were presented to the Sētupati, not for the confirmation of their title, but to obtain from him, as the great chieftain of the district, a recognition of it, and to secure his protection and support.[54]

But he dismissed the case on the grounds that the Sētupati had nowhere proved his role in the "appointment" of pantarams.

A second protracted, yet highly charged, court case in which the Sētupati was a litigant was popularly known as the "Kamuthi Temple Case."[55] Subsequently touted as the first temple-entry case, it represented an unsuccessful attempt by a mobile group of former toddy-tappers then known as Nadars, to enter and to receive honor in a Maravar controlled temple. As the "hereditary trustee" of the Śrī Mīṉākṣi Sundarēsvarar Temple in the town of Kamuthi, the Sētupati charged that Nadars had violated custom and usage by forcibly entering the temple. In their 1908 decision, the Judicial Committee of the Privy Council supported the Sētupati's charges. According to the decision, Nadars had been, and therefore, should continue to be, excluded from worship in the temple.

As in the Ramesvaram Temple Case, this decision of the courts undermined the constitutive capacity of the Sētupati as king and as protector of transactions in his domain. In demanding fixity with respect to their interpretation of custom and usage, the court deprived the Sētupati of his role as grantor of privileges, a role which permitted innovation and alteration in the distribution of temple honors. The Sētupati sought recognition of his role from the Nadars. There is every suggestion that had he received it, Nadars could have "come forward" (*munta vā*) through established procedures, namely by recognizing the Maravar Sētupati as higher in rank than they were. Nadars, however, argued that the Brahmanical character of some of their customs made them superior to Maravars whose customs constituted a departure from the practises of most caste-Hindus.

Before discussing the relevant details in this case, the context in which it

[54]*The Revenue Register*, *op. cit.*, p. 178.

[55]*M. Bhaskara Setupati Avergal vs. Irulappan Nadan*, Original Suit 33 of 1898, Court of the Sub-judge, Madura (East); Appeal Suit 11 and 77 of 1900, High Court of Judicature, Madras. Judgement, 14 February 1901. Also see Robert Hardgrave, Jr., *The Nadars of Tamilnad: The Political Culture of a Community in Change*, University of California Press, Berkeley, 1969.

occurred is noteworthy. In Ramand, the late nineteenth century was a period in which the cultural markers of kingship, namely donation and protection of temple ritual and endowments, received renewed attention. Symptoms of kingship were to be seen everywhere. Navarātri was celebrated with pomp and ceremony; non-Brahman monastic institutions and feeding houses were being endowed; and attempts were being made to protect temples from the inroads being made on them by mobile groups.

That the Sētupati chose to engage in kingly activities at this time may appear to be surprising, if not paradoxical. At this time the Samastāṉam was experiencing great difficulties. It was heavily indebted; famines and cyclones occasionally caused water shortages in the already parched land; prices rose considerably; and finally, "rioting and looting" invited the punitive measures of the Madras Special Police. Other changes disturbed the economic and social order. Migration of labor to plantations in Ceylon and Mauritius under Kāṇkani recruitment was on the increase; resident mobile groups argued for honors equal to, if not higher than, that of the Sētupati; and conversion movements of Hindus to Christianity, and more curiously, of Hindus to radical Islam, disturbed the peace.

The apparent paradox of the Sētupati's active engagement in kingly activities, during a period of immense stress, can be dissolved. It was precisely in such potentially explosive periods that the Sētupati appears to have historically affirmed his kingship through massive gifting activities to temples and choultries and through ritual celebrations in which he was invoked as a royal personage.

It was in this context of renewed king-like activity that the Sētupati, designated in Anglo-Indian law as hereditary trustee, took the Kamuthi Temple Case to court. Although not framed in terms of temple honors, honor and its misuse was of central concern to both the plaintiff and the defendants. A violent incident provoked the case on 14 May 1898. A group of fifty to sixty Nadars, accompanied by drummers and torches, forcibly entered the Kamuthi Temple in order to honor the presiding deities of Śrī Mīṉakṣi and Sundarēsvarar with their offerings of coconuts, camphor and garlands. The priest, on behalf of the divine couple, refused to accept these offerings. Bypassing the priests, the Nadars themselves entered into the inner *sanctum*, and themselves honored the deity. The Nadars were not content with a mere act of physical entry into the temple. Rather, they were intent on engaging in a transaction with the presiding deities, ultimately the source of the highest honors.

Arguing that disgrace had been brought to both the temple and to its community of devotees, the Sētupati claimed substantial material damages. The case was valued at about Rs 3,000. Of that, he claimed half of the total valuation of the case, for "loss of honor and reputation to the temple caused by unlawful acts."

Moreover, in the depositions given by over one hundred witnesses, honors exchanges and transactions as constitutive of rank, authority and resource control, were a recurring concern. A Vaiṣṇavite Brahman astrologer and *purōhita* in the temple recalled the manipulation of symbolic paraphernalia and actions by Nadars.[56] He observed that the carriage by Nadars of both *kāvatis* and marriage palanquins around the agraharam and the temple had been on the increase. But, he made a distinction between these two activities. The carriage of a *kāvati* was "considered a religious duty or vow," with the implication being that it was an acceptable activity for Nadars. The perambulation of a palanquin, however, when the community celebrated a marriage, he charged, was "an assertion of equal social status."

Another witness recited an incident in which Nadars withheld honors from a Maravar cultivator. In return, Maravars sought to have honors withheld from Nadars. The recital of events read:

> Vellachami Tevan of Pasumbone, a well-to-do ryot, led a combination about 1885 against the Nadars. He used to come to Ramnad often where he was honored by all classes. They used to take off their upper cloths and give him betel-leaf. Nadars refused him this. Vellachami Tevan got together the other classes to combine and boycott the Nadars. They denied them fire and water. The idol was not taken in the direction of their streets at Mahanavami. The other classes were told not to associate with Nadars.[57]

Nadar refusal to honor Vellachami Tēvan might be interpreted as a claim to a position of honor at least equal to his. This pretention invited a counter-response. Śri Mīṉākṣi and Sundarēsvarar were not processed through those neighborhoods where Nadars resided. Rerouting this critical processional of the deities and the Sētupati on *vijayadasami*, the tenth day of Navarātri when the arrow-shooting contest was celebrated, so as to avoid Nadar streets, insured that Nadar householders would be boycotted in the deity's distribution of honors. Normally, Nadar householders would present offerings to the processional deities from temporarily constructed thatched sheds in front of their homes. These offerings would be received by the deity and a portion of them returned to the worshipper in a ceremony known as *tirukkan*. For Nadars, this was critical since, at this time, they could not enter into the *sanctum* of the temple for the receipt of other honors.

Up until 1898, Nadars had been considered a service, and hence unprivileged, community, dependent on the commands of privileged groups like the Ceṭṭiyārs and Vellalas. In various ways, they vicariously and symbiotically partook of the honor afforded them by the temple. They did so through proxies who themselves received honors distributed by the deity in ritual contexts

[56] Original Suit 33 of 1898, Judgement, 20 July 1899, plaintiff witness no. 20, p. 18.
[57] *Ibid.*, plaintiff witness no. 4, p. 30.

which had been generated by Nadar gifting activity. Proxies then redistributed these honors to Nadars. In the Tirupparankundrum Temple (Madurai District), for example, "flower canopies were placed in the arthamandapam by Vellalas, while Nadars [paid] the cost." Similarly, in the Śrī Mīṉākṣi Sundarēsvarar Temple at Madurai, the stanikar claimed that temple honors were indirectly distributed to Nadars:

> Even castes who are denied entry, perform thirukkans or mantagapadi[58] which is conducted by their mahamai kannakan [accountant] while they worship from a distance. . . the holy cloth is not tied and vibhuti or prasadam are not given directly to Shanars at this mantagapadi.[59]

The Judge in the original suit of 1898 was astute and methodical in elucidating most aspects of transactions in South India. But, although he was puzzled that witnesses did not refer to the Nadars as polluting, he nowhere seems to have understood the place of temple-honors and the relationship of the Sētupati to them in determining relations between communities. After amassing an impressive body of information, he determined that it was the custom in the Kamuthi temple to exclude Nadars from worship. The case then went to the High Court, and subsequently to the Privy Council.

Of particular interest in light of the Judge's determination that Nadars had customarily been excluded from the temple was an attempted compromise in the year 1901. The Nadars and the Sētupati announced their proposed agreement. The Sētupati agreed to allow Nadars to worship in the temple, with one qualification. They were to worship "in the same manner and to the same extent as the Vellala, Chetty and other sudra sects of the Hindu community. . ." Nadars were to have "no rights of access and worship other than those enjoyed and exercised by the aforementioned."

A clue to why this agreement may have been reached lies in a marginal note written by the Judge. In the column of his own printed copy of the compromise proposal, the Judge wrote: ". . . no mention in the compromise of the benefit to the temple of presents by Shanars." He intimated that he considered the prospective "presents" offered by the Nadars (then called Shanars) to be bribes. But, another construction can be placed on the giving of "gifts" by Nadars. Such gifting activity would have placed Nadars in a direct transactional relationship with the presiding divine couple, Śrī Mīṉākṣi and Sundarēsvarar, from whom they would have received temple-honors. The privilege of so doing required the intervention of the Sētupati who, presumably, caused

[58] A ritual celebration embedded in a ten to twelve day festival in which the donor invites the deity to come, sit-in-state and be entertained in a hall (*maṇṭapam*) constructed for this purpose.

[59] Original Suit 33 of 1898, Judgement, plaintiff witness no. 32, p. 42.

them to be appropriate to engage in temple transactions. In this particular case, his intervention may have been necessary both from the perspective of the Sētupati and from that of other, potentially competitive, communities. Hence, limits were to be placed on the appropriateness of the Nadars. They were to be bound by those rules of exchange and prestation which operated for other specified communities.

Having considered the joint proposal of the Nadars and the Sētupati, the Judge concluded that it was unacceptable. The lower court judge had found that the prevailing custom in the Kamuthi temple had been to exclude Nadars from worship therein. In light of this custom, therefore, the Sētupati, according to the High Court Judge, did not have the power to enter into a compromise which would "alter the fundamental character and uses of the temple as ascertained by judicial authority." Seven years after this proposed compromise, the decision of the Judicial Committee of the Privy Council sustained the decision of both lower courts. The Sētupati's original charge that Nadars had been, and ought to continue to be, excluded from worship in the Kamuthi temple was supported.

But, it might be argued, what the Sētupati had hoped to achieve in the original case could have been accomplished in the compromise agreement had it been enacted. His concern with Nadars' access to worship in the temple was a concern with respect to their aspirations to be superior to Maravars, the community from which the Setupati came. More specifically, he was preoccupied with his constitutive role with respect to worshippers and priests. That would have been honored in the enactment of the compromise solution.

In his decision, the Judge not only overlooked the place of temple honors in this dispute, but he also misjudged the place of "custom and usage" in determining human behavior. Custom had not had the fixity which courts of law preferred to believe it had. By refusing to give effect to the proposed 1901 compromise, the Judge was creating, and not sustaining, custom and usage. Custom would have permitted the Sētupati to find Nadars appropriate to enter the temple. Instead, the Judge made the courts the arbitrators of custom, if not the innovators of it. This position of the courts is not surprising since they had been self-consciously assuming this role. In Sivakasi, a town neighboring Kamuthi, another Śaivite temple had been closed due to Nadar (there called Shanar) and Maravar disputes. The government investigator reported, in a personal letter to his superior, that:

> So long as the position of the Shanars is what it is viz. that of a caste claiming higher privileges than that their neighbors will allow them, so long must the administration of this district be extremely difficult. . . . No arbitration, and no order will put an end to the present state of tension. Gradually, the civil courts will, by their decisions, determine the actual

> status of these Shanars, and gradually they will accept the position assigned them.[60]

In conclusion, he continued: "We are dealing with thousands of rascals all longing to go at each others throats, who respect nothing but the strict enforcement of the law."

In the post-1864 period, court decisions systematically reinterpreted both the Sētupati's role with respect to Hindu temples, and the role of the Hindu temple with respect to the kingship of the Sētupati. The Sētupati was considered a donor to the temple who had ceased to possess sovereign rights This reinterpretation was in part rooted in the notion that the Maravars were a "low caste." Even the distinguished lawyer, J.B. Norton, allowed the perceived status of the Maravars in relation to temple pantarams to influence the way in which he framed legal issues:

> The zemindars of Ramnad are of a low caste—the Maravar caste—and the eaters of animal food—the pandarams are of the pure Shiva caste. Therefore, it is contrary to all precedent and religious usage and propriety that the zemindar should personally invest the pandaram with the *cashayem* or red cloth, the beads and the ear-rings, the symbols of the sacred office. Vencatachellum must have been regarded by the zemindar Ramasvami Setupati as duly appointed, otherwise, the latter would not have allowed him to perform the ceremony of tying the parivattam, or cloth of honor, round his head on the day of his installation.[61]

But the logic of caste relations could not fully explicate the relationship of the Sētupati to presiding deities in Hindu temples, temple priests and other donative groups. Kings are kings by virtue of what they do, and not necessarily through fulfillment of ascriptive criteria.

CONCLUSION

Ritual changes were among the many innovations initiated in late nineteenth century India. Ritual was reformulated and the past reinterpreted in keeping with ideas which motivated a rapidly expanding imperial system.[62] But even in this changing imperial context in which an English queen was entitled "Queen Empress of India," the Rājā of Ramnad continued to generate rituals in which he was celebrated as a king. How is this performance of rituals,

[60]Loose letter included in *Disturbances in Madura and Tinnevelli*, Madras Government Press, 1899.

[61]Moore's *Indian Appeals, op. cit.*

[62]In this respect, we are indebted to the work in progress of Bernard S. Cohn.

which appear to have been inconsonant with an imperial system in which authority was increasingly centralized in an imperial capital, to be interpreted?

The celebration of the royal ritual of Navarātri in 1892 might be interpreted to have been an effort by the recently installed Sētupati to revitalize Hindu kingship as it had flourished in the seventeenth and early eighteenth centuries. Symptomatic of his kingship was his sponsorship of ritual events which placed him in a direct transactional relationship with temple-deities. It was this relationship which had been the source of royal authority. In this symbiosis, the deity was the source of the king's royal honors; and the Sētupati was the source of the deity's royal privileges, privileges which included the distribution of honors.

Such revitalization, however, in 1892 occurred in a hostile, if not antagonistic, context. Having been deprived of such kingly activities as conquest and conflict-resolution, he was also deprived by court decisions of contexts in which his constitutive authority could be invoked. In 1874, the pantaram was unambiguously, and without engaging in ritual transactions with the Sētupati, made the manager of the prominent pilgrimage center at Rāmēsvaram. The Sētupati was recognized only as a donor in, and not a protector of, the temple. Similarly, eight years after his majestic celebration of Navarātri in 1892, he was deprived of another context in which to invoke his authority. The issue of the incorporation of Nadars as donors in the temple was decided by the courts and not by the Sētupati, the temple's hereditary trustee. In this context, the key fact is not that the court ultimately decided against the Shanars, but rather that this decision was made solely through legal fiat, instead of being decided by the royal authority of the Sētupati.

How is the effort of the Sētupati to revitalize Hindu kingship in the late nineteenth century to be assessed? In relation to the pre-British royal behavioral model of the Sētupati, this effort must be deemed to have failed. As the Sētupati had come to be deprived both of his capacity to wage war and his capacity to allocate temple-related privileges, both crucial aspects of his previous royal role, in effect, the Sētupati was reduced to a mere donor in the temple. The grand celebration of the Navarātri festival in 1892 was an effort to claim his full royal status. But given the erosion of this royal status by other forces in the late nineteenth century, this was an unrealizable claim.

This is not to imply, however, that the 1892 Navarātri celebration was the last royal gesture of the Maravar royal family. In the twentieth century, such royal rituals were perpetuated, participation in colonial ritual contexts eagerly pursued, and temple management and donation vigorously continued. But in the changing bureaucratic and political contexts of the twentieth century, no such strategies could fully revive the kingship of the Sētupatis.

What can be said of the role of temples in relation to this major and perhaps irrevocable shift in the royal status of the Sētupati lineage? It has been the argument of this essay that, throughout the period under consideration, temples were primary contexts for the definition of the royal role of Sētupatis, as well as a sensitive index of changes in this role. In the seventeenth and early eighteenth centuries, the Sētupati had been a generous donor, a kingly protector and an authoritative source of temple privileges. By the end of the nineteenth century, while the Sētupati continued to be a central donor, his authoritative and constitutive role in relation to temples had given way to a competitive situation in which the Sētupati became one among many aspirants to temple control.

Śiva, Mīnākṣi, Viṣṇu—
Reflections on a Popular Myth in Madurai[1]

DENNIS HUDSON

Every year in the month of Citrā (April-May) two Hindu festivals take place in the South Indian city of Madurai, timed with reference to the same full moon. One is the wedding of the gods Śiva and Devī conducted at the major Śaiva temple in the center of the old city, which concludes with a procession of the bride and bridegroom in their image forms around the outskirts of that city. The other is the journey of the god Viṣṇu to the Vaigai River bordering on the old city, which concludes with his return to his Vaiṣṇava temple twelve miles to the north of Madurai. The wedding of Śiva, known locally as Sundareśvarar (The Beautiful Lord), with an *avatār* of Devī, known locally as Mīnākṣi (The Fish Eyed), is, according to their temple tradition, the result of Śiva's conquest of this queen of Madurai after her own conquest of the universe. The wedding establishes their joint rulership over the city. The journey of Viṣṇu, known locally as Aḻagar (The Beautiful Lord), to the river is said by his temple tradition to be for the benefit of his devotees and for the sake of fulfilling a promise he once made to the *ṛṣi* Maṇḍūka to bestow *darśana* upon him and grant him eventual release from *samsāra*. The journey also establishes his rulership over the region between his temple and the river.

Aḻagar sets out for the river in time to enter it on the morning of the Citrā full moon day, usually leaving his own temple after the wedding ceremonies for Śiva and Mīnākṣi have been completed and shortly after they have begun their procession around the old borders of the city. Both the wedding and the journey are ordinary festivals prescribed by the *āgamas* of their respective traditions and at the high point of each a crowd estimated to number about

[1]The following reflections represent a further working out on my part of the conclusion to my paper, "Two Citrā Festivals in Madurai," forthcoming in *Interludes: Religious Festivals in South India and Ceylon*, ed. by G.R. Welbon and Glenn E. Yocum, New Delhi, Manohar. An earlier version of this paper was presented at the All-India Oriental Conference, Kurukshetra University, 26-28 December 1974. This version has been shaped in part by discussions with R.N. Sampath, Professor of Sanskrit, Presidency College, Madras, and with Professor Alan Babb, Department of Anthropology and Sociology, Amherst College. I am grateful for their criticism and suggestions.

500,000 people gathers to participate in the auspicious presence of divinity in its midst.[2] It is quite clear from the myths and rituals of the two temples that from their respective official perspectives, these two festivals have nothing to do with each other, sharing only geographical proximity, timing with reference to the same full moon and thousands of the same devotees.[3]

What is intriguing, however, is that in the minds of these many devotees these two festivals are not separate and distinct, but form a single festival, the "Cittirai Festival" (*Cittirai peruviḻā*), in which the wedding of Śiva and Mīnākṣi and the journey of Aḻagar are fused into a unified drama consisting of two scenes enacted by the priests and servants of the two temples. This fusion is expressed in a pervasive oral myth, the main outline of which is the following.[4]

Aḻagar, through his identity as Kṛṣṇa, is Mīnākṣi's brother and is naturally expected to attend her wedding with Śiva.[5] In fact, though the popular myth does not say this, the essential part of the marriage is the *dhāra vār* ritual in which he gives her away to Śiva to be his property. For some reason, however, the exact time of the wedding is not made clear to Aḻagar so that while crossing the Vaigai River to enter the old city for the wedding he learns from another form of Viṣṇu (Kūḍalaḻagar) whom he meets in the riverbed that the wedding has already taken place. This performance of the wedding without him, the brother of the bride, he regards as an extreme insult and therefore refuses to enter the city, though he sends his wedding present on to his sister through Kūḍalaḻagar. From this it appears that his anger is directed towards Śiva, the king of the city and his new brother-in-law, rather than towards his sister, Mīnākṣi. Angrily Aḻagar turns around and proceeds along

[2]Census of India, 1961. *Madras: Fairs and Festivals*, ed. by P.K. Nambiar and K.C. Narayana Kurup, Madras, Government Press, 1968, pp. 32-33.

[3]Each of these festivals has been described at length by me in the aforecited study, "Two Citrā Festivals in Madurai."

[4]This popular oral myth was the only explanation ever given to me when I resided in Madurai between 1960 and 1962, and my awareness of the fact that there were two distinct festivals only arose after I began to study the 'Cittirai Festival" in 1970. Despite the fact that W. Francis in *Madura: Madras District Gazetters* (I, Madras, 1914, pp. 285-86) describes this popular myth and notes that it has no canonical authority, few have been aware of this. See, for example, J.P Jones, "Madurai," *Encyclopedia of Religion and Ethics*, ed. by James Hastings, Vol VII, pp. 239-40; Lowell Thomas, *India: Land of the Black Pagoda*, New York, Collier and Son, 1930, pp. 160-61; and N. Padmanabhan, "Chithra Festival," *Sunday Standard Magazine, Section*, Madras 12 May 1968.

[5]According to K.A. Nilakanta Sastri, Durgā is identified in one part of the *Mahābhārata* as the virgin sister of Kṛṣṇa, while in another part as Umā, the wife of Śiva. He also notes that in the Smārta Pañcāyatana Pūjā, two Śaiva and two Vaiṣṇava male images are used, and the fifth, the Goddess, is common to both, "as mythology makes her the wife of Śiva and the sister of Viṣṇu." See *Development of Religion in South India*, Bombay, Orient Longmans, 1963, pp. 61 and 65. This iconographic fact is suggestive of the role Mīnākṣi plays as mediator between Śiva and Viṣṇu as will be discussed below.

the north bank of the river to the nearby hamlet of Vaṇḍiyūr where he spends the night with Tulukka Nācciyār, his Muslim consort who was once the daughter of a Sultan in Delhi.[6] The next morning he processes to a *maṇḍapa* on the riverbed where he bestows *darśana* on the *ṛṣi* Maṇḍūka. Then he spends the night on the northern bank of the river, opposite the old city, portraying his ten *avatār* forms to his assembled devotees, after which he makes the twelve-mile journey back to his own temple, still angry about the wedding.

This popular oral myth fits the two festivals together so that the transition from the wedding to the journey in the five or six days around the Citrā full moon is perceived as a change of scene in a single divine drama—a drama in which the actors in the form of images tended by the priests behave like royal human beings. The myth blurs the distinctions which are quite clearly articulated in the actual performance of the two festivals by changing the motivation for Aḻagar's journey and by explaining the crucial ritual events of that journey in terms different from those expressed in the story told by his own temple. The popular myth presupposes the wedding myth of the Śaiva temple, but for it the important facts are that Aḻagar never even enters into the city, much less participates in the wedding, and that he is angry.

Why has such a popular myth developed and why has it remained the dominant means by which most of the half-million participants understand this conjunction of two distinct festivals? This question intrigues me and I would like to make some contributions here towards an answer in the form of suggestions for further research and reflection. It will seem to some, I suspect, that I read too much out of what can be understood simply as an etiological myth arising out of "mythic consciousness" to answer the logical question of why these gods behave as they do at this time every year. But I think it is worth probing this popular myth a bit to see whether the reasons for its perception of the gods as belonging to one another, for its concern to unify the two festivals into one, and the form this unification takes has been created by "mythic consciousness" for more profound reasons. These reasons may partially account for the vitality with which Hindus in the region have been participating in the "Cittirai Festival" for centuries. Such a probing may also shed some light on the general question of the origins and meanings of myths in Hindu culture.

[6]This aspect of the popular myth is probably derived from the Tulukka Nācciyār tradition of the Śrī Rangam Temple about eighty miles to the north on the Kāverī River. See two studies by V.N. Hari Rao, *Koil Olugu: The Chronicle of the Srirangam Temple with Historical Notes*, Madras, Rochouse and Sons, 1961, pp. 24-31, 33; and *The Śrīrangam Temple: Art and Architecture*, Tirupati, The Sri Venkateswara University, 1967, p. 104. The Śrī Vīrarāghava Perumāḷ Temple in Vaṇḍiyūr provides no physical evidence, however, that the Nācciyār with whom he spends the night is Muslim, though I was assured that she was by devotees at that temple in 1969.

It is impossible to determine who originated this popular myth, of course, and therefore I will call the creator "mythic consciousness" or the "popular mind" for want of more accurate terms. The origin of the myth, however, could not have been before the juxtaposition of the two festivals around the same full moon and, as we will observe, this appears to have occurred in the early seventeenth century under the rule of the Hindu ruler of Madurai, Tirumala Nāyak.

The form of the myth—antagonisms between brothers-in-law at the time of a wedding—probably derives from at least two intentions "mythic consciousness" had in creating the myth. The first intention was to express a unity between Śiva and Aḻagar by bringing them together into one family through the marriage of one to the sister of the other. This is easily done since it is logical that if one festival is a wedding and the other is a journey, the journey is to the wedding, especially since the traveller, Aḻagar, is already assumed by the wedding myth to be the brother of the bride, Mīnākṣi. In fact, according to the ritual of the Śaiva temple, Viṣṇu is actually present at the wedding in the form of an image processed from Tirupparaṅkuṉṟam, a Śaiva temple about five miles southwest of Madurai. The effect of this marriage theme in the popular myth is to bring the temple of Aḻagar, twelve miles to the north, into relation with the Mīnākṣi-Sundareśvara Temple of Madurai as the palaces of two kings who are brothers-in-law and thus members of the same family or sub-caste (*kulam*). The nature of this *kulam* will be discussed shortly.

The second intention, however, is to express a tension and antagonism within this family (*kulam*) which makes the unity of the relatives aligned through this marriage precarious. The timing of the two festivals means that that if the wedding is chosen as the explanation for his journey, Aḻagar will inevitably arrive at the river after the ceremony has been completed. This fact indicates, I suggest, that in choosing this motivation for the journey, "mythic consciousness" intended to point up an antagonism between Śiva and Aḻagar and between their respective palaces and retinues. The popular myth intends, I suggest, to symbolize a tension-ridden unity by portraying two divine kings who are rivals and yet are members of the same family or sub-caste (*kulam*) through marriage. The motivations for and meanings of this dual symbolism may be partly understood by investigating aspects of Madurai history and Tamil Hindu social organization.

History

When looking at the history of the city of Madurai and the region around it, four aspects seem relevant for an understanding of this myth. First, Madurai was the traditional capital of the Pāṇḍyan kingdom which, like the other Tamil kingdoms, experienced a long history of rivalry between the traditions of Śiva and of Viṣṇu. This rivalry extends at least from the Hindu *bhakti* movements of the eighth and ninth centuries and Madurai has been associated with the Śaiva tradition although the Pāṇḍyan kingdom also contains important ancient Vaiṣṇava temples and pilgrimage centers, one of which is the temple of Aḻagar. The Vaiṣṇava tradition in the Pāṇḍyan region may be characterized as a vigorous and defensive minority in a predominantly Śaiva, or at least non-Vaiṣṇava, Hindu society.[7]

Second, Tirumala Nāyak (1623-1659) was probably the ruler who brought the wedding and journey festivals together and expanded both to their present forms.[8] He was the last of a series of rulers representing the Vijayanagara Empire whose emperors had been active in expanding the temples of the region, both Śaiva and Vaiṣṇava. Tirumala Nāyak expanded the Mīnākṣi-Sundareśvara Temple and in the process constructed two large cars (*tēr, ratha*) in which the images of the bride and bridegroom would be pulled around the borders of the city. At that time, however, the wedding festival was timed to take place two months earlier, with reference to the full moon of Māci (February-March) and not to the full moon of Citrā (April-May). Moreover, the month of Māci was harvest time and therefore there was not enough manpower available to pull the huge newly constructed cars.

The month of Citrā, on the other hand, fell during the hot season when agricultural work was dormant aud people were plentiful at the time of Aḻagar's journey from the Aḻagar Temple to the Vaigai River at the Citrā full moon. Tirumala Nāyak therefore switched the time of the wedding from Māci to Citrā and moved the then existing Citrā festival to Māci. In addition, he expanded the wedding festival to include the *līlā* of Mīnākṣi's coronation as queen of Madurai and expanded the journey festival by bringing the goal of Aḻagar's journey closer to the border of Madurai at its present site in the riverbed. Large numbers of people were now able to come to both festivals to pull the enormous new cars for the wedding, to conduct profitable cattle markets, to mingle with one another and to provide the splendid celebrations the Nāyak desired. Incidentally, Tirumala Nāyak also demonstrated in these changes his power to shift festivals around even when doing so went against the explicit prescriptions of their ritual texts.[9]

[7]For documentation of this history of rivalry and of the minority position of the Vaiṣṇavas in Tamil Nad, see the study by Burton Stein included in this volume.

[8]The following account is based on A.Ki. Parantāmaṉār, "Tirumalai Nāyakkar Tiruppaṇikaḷ 1623-1659," P.T. Rajan, ed., *Madurai Sri Meenakshi Sundareswarar Mahakumbabhishekam Souvenir*, Madurai, The Thiruppani Committee, Sri Meenakshi Devasthanam, 1963, pp. 91-95.

[9]In discussion Prof. R.N. Sampath observed that the *āgamas* make clear that the Vaiṣṇava festival of the Lord processing to a river (*ūṟal*) is to take place in the month of Citrā (April-May) or Vaikāci (May-June), while the Śaiva wedding festival (*tirukkaliyāṇam*) is to occur in Māci (February-March) or Paṅkuṉi (March-April). Carol Breckenridge's study of the role of the *sthānikar* in the temple as the mediator between the patron and the god

Third, the journey of Aḻagar over the twelve miles from his temple to the river is closely connected with Ambalakkārar division of the Kaḷḷar, a caste politically dominant in the region traversed, and this connection probably goes back at least to the reign of Tirumala Nāyak, if not before. The documentation of the history of this connection, however, is difficult.[10] The Kaḷḷar are a caste noted for their warrior traditions and connected historically with both guardianship and thieving in the region north of Madurai and around the hills in which the Aḻagar Temple stands. Any ruler of Madurai would have secure communication with the cities north of Madurai only if he had control over the Kaḷḷar.

Today the caste-deity (*kuladevam*) of the Kaḷḷar, Kaṛuppaṇṇacāmi, is regarded as the guardian of the Aḻagar Temple, where his main shrine is the door of the main gate.[11] How far back this connection goes is not at all clear, but it is old: there is a ritual at the beginning of the journey in which Aḻagar "conquers" the Kaḷḷar as he enters their territory and they then become his guardians all along the way to the river and back. Aḻagar in turn disguises himself as a Kaḷḷar and carries their traditional weapon. The festival image which is processed in this journey is therefore known as Kaḷḷaḻagar, "The Beautiful Lord of the Kaḷḷar." It would be important to find out when this relationship between the Kaḷḷar and Aḻagar developed: if it developed prior to the reign of Tirumala Nāyak or during it, the relationship may provide another explanation of why the Nāyak expanded this festival and juxtaposed it to the wedding festival, i.e. he wanted to symbolize his political unity with the Kaḷḷar by linking a festival symbolizing their identity (a caste ruled by Aḻagar) with a festival symbolizing the identity of Madurai (a city ruled by Śiva and Mīnākṣi).[12]

---

provides insight as to how such changes in these festivals were implemented by Tirumala Nāyak who was patron of both temples.

[10]The following discussion of Kaḷḷar history and social organization is based on Louis Dumont, *Une sous-caste de l'Inde du Sud: Organisation sociale et religion des Pramalai Kallar*, Paris, Mouton, 1957; B.S.Baliga, *Madurai: Madras District Gazetteers*, Madras, 1960, pp. 329-30; Francis, *Madura*, I, pp. 86-96; J.H. Nelson, *The Madura Country: A Manual*, Part II, Madras, 1868, pp. 44-56; Edgar Thurston, *Castes and Tribes of Southern India*, Vol. III, Madras, 1909, pp. 53-91; and the letters of French Jesuit missionaries of the seventeenth and eighteenth centuries translated in Sathyanatha Aiyar, *History of the Nāyaks of Madura*, Madras, University of Madras, 1924, pp. 252-53, 289, 305.

[11] The most complete discussion of the Alagar Temple to date is given by K.N. Radha Krishna, *Thirumalirunjolaimalai* (*Sri Alagar Kovil*) *Stala Purana*, Madura, Sri Kallalagar Devastanam, 1942. Kaṛuppaṉṉacāmi and his shrine are described on pp. 210-15.

[12]Assuming that the Ambalakkārar Kaḷḷar have "always" regarded Kaṛuppaṉṉacāmi as their *kuladevam*, Tirumala Nāyak, or another nāyak, may have elevated him to the position of guardian of the Alagar Temple and in turn solidified the relation by having Alagar dress as a Kaḷḷar. Theologically such an identification would express the Lord's graciousness (*saulabhyam*).

Such a desire would be consonant with his own religious tradition, for he was a Vaiṣṇava personally devoted to his Lord and would not eat his main meal, it is said, until Kṛṣṇa residing in the temple at Śrīvilliputtūr some forty miles to the southwest, had eaten his. Furthermore, the ritual "conquest" of the Kaḷḷar by Aḻagar may have been intended to symbolize his own political conquest of, and unity with, the Kaḷḷar—a possibility strengthened by the fact that as devotees to Aḻagar, he and the Kaḷḷar would be servants of the same Lord, though he would serve as temporal ruler and they as his servants. Information about the history of this ritual is necessary, however, before this speculation can be confirmed.

Fourth, Tirumala Nāyak may have desired to strengthen *dharma* in his kingdom through the stimulation of these festivals. Fulfilling his royal duty to patronize festivals for the spiritual and material well-being of his kingdom would, in his Hindu perspective, win him personal merit and strengthen *dharma* for all, giving his rule a metaphysically solid foundation which would be expressed devotionally in the increase of *bhakti* among both Śaivas and Vaiṣṇavas and politically in their strengthened allegiance to him as ruler. Such a concern for *dharma* in the kingdom would be particularly relevant to Tirumala Nāyak since he was the first nāyak of Madurai to break away from the Vijayanagara Empire and to re-establish the ancient political independence of the Pāṇḍyan kingdom. It would also be a way for him, a ruler of Telugu origin and thus to some degree a foreigner to Madurai, to legitimize himself as the king of an ancient Tamil kingdom.

Whatever the factors were that led to it, the yearly celebration of two such massive festivals meeting on the borders of the same full moon and of the same city would, it seems, inevitably produce a cultural drama articulating some relation between the gods and the people who met at these borders, particularly since, though they were ruled respectively by Aḻagar and by Śiva and Mīnākṣi on the divine level, the people were ruled on the socio-political level by the same temporal ruler. The popular myth expresses this relation between the gods and between the people as one of unity, but a unity that is defective. Moreover, it uses the symbol of a marriage alliance to do so. Why?

Social Organization

The unity of the gods and of the people expressed by the popular myth derives in part, I suggest, from the political facts discussed above and from the popular Hindu interest in all the gods as relevant to one's life rather than in an exclusive allegiance to one god at the expense of others. To see them as parts of a single family or sub-caste (*kulam*) is a way of expressing the unity of the *devas* over against the rival family or sub-caste (*kulam*) of the *asuras* or *rākṣasas* who are their perpetual enemies. It is also a way of saying that the people who belong to these two male gods—ruled respectively by Aḻagar and by Śiva—and who attend their "palaces" or temples twelve miles apart are related to each other as parts of a whole. The whole is the Pāṇḍyan kingdom, or at least a northern portion of it, the socio-political realm this *kulam* composed of the "lineages" of Śiva and Aḻagar occupies.

The myth says, however, that the unity is defective: every year Aḻagar is insulted by Śiva, refuses to enter his kingdom, and goes away angry. This antagonism between brothers-in-law is a realistic fact in ordinary Tamil families and it does express certain social tensions within this region of the Pāṇḍyan kingdom. First, there has been a long-standing rivalry between the "lineages" of Śiva and Viṣṇu in the area. Second, as has already been noted, the Kaḷḷar were an important threat to the city and relations with them was long a source of anxiety on the part of the people in the region. Third, the retinue which accompanies Aḻagar to the river is dominated by the low-caste villagers who are in the majority in the villages north of Madurai, especially by the Kaḷḷar and the Gōṉār, or herdsmen. These people assemble in the riverbed where they camp for several days, dress in costumes which apparently identify them with Kṛṣṇa, and observe rituals and vows which are typical of local and family customs (*deśācāra, kuladharma*) followed by Tamil non-brahmans. These include the first tonsure of children, god-possession and animal sacrifices, among others. The retinue of Śiva and Mīnākṣi, on the other hand, is dominated by the people of the city itself who have a larger high-caste component and who, during the wedding festival, follow the classical Sanskrit rituals (*śruti, smṛiti, āgama*) conducted by the vegetarian ritualists of the Mīnākṣi-Sundareśvara Temple.[13] The contrast between the retinues is not absolute, however, because many Hindus participate in aspects of both festivals and the tone of the "Cittirai Festival" today is one of cooperation on the part of all. But this has not always been the case and the antagonism between the two retinues has been explicit in the past. For example, earlier in the century many of those who came with Aḻagar to the river were not allowed into the inner shrines of the Mīnākṣi-Sundareśvara Temple either because they belonged to an "unclean" caste or because their local and family rituals were deemed "unclean."[14]

In sum, the antagonism expressed by the myth seems to symbolize a real social antagonism in this geographical region: politically between the Kaḷḷar and the ruler of Madurai, sociologically between the local low-caste village people and cults and the more classical high-caste city people and cults, and historically between two "lineages," the Vaiṣṇavas and Śaivas. In light of

[13]In making this distinction between *deśācāra-kuladharma* and *śruti-smṛiti-āgama,* I am following the lead of Milton Singer, *When a Great Tradition Modernizes*, New York, Praeger, 1971, pp. 187ff.

[14]See C.G. Diehl, *Instrument and Purpose: Studies on Rites and Rituals in South India*, Lund, 1956, p. 177, n.4

this, it is interesting to note that the anger is on the part of A̲lagar. Does this mean that the members of his retinue are angry about their relatively powerless position as low caste villagers aligned with A̲lagar over against the members of Śiva's retinue who belong to the city?

All members of both retinues, however, do relate positively to Mīnākṣi. As the queen of the city she can be viewed either as the wife of one's lord, Śiva, or as the sister of one's lord, A̲lagar. In fact, for the people of the city and for those who come to it throughout the year, she is the main focus of devotional attention. When they visit the "palace" of Śiva and Mīnākṣi most people give her rather than Śiva the primary attention, and the temple is commonly known simply as the "Mīnākṣi Temple." As a bride, Mīnākṣi is the means by which Śiva and A̲lagar are linked together as members of a single *kulam*, and those who "descend" from either "patrilineage" belong to her—and to each other, even though that belonging may be expressed as tension-ridden unity.

The reason "mythic consciousness" has chosen the alliance of brothers-in-law as a symbol of unity and antagonism is, I suggest, because of the nature of the family or sub-caste (*kulam*) in Tamil Hindu society.[15] The Tamil Hindu family is patrilineal and usually patrilocal, but employs cross-cousin marriage as a means of aligning successive generations of its patrilineages into a large *kulam* which serves as an endogamous sub-caste. This *kulam* is composed of various individual households (*kuṭumbam*) made up of husband, wife and children, but this is not the basic social unit in the society—the basic unit is the *kulam* within which individual *kuṭumbams* tend to intermarry generation after generation. The *kulam* is thus an apt symbol for a unity of contending parts.

Within this social context, a woman at her marriage is the means by which unity is sustained: she aligns two patrilineages through her roles of wife and of sister, and as a mother will produce children, one of whom, as representative of her husband's lineage, will ideally marry a representative of her own lineage, e.g. her brother or his child. Thus as a wife, sister and mother the married woman can be said to stand at the center of the *kulam*, the composite patrilineages she unites symbolized by her husband on one side and her brother on the other. As Louis Dumont has pointed out, this trio is a common

[15]A description of the structural tensions implicit in kinship systems which employ cross-cousin marriage is given by David M. Schneider and Kathleen Gough, eds. *Matrilineal Kinship*, Berkeley and Los Angeles, University of California Press, 1967, pp. 1-29. The details of the Hindu systems given here are based on Iravati Karve's description of the differences in kinship organization between the "Northern Zone" and "Southern Zone" of India in her *Kinship Organisation in India*, Poona, Deccan College, 1953. Brenda E.F. Beck gives a very useful detailed analysis of one regional version of the Tamil Hindu family structure in *Peasant Society in Konku: A Study of Right and Left Subcastes in South India*, Vancouver, University of British Columbia Press, 1972, Chapter 5.

iconographic motif in the Brahmanical temples of South India: Viṣṇu is shown giving his sister in marriage to Śiva and "a pair of brothers-in-law is there made to sum up Hinduism as a whole (in Madura and elsewhere)."[16]

It is interesting to observe by way of contrast that what is here a living symbol for unity in South India would be lifeless in North India. The cross-cousin marriage custom of South Indian society is expressly forbidden as incest by the dominant kinship system of the North. If a family were to be used by northern Hindu "mythic consciousness" as a symbol of unity among the gods, it would probably be a version of the joint-family composed of the male members of a single patrilineage and their wives and children, i.e. in Tamil terms a *kuṭumbam* rather than a *kulam*. Any representative of the wife's patrilineage would hold only a peripheral position in the symbol for in the ritual of marriage she has been given to her husband's family and her own family has relinquished all claims on her. Her husband's family is not expected to return a bride in the next generation and the two families tend to maintain a formal distance from one another. The power of the icon and myth of Śiva, Mīnākṣi and Viṣṇu to express antagonism within unity thus derives from a particular mode of Hindu social organization and is not a universally Hindu phenomenon.[17]

Given these differences in kinship systems there is, as Iravati Karve has pointed out, a difference in experience on the part of the woman who becomes a wife in the two systems.[18] This difference in experience as a woman may indicate that there are significant differences between the North and the South in the meaning of symbols used for Devī. In the North the bride enters a house of strangers where she experiences herself as powerless before the

[16]*Contributions to Indian Sociology*, Vol. VIII, October 1965, p.93. This comment, illustrating the stress on renewed affinity in the South Indian kinship system, is the origin of my attempt to understand this popular myth from the point of view of family structure.

[17]One example which brings out the difference is the account of Śiva's marriage to Pārvati in the Sanskrit *Śiva Purāṇa: Rudrasamhitā*. There Pārvati's patrilineage is represented by her father Himavat who gives her to Śiva by placing her hand in Śiva's hand and reciting mantras. He and his wife, Menā, then recede into the background and are of little importance in subsequent Śaiva myths. Viṣṇu in this event is present as "the officer-in-charge of the marriage-party of Śiva and a great favourite of Śiva," but he and Brahmā are both portrayed as Śiva's creatures. The unity of all the gods is here portrayed as a king, his bride and his friends and servants—not as two kings and a sister-bride. See Chapters 42-49 of *Śiva Purāṇa: Rudra Samhitā*, Vol. II of Ancient Indian Tradition and Mythology Delhi, Motilal Banarsidass, 1969, pp. 648-84, especially 43: 37-39; 44: 90-93; and 48: 37-43. The Tamil *sthala purāṇa* of the Mīnākṣi-Sundareśvara Temple, by contrast, presents a similar scene when describing the marriage of Śiva and Mīnākṣi except that Viṣṇu is the one who places the bride's hand into Siva's hand and this suggests that Viṣṇu's relation to Śiva is more than "the officer-in-charge of the marriage party of Śiva and a great favourite of Śiva," but in fact his brother in-law, which in the Tamil context suggests a relationship of interdependence and possible rivalry between the two.

[18]Karve, *Kinship Organisation*, pp. 228-29.

authority of her husband and his family and where she is expected to conform entirely to that family's needs and patterns. The tensions she experiences will be between her own self and all other members of the family who have authority over her, or, in cases where her husband is in conflict with his father or brothers, between her loyalty to him and the authority of his antagonists. In the South the experience can be qualitatively different. Ideally the bride enters a house not of strangers, but of relatives—her mother-in-law may also be her aunt—and she is not totally subject to her husband's family, for they are indebted to her patrilineage, owing them a bride. Her contacts with her own patrilineage will be frequent and ritualized. The wedding festival thus articulates the continuing unity of the family or sub-caste (*kulam*) for which she acts as a crucial link. Her experience as a bride will consequently be one of greater importance and independence in the life of her husband's patrilineage than that of a comparable bride in the North, for as wife and mother she is a means by which her husband's patrilineage is aligned with another patrilineage, ideally her own through her children, to form the larger and more important unit of the *kulam*.

What implications does this difference in experience have for the meanings of various Devī symbols used in the North and the South? This question requires further investigation, but I suggest that in the case of the popular myth of the "Cittirai Festival," Mīnākṣī, the Goddess, is portrayed as the one who holds things together in both the divine and human realms. As "Mother of the Universe," she is crucial to the unity of all things. Without her mediating link, the two lineages of Śiva and Viṣṇu, which compose the divine *kulam*, would divide the gods into disunited and antagonistic camps which would thereby be rendered vulnerable to the onslaught of the ever watchful *rākṣasas*. The well-being of the entire universe, therefore, depends upon her linking role as the wife-sister who annually becomes the bride. As "Queen of Madurai," her annual marriage repeatedly pulls together the two human "lineages" descending from Śiva and Aḻagar into a single social *kulam* which comprises the society of the Pāṇḍyan kingdom. The northern portion of this social "family," however, experiences antagonism within its unity, greater perhaps than experienced in other portions of the "family," and the "Cittirai Festival" re-enacts this fact year after year. But its repeated enactment does affirm the ideal and hope of unity while recognizing at the same time its flawed nature.

Concluding Remarks

Given the Hindu framework within which this popular myth exists, there are certain metaphysical implications embedded within it, I think, which remain latent in popular thought. The manifest realm, *samsāra*, is compounded of parts, is in dynamic flux, and is flawed by ignorance and desire, but the myth suggests that on every crucial level of it—the family, the society, the gods—there is a basic unity. When the component parts of this unity operate harmoniously, there is well-being at each level for all constituent members. The crucial mediator, moreover, between the contending parts is in each case a woman: the wife-sister-mother in the family or sub-caste (*kulam*), the "Queen of Madurai" in the Pāṇḍyan kingdom, and Devī in the cosmos. Without her mediation the whole on each level will disintegrate through the natural rivalries of the respective "patrilineages," and anyone who aspires for prosperity on any or all of these levels will lose out in the disintegration of unity and stability. Only the person who ardently seeks to transcend all of these levels of the manifest universe, such as the *ṛṣi* Maṇḍūka, can be indifferent to this crucial role of the woman, for which the paradigm is Mīnākṣi. It is only as a result of her mediating and unifying role as wife and sister that hundreds of thousands of Hindus of all castes and cultural levels can participate every year in some portion of what they perceive to be a single drama enacted by those three gods at the full moon of Citrā.

Ideology and Cultural Contexts of the Śrīvaiṣṇava Temple[1]

FRIEDHELM HARDY
King's College, University of London

INTRODUCTION

> In vain are Hindu idols decked with rich ornaments; they are not rendered thereby less disagreeable in appearance. Their physiognomy is generally of frightful ugliness, which is carefully enhanced by daubing the images from time to time with a coating of dark paint. . . . The attitudes in which they are represented are either ridiculous, grotesque, or obscene. In short, everything is done to make them objects of disgust to any one not familiar with the sight of these strange monsters.[2]

What is of interest in this devastating judgement, which in about 1800 the French missionary Abbé Dubois made, is the standard of reference to which he resorted. In reality, the good Abbé was undoubtedly upset by the fact that these Hindus worshipped gods other than his own, and thus were "idolaters,"[3] and yet, he evaded a direct theological (and thereby axiomatic) condemnation by appealing to aesthetic standards.[4] After all, even "obscene" is as much an

[1]The present paper represents an initial assessment of the research which I have been carrying out on Vaiṣṇava temple culture. My visits to many of the temples during an extensive journey through Tamil Nadu in the summer of 1975 was made possible through a grant from the Central Research Fund, University of London. I wish to express my thanks also to Pandit Gopālacakravartī Aiyaṅkār of Triplicane/Madras who has been of invaluable assistance to me, particularly during my travels, and to all those *pūjāris*, trustees and officials who showed a positive attitude towards my interest in their temples.

[2]*Hindu Manners, Customs and Ceremonies*, by the Abbé J.A. Dubois, translated by H.K. Beauchamp, 3rd edition, Oxford, 1906, p. 581.

[3]It is an amazing accident in the history of words that in spite of the Abbé's (and his kind) blatant impotence to grasp the significance of the temple cult for the *bhakta* himself, even pious Hindus nowadays speak of the "idol" when referring to the *vigraha* in the temple.

[4]In another passage, the Abbé resorts to a different standard of judgement, viz. to hygiene. "The low elevation; the difficulty with which the air finds a way through a single

aesthetic as a moral category. Perhaps unknown to himself, he did actually follow in this the way in which Hindus themselves interpreted the significance of the temple, viz. through aesthetic categories (which obviously in their case were positive). There exists a cultural and artistic forecourt which surrounds the abstract theological concept and represents the concrete expression of what the temple signifies to the devotee. As the quotation shows, it is precisely here that cultural and artistic prejudices—long before any *religious* bias has the opportunity to enter—prevent a genuine understanding and appreciation of the underlying meaning. Because the aesthetic side did not appeal to Dubois, he considered it unnecessary to investigate any possible religious significance, and in fact judged the latter in terms of the former.

I believe that any attempt to explore what the temple meant to the worshipper ought to concern itself as much with the dogma, as with these areas of cultural and artistic expression which illustrate in material terms the motivational force of the dogma. At the same time, it must not be forgotten that the development of this dogma was itself partly influenced by these same areas. Thus I shall delineate in this paper how a basic theological concept, which was linked to a particular institution (the temple), was treated, interpreted, and given concrete expression in various ideological and cultural contexts. The feedback of the cultural treatment on the ideological developments will incidentally be touched upon. My observations restrict themselves to one area of Indian temple culture, viz. the Śrīvaiṣṇava temples in the Tamil South,[5] mainly during the period of the Āḻvārs and Ācaryas (c. sixth to sixteenth century A.D.); later material will, however, also be included.

Applying the theoretical observations made so far to this area, I propose to investigate, firstly, the conceptual understanding of the temple in the Āḻvārs and its systematic formulation in the later Ācāryas Secondly, I explore the pattern of response to it which evolved in Tamil society and which falls into three well-defined themes. Under the first heading we shall be analyzing the original concept and the rational, intellectual reaction to it in terms of an ideological structure in which it became embodied, while under the

---

narrow and habitually closed passage; the unhealthy odours rising from the mass of fresh and decaying flowers; the burning lamps; the oil and butter spilt in libations; the excrements of the bats that take up their abode in these dark places; finally, and above all, the fetid perspiration of a multitude of unclean and malodorous people;—all contribute to render these sacred shrines excessively unhealthy. Only a Hindu could remain for any length of time in their heated and pestilential precincts without suffocation." (*Ibid.*, p. 581). But unlike aesthetic values, hygiene is open for objective assessment; already the translator had to remark: "The Abbé nowhere remarks on the burning of camphor, which plays so conspicuous a part in all Hindu worship, and which acts at the same time as a disinfectant" (note, p. 581)—I may take this opportunity to express my extreme gratitude to those bats mentioned by the Abbé, for thanks to them there were no mosquitoes to torture me in the temples.

[5]For a precise definition of the *divyadēśaṅkaḷ* see below under "the many temples."

second heading patterns of behavior and emotional attitudes are explored. I shall then, thirdly, turn to a different structure of meaning by which, from the point of view of the devotee, an individual temple complex is explained and justified by reference to (mythical) history. The material relevant to this is contained in the various *sthala-purāṇas*.

I. The Institution and the Concept of Viṣṇu's Presence in the Temple

(1) *The situation in* caṅkam *literature*. The earliest sources about Southern religion, the so-called *caṅkam* literature, express a simple conception of the local presence of a god. Phrases like "Neṭuvēḷ who lives in the *kaṭampu* tree"[6] or "where [Viṣṇū] reclines on the serpent couch"[7] are typical of it. There is no indication of whether or not it was felt to be a problem that there exists only one Murukaṉ or Viṣṇu, but many *kaṭampu* trees and temples. Again, it is impossible to determine the extent to which in this early period the institutions surrounding these divine presences had been developed. While we hear frequently of simple offerings like flowers made at the trees,[8] rare mention is also made of a more complex institution, viz. the "public hall" (*potiyil*) in which worship took place before a pillar (*kantu*):

> . . . the public hall with the "pillar" where travellers would rest; where captive girls, after bathing in the fresh-water tank, would light the "perpetual" lamp at twilight, and where many people would cross over the ground prepared with cowdung, and, beautified with flowers, would worship.[9]

The *Paripāṭal*, presumably composed and compiled during the earlier first millennium A.D. in Madurai, represents the next stage in the development. Song XV, dedicated to Tirumāliruñcōlai, is of interest in the present discussion. There is a clear awareness that Viṣṇu is the transcendental god beyond space and time, but the phraseology about his local presence in the temple remains simple. He is called the "owner of Iruṅkuṉram" (which refers to the temple at the foot of the hill),[10] and is said to "hold on to it in affection,"[11] to have "united, and to remain in close union"[12] with it. Once we also hear

[6] *Perumpāṇārruppaṭai*, line 76.

[7] *Ibid.*, 373.

[8] See F.E. Hardy, *Emotional Kṛṣṇa bhakti*, D. Phil. thesis, Oxford, 1976, pp. 190-93 (manuscript).

[9] *Paṭṭiṉappālai*, lines 246-49; see Hardy, *op. cit.*, pp. 189f for a more detailed discussion of the passage.

[10] *Paripāṭal* XV, line 53: *Iruṅkuṉrattāṉ*

[11] *Ibid.*, line 14: *tāṅku*.

[12] *Ibid.*, line 28: *puṇarnt' amar*.

that he "manifested himself"[13] there. As motive for this manifestation is given: to be visible to man, whose sins are destroyed when he sees the god.[14]

But on the whole the Viṣṇu temples are of marginal importance in the *caṅkam* corpus. This changes radically when we turn to the Āḻvārs (c. sixth to nineth century A.D.), the great Viṣṇu *bhaktas* and Tamil poets, who sang about a large number of Viṣṇu temples in the South and in whom temple religion appears already in a complex form. However, in their phraseology the archaic and simple conception of divine presence remains unchanged.

(2) *The phraseology about Viṣṇu's presence employed by the Āḻvārs.*[15] The formula "Viṣṇu is in the temple" may conveniently be used to illustrate the phraseology of the Āḻvārs, it provides three slots which will be discussed separately.

"Is in." In its simplest form, this appears as "in,"[16] and also as "he who is inside."[17] But more frequently this is specified through verbs denotative of human action: "lives, dwells, abides in, stays, remains, holds on to, is resident, is united with, etc."[18] Often a more specific reference is made to the particular posture of the *vigraha* in the individual temple: "who reclines on the serpent couch in. . . ,"[19] "who sleeps in. . . ,"[20] "whose form is that of a dwarf brahmin in. . . ."[21] Particular mention must be made of the verb "resides, is enthroned, sits in state or majestically."[22] It implies a symbolism which will be discussed below, viz. Viṣṇu as king. Viṣṇu's presence in the temple is by no means accidental, for he is the owner of it, and of the whole village or town that surrounds it. This is expressed by the simple genitive: "he of Araṅkam,"[23] or by the possessive noun derived from the temple name: "Araṅkaṉ, Vēṅkaṭattāṉ, TirukKuṭantaiʸ ūrāṉ,"[24] or by words denoting "lord, owner, master."[25] The act of "abiding" is often connected with a "going

[13] *Ibid.*, line 51: *tōṉri:* this verb refers frequently in the Ālvārs to the classical *avatāras.*

[14] *Ibid.*, line 37.

[15] For a detailed study of the Ālvārs and their religion see Hardy, *op. cit.*, pp. 307-553.

[16] *Perumāḷ-Tirumoli* I, 1; X, 1 Here and in the following notes only some selective references to the works in the *Divya-Prabandham* are given.

[17] *2nd Antâti*, stanza 28.

[18] Urai (*Tiruvāymoli* V, 9, 1); nil (*ibid.* 2); iru (*ibid.* 7, 3); vāl (*ibid.* 8); payiru (*2nd Antâti*, 46); mēyāṉ (*1st Antâti* 6); parriyāṉ (*ibid.* 27).

[19] *Perumāḷ-Tirumoli* I, 3. 7.

[20] *Tiruvāymoli* V, 8, 2.

[21] *Ibid.* V, 9, 1.

[22] *Ibid.* V, 7, 1: *Vīrr'iru.*

[23] *4th Antâti*, stanza 30: *Araṅkatt' avaṉ.*

[24] *PerumāḷTM* II, 1-4; *2nd Antâti* 28; *TiruvāyM* V, 8, 10.

[25] Kōṉ (*TiruvāvM* V, 9, 1); nātaṉ (*ibid.* 7); nampi (*ibid.* 5, 1); ūraṉ (*ibid.* 8, 10).

there, arriving there, entering"[26]; compare also: "he turned into his abode. . . ."[27] On the other hand, this residence is not understood as merely temporary, as is illustrated by phrases like: "abiding for a long time, permanently, for many days"[28]—phrases which in Tamil approximate the idea "for all eternity" and are rendered thus by the commentators.[29]

"The temple." The terms used to denote the actual abode of Viṣṇu are *i.a.*: *iṭam* "house, residence, place,"[30] *ūr* "village, town,"[31] *nakar* "temple town,"[32] *tāḻvu* "resting place,"[33] *kōvil* (from which the much more common *kōyil*) "palace, temple,"[34] and *iraipāṭi* "palace."[35] In the last two words we notice once again the royal symbolism which will be discussed below. For certain temples which are situated on or by a mountain or hill, we find in the same position as these words "hill, mountain."[36]

I have not been able to trace in the *Prabandham* any of the terms which in later literature denote the actual image of the god, viz. *arcā*, *vigraha*, *mūrti*, *bera*. One might well conclude from this that the Āḻvārs regarded the figure in the temple simply as (a manifestation of) Viṣṇu, thereby betraying an archaic realism similar to their not drawing a conceptual distinction between the absolute Viṣṇu and his *avatāras*. When Nammāḻvār uses the word *kōlam*,[37] he is referring to the "appearance" or "posture" of Viṣṇu's body, and does not use the word in the sense of *vigraha*.

"Viṣṇu." One might think that the iconographic peculiarities of the *vigraha* would impose specific limitations on the Āḻvārs' description of the individual temple god. But this is the case only to a limited extent, usually with reference to the posture of the *vigraha*, e.g. "Viṣṇu who reclines in Kuṭantai on the serpent couch."[38] On the whole, the Āḻvārs felt unrestricted by such formal considerations. For instance, Kulaśekhara composed a poem about Cittirakūṭam in which he gives a summary of the *Rāmāyaṇa*, while Kalikaṉri, in a poem about the same temple, provides an account of the various Vṛndāvana

[26] Eri (*TiruvāyM* V, 7, 4); muṉṉi vantu (*ibid.* VII, 3, 5); ceṉru cēr (*ibid.* VIII, 9, 6); maruvi (*PeriyatiruM* VII, 5, 1).

[27] *3rd Antâti*, 32: *iṭam āka koṇṭāṉ*.

[28] Nīṭu urai (*TiruvāyM* V, 9, 3); maṉṉu (*ibid.* VI, 3, 10); pal nāḷ payiṉratu (*2nd Antâti*, 46).

[29] *3rd Antâti*, 61: *paṇṭu ellām*.—For *pal nāḷ* (see previous note) Aṇṇaṅkarâcāriyar says: *an-ādi-kālam* "since beginningless times."

[30] *1st Antâti* 38.

[31] *TiruvāyM* VI, 3, 2.

[32] *PerumāḷTM* I, 1.

[33] *3rd Antâti*, 62.

[34] *PerumāḷTM* II, 3.

[35] *3rd Antâti*, 30.—The word is not mentioned as a compound in the Madras Tamil Lexicon; literally it means "town/village of the king/chieftain." Aṇṇaṅkarâcāriyar renders it *rājatāṉikaḷ* "a king's residence; capital: palace."

[36] *1st Antâti*, 40; *3rd Antâti*, 68. 71; *4th Antâti*, 48.

[37] *TiruvāyM* V, 9, 1: *māṉ kuraḷ kōla*.

[38] *4th Antâti*, 36.

episodes of Kṛṣṇa.[39] The *mūla-vigraha* in that temple actually shows Nārāyaṇa reclining on the serpent Ananta. In fact, many of the Āḻvār songs about temples are motivated by the desire to establish or stress that the local god is no other than the universal, transcendental Viṣṇu. The poet could therefore use the full repertoire of Viṣṇu mythology when speaking about a specific *vigraha*. But this must not be understood as an attempt to dissolve the individuality of the local god altogether. Not only did the Āḻvārs take great care in describing the local setting of the individual temple, but they also began a trend which then in the course of Śrīvaiṣṇava history became standardized: to address the local god by his own, specific name. For example, Nammāḻvār addressed the god in Tiruviṇṇakar as *Oppar-il appaṉ* "master who knows no equals," and today the temple is known by the name Uppiliyappaṉ-temple.[40]

The Āḻvārs do not display any amazement about the fact that Viṣṇu on the one hand is the transcendental lord of Vaikuṇṭha, and on the other abides on earth. Thus they simply say: "Kaṭikai is indeed the palace (*kōyil*) of him who abides in Vaikuṇṭha."[41] Similarly they are not aware of the *avatāra* notion of Sanskritic theology.[42] We shall presently see how this situation was specified through the *arcâvatāra* concept of the later Ācāryas. The Āḻvārs do, on the other hand, reflect on the related problem of the *many* temples, and some observations on this may be added here.

(3) *The many temples*. The Āḻvārs were clearly aware of the fact that Viṣṇu was present on earth in a number of different temples. In the early strata of the *Prabandham*, the emphasis is on relating a particular temple to the universal Vaiṣṇava material; the following stanza may illustrate this:

> In the past he lifted the mountain [Govardhana] and defeated Kaṃsa.
> Vēṅkaṭam is where he stands.[43]

The god in the local temple (Vēṅkaṭam) is identified with Viṣṇu who in his *Kṛṣṇâvatāra* lifted the mountain Govardhana and killed Kaṃsa. However, the *plurality* of these local temples could not be ignored, and thus we hear: "He stands, sits, reclines, and walks in Vēṅkaṭam, Viṇṇakar, Vehkā, and

[39] *PerumāḷTM* X and *PeriyaTM* III, 3.

[40] *TiruvāyM* VI, 3; Nammālvār calls the temple simply Tiruviṇṇakar, but in stanza 9 he refers to the god as *oppilar appaṉ*. Tamil folklore has given its own interpretation of this somewhat abstract title. It changed it into *upp' ili*, lit. "without salt," and explained it by a charming story. Viṣṇu wanted to marry Bhūmi; when in the form of an old man, he asked permission from her guardian Markaṇḍeya, the sage tried to evade the issue by pointing out the very young age of the girl. He said that she did not even know anything about cooking and thus might forget to put salt into his food. But Viṣṇu replied that he did not want any salt in his food, and thus came to be known as "lord without salt." As a consequence, the food prepared nowadays in the temple does not contain any salt.

[41] *3rd Antâti*, 61.

[42] See Hardy, *op. cit.*, pp. 289f; 529-31.

[43] *1st Antâti*, 39.

Kōvalūr."[44] Here it is still possible to attempt a functional differentiation (through the four different postures) for a small number of temples (here: four), but it becomes impossible when a larger number is considered.[45] The variety of the temples has then to be regarded as the inexplicable expression of Viṣṇu's *līlā* and his eagerness to be in the vicinity of as many people as possible. But at least externally this variety can be contained in a wider structure; Kalikaṉri (8th century A.D.) offers the most extensive lists of temples, viz. c. 85, among the Āḻvārs, and his *Periyatirumoli* follows the pattern of a pilgrimage,[46] which as a *pradakṣiṇa* through South India imitates the stereotyped *digvijaya* of a king. At a later stage, certainly from the time of Rāmānuja onwards,[47] another pattern is added to this in the form of the sacred number 108. A somewhat forced count of all the different temples mentioned in the whole *Prabandham* yielded the figure 108. For the Śrīvaiṣṇavas, these 108 temples surpass in sanctity all other places of pilgrimage, and are known as the *tiruppatikaḷ* or, in Sanskrit, *divya-deśams*, other temples are called for instance *abhimāna-sthala*. Not only do these 108 temples constantly appear, as a fixed group, in literature,[48] but many individual temples also draw attention to the group in various ways. For instance, in Naṟaiyūr a show-case displays miniature copies in bronze of all the 108 *utsava-vigrahas*, and the temple in Śrīvaikuṇṭham has in the inner *prakāram* a series of very beautiful and relatively old frescoes which depict the 108 Viṣṇus individually. Among these temples, 97 belong to South India, and 82 to Tamil Nadu. The present paper is based on material which has been selected from among that concerning these 82 Tamil temples.

In the course of Śrīvaiṣṇava history, a certain hierarchical structure evolved which allowed certain temples among the 108 to figure in a more important position than others, because of alleged special sanctity, popularity, imposing size, etc. While with the earlier Āḻvārs Veṅkaṭam figured as the most important temple,[49] from the time of the later Āḻvārs onwards Śrīraṅgam began to

[44] *Ibid.*, 77.

[45] In the *Antâtis*, up to eight temples are listed in one and the same stanza: *3rd Antâti*, 62. In *Periyatirumaṭal* 53-68, a series of thirty-six temples is given.

[46] Probably *2nd Antâti* 14 refers already to the custom of pilgrimage: *pēr ōti tirintu tīrttakarar āmiṉ* "praise his names, walk (through the country—comm:=visit the shrines), and become *tīrthaṅkaras!*" The last word appears to play with the two meanings of *tīrtha:* place of pilgrimage, and (with *-kara*) saint.

[47] See Periya Nampi's *Tiruppatikkōvai*, Vaṅkippuratt' Ācci's (Nālāyira-ppāsura-ppaṭi) *Nūṟṟ' eṭṭu ttiruppati-kkōvai*, etc.

[48] In verse 18, canto XII, of the *Divyasūricarita* (ed. in Telugu characters by Śrīnivāsâcārya Kāñcīpuram, 1953), Periyâlvār explains to Āṇṭāḷ, for whom he has arranged a *svayaṃvara*, where the 108 Viṣṇus who have arrived live. Vs. 34-79 mention and describe many of these temples.

[49] I have counted 37 references in the four *Antâtis*, and 51 to all other temples mentioned. For the whole *Prabandham* the figures are: 104 to Veṅkaṭam, 56 to Śrīraṅgam (first and

tower over all others. Thus already the *Tirumālai* indicates almost an apotheosis of this shrine: "If people called out but 'Araṅkam!', hell would perish. . . ."[50] In medieval literature lists of the three or four most important and sacred temples are found, in which the Varadarājapperumāḷ temple in Kāñcīpuram takes the third place, behind the two mentioned above.[51]

A few remarks on the importance of these temples for Śrīvaiṣṇava theology may be added here. The majority of the songs in the *Prabandham* are addressed to, or deal with, Viṣṇu in a specific temple. This custom is continued by many of the Ācāryas. A considerable *stotra* literature, among whose authors figure some of the most distinguished Śrīvaiṣṇava theologians,[52] gathers abstract theological thought and poetic imagination around the individual *vigraha*, and derives its inspiration from that concrete temple situation. One of the concepts which thus developed with these Ācāryas, viz. the *arcâvatāra*, will now have to be discussed in detail.

4) *The* arcâvatāra *concept*. From a critical, philosophical or theological, point of view, the phraseology which we found in the Āḻvārs, and its underlying conception, had to appear simplistic to the Śrīvaiṣṇava theologians. It was only natural that attempts were made to specify in philosophically satisfactory terms the manner in which the same being could be transcendent and yet, at the same time, be present in many different temples. A similar problem had already presented itself in an earlier period concerning Viṣṇu's mythical manifestations, and the concept of the "*avatāra*" had been developed to cope with this.[53] According to this model, presumably in Pāñcarātra circles, another concept evolved concerning Viṣṇu's presence in the temples. This was the *arcâvatāra* notion, which means: Viṣṇu "incarnates" himself in the temple image (*arcā*) in the mode of a mythical *avatāra*. Thus in that sense, each temple image contains a full *avatāra*, with the difference that unlike the mythical ones, which were distributed over different periods in the past, these *avatāras* are spatially distributed and in the present time. Although already

---

second position in a table of frequency). Many of the later references are, however, of a stereotyped and conventional nature and thus do not suggest the superior position of Veṅkaṭam in the later Āḻvārs.

[50]Stanza 13. Āṇṭāḷ (see note 48 above) chose Raṅganātha as her husband, and most Ācāryas were associated with Śrīraṅgam.

[51]It is needless to add that from the point of view of other temples, *they* were the most important one in the list. E.g.: "There are 108 *kṣetras* of Viṣṇu on earth. Among these the great Nandināthapuram is the foremost." (*Nāthaṉ-kōvil-sthalamāhātmyam*, chapter IV, verses 2f; Tanjore Sarasvati Mahal Library, Descriptive Catalogue No 10029, manuscript.)

[52]Thus we have the *Devarājâṣṭakam* by Tirukkacci Nampi, the *Sundarabāhustava* by Kūratt' Āḻvāṉ, the *Śrīraṅgarājastuti* by Parāśara Paṭṭar, a whole group of *stotras* and Tamil *prabandhams* by Veṅkaṭanātha, and the *Devarājamaṅgalam* by Maṇavāḷa mā muṉi.

[53]On the formation and history of the notion "avatāra" see P. Hacker, "Zur Entwicklung der Avatāralehre" in *Wiener Zeitschrift für die Kunde Süd- und Ostasiens*, vol. 4, 1960, pp.47-70.

Yāmunâcārya had integrated the Pāñcarātra into Tamil Vaiṣṇavism,[54] even in Rāmānuja this concept does not yet appear to be operative.[55] However, with the post-Rāmānuja thinkers it appears fully accepted and plays the central role in their theology of the temple. Piḷḷai Lokâcārya gives the following definition :

> [The concept] "*arcâvatāra*" denotes [Viṣṇu's] state of permanently abiding in the temples and in the houses, of coming close [to man] in objects which are attractive to people, without restrictions of space, time, or privileged persons [being in these points] unlike the special (=mythical) manifestations.[56]

Similarly Veṅkaṭanātha:

> [The concept] "*arcâvatāra*" denotes [Viṣṇu's] abiding, according to the desires of those who resort to him and for their sake, in the manner that has been described in this verse[57] : "Taking on the form of the image, he enters into and abides with his *ātman* in the image".[58]
>
> . . .Emperumāṉ (=Viṣṇu) who came in delight and turned himself into the *arcâvatāra*, being totally dedicated to one purpose and instituting his (temple) presence for the sake of a particular devotee . . . .[59]

Thus the *arcâvatāra* is Viṣṇu himself, in so far as his "*ātman*"[60] abides in the image, which is an object initially created or chosen by man according to his own liking, but accepted by Viṣṇu for the sake of man, in order to be close to him everywhere and always. But although man creates the abode and the image for Viṣṇu, it is the latter's free will which decides on his taking residence there; neither *karma* nor any (magical) act of man has the power to force him into it.[61]

[54]See J. van Buitenen, "On the archaism of the *Bhāgavata-Purāṇa*" in *Kṛṣṇa: Myths, Rites, and Attitudes*. ed. M. Singer, Chicago, 1966 (reprinted 1968), pp. 26-33

[55]See J. Carman, *The Theology of Rāmānuja*, New Haven and London (Yale University Press), 1974, pp. 180f; 298f.

[56]*Tattvatraya* (ed. with Maṇavāḷa mā muṉi's commentary by Aṇṇaṅkarâcāriyar, Kāñcīpuram, 1966), *sūtra* 200.

[57]The editor identifies the quotation as: *Sātvata-saṃhitā* VI, 22.

[58]*Rahasyatrayasāram* (ed. with a Tamil commentary by Narasimmācārya-svāmi, Madras, 1920; Tamil and Grantha characters), chapter V, p. 254.

[59]*Ibid* , chapter XV, p. 510.

[60]*Ibid.*, chapter V, p 260. Veṅkaṭanātha says that the *pēraṇi* (comm: =*mūla-kāraṇam*) "material cause," of the *arcâvatāra* is Viṣṇu in his most transcendental form of existence, viz. as *para*.

[61]*Tattvatraya sūtra* 194: Free will is the cause of the *avatāras*; 196f: One could object that *karma* must be assumed as the cause of the *avatāras*, because it has been stated in many

Unlike gnostic or idealistic theologies, medieval Śrīvaiṣṇava thought does not regard the *arcā* manifestations as the "lowest" form of divine emanation but, on the contrary, as a complete representation of Viṣṇu's essential nature.

> That he gives rise to bliss, that he is a splendid refuge, that the whole world must resort to him, and that he can be experienced [by the whole world]—all this *finds its fulfilment* in the *arcâvatāra*.[62]

Here in the *arcā* Viṣṇu proves in the most obvious manner that he is concerned with man and that he wants to be near him. This attitude of Viṣṇu was formulated by the Ācāryas in the term *saulabhya*, "easy accessibility."[63] When discussing the phrase "Lord of Vēṅkaṭam" in a song by Nammāḻvār, a commentator paraphrases "who possesses perfect *saulabhya* by being present on the Sacred Mountain (viz. Tirumalai,=Vēṅkaṭam)."[64] The *Īṭu* is more elaborate on the same phrase :

> *Saulabhyam* is indicated by the phrase "you who are Lord of Vēṅkaṭam which is liked by gods and sages. . . ." They like [the temple] because they can find here something that is not found there [in heaven], since [the auspicious qualities] *śīla* etc. are present here, assuming visible form even for the lowest persons, more so than even in the highest heaven, like a lamp[65] in a dark place.[66]

That Viṣṇu opens himself up to man and is eager to be close to him, mani-

---

scriptural authorities that he was born in consequence of the curse of Bhṛgu etc. [The answer to this is that] in those [places] the curse is merely a pretext (*vyājam*), and it is therefore confirmed that the *avatāra* originates by an act of free will.

62 *Ibid* , *sūtra* 201.

63 On the connotations of this term see Carman, *op. cit.*, pp. 77-87; also pp. 11f; 173ff; 223ff

64 The 12000 (ed. in *Pakavatviṣayam* by Kopālakiruṣṇamācāriyar etc., Triplicane 1923-30), p 474, on *Tiruvāymoḻi* VI, 10, 10.

65 The simile of the lamp is explained by Piḷḷai Lokâcārya in his *Śrīvacanabhūṣaṇam* (ed. by Aṇṇaṅkarâcāriyar with the commentary of Maṇavāḷa mā muṉi Kāñcīpuram, 1966, *sūtra* 37: "The [qualities] easy accessibility etc., which are relevant to devotion (*prapatti*) are fully brought out here (in the *arcā*), like a lamp in a dark room." Maṇavāḷa's comment: "Although all these qualities are found also in the *paratva*, they do not light up—similar to a lamp during the day—, because they are found in something which is directed to those endowed with supreme perfection (literally, "likeness to Viṣṇu)." But in the material of the *arcavatāra*, they shine brightly—like a lamp during the night—because they are directed towards the people in *saṃsāra* who are infinitely base-and-low (*taṇmai*)." In other words, the *arcâvatāra* does not in itself possess qualities which are different from those found in the transcendental Viṣṇu; but owing to the darkness of contingent human existence, they shine forth in an accentuated manner.

66 The 36000 (ed. in *Pakavatviṣayam*, see note 64), p. 494.

fests itself most strongly in an aspect of the *arcā* which particularly amazed the Ācāryas.

> Taking off his perfection and relinquishing his total freedom, he abides in it (=the *arcā*) by showing great love even to those who do not love him.[67] Hiding his own lordship, he pretends to be ignorant, powerless, without independent will; becoming enslaved to boundless compassion, he grants all that is desired [by man].[68]
>
> *Saulabhya* means to be dependent on the *arcaka* who is easily accessible to all without distinction of high and low people.[69]
>
> . . .total dependence on the devotee—something that evades mental understanding and verbal definition.[70]

The post-Rāmānuja theologians grouped together Viṣṇu's attributes under two headings: *paratva* and *saulabhya*, "transcendence" and "easy accessibility."[71] By stating that the *arcā* illustrates the group of *saulabhya* qualities, they do not mean to say that the transcendent Viṣṇu is qualitatively different. This is important particularly with reference to his form or body. Even the transcendent Viṣṇu in his *svarūpa* "possesses a wonderful form (*vigraha*)"[72]; "that *vigraha* is infinitely more pleasurable than the qualities of his *svarūpa* [which are knowledge and bliss]. . . . It consists of unlimited splendour, is a storehouse of a series of auspicious qualities like youthfulness etc.; it infatuates all people and causes disgust with all other pleasures; it is the substratum of the many *avatāras*. . . ."[73] Since Viṣṇu in his essential nature possesses a form, and since he is fully present in the *arcā*, the latter thus displays—in its limited man-made shape—the qualities of the divine body. The *Īṭu*, when commenting on the phrase "at your feet" (which refers to the lord of Vēṅkaṭam), says:

> This phrase indicates that [the lord of Vēṅkaṭam] possesses a *vigraha*. . . . Because it is a *vigraha*, it can be a substratum for splendour (or: beauty), can give rise to love towards himself along with a dislike of other sense-objects.[74]

Veṅkaṭanātha speaks of "the alluring power"[75] of the *arcâvatāra*. Thus divine

67 *Śrīvacanabhūṣaṇa*, *sūtra* 38.
68 *Tattvatraya*, *sūtra* 202.
69 The 36000, vol. VI, p. 494.
70 *Rahasyatrayasāram*, chapter XV, p. 512.
71 See Carman, *op. cit.*, pp. 77-87.
72 *Tattvatraya*, *sūtra* 141.
73 *Ibid.* 181.
74 The 36000, p. 495, on: *uṉ aṭi kīl* (*TiruvāyM* VI, 10, 10).
75 *Ākarṣakatva*, *Rahasyatrayasāram*, chapter XV, p. 512.

beauty pervades both the transcendent and the *arcā vigrahas* of Viṣṇu; it is that element which links the different forms of his existence. Made available to man (who tries to increase its impact by beautifying the *vigraha* further through flower-garlands, clothes, and ornaments), this beauty has the most immediate and spontaneous appeal. As Piḷḷai Lokâcārya says:

> This [arcâvatāra] redirects the attention of man who, engrossed in sensual pleasures, had turned away from him; he is capable of increasing his love—something the *śāstras* (the scriptural injunctions) are not able to achieve.[76]

Who is this "man" spoken about here? That the Ācārya is by no means thinking only of the humble, ignorant but pious worshipper is made clear in the following *sūtras:*

> Three types of persons are privileged to surrender themselves to it (=*arcâ-vatāra*): the ignorant, the wise, and those absorbed in *bhakti.* Those who do this out of ignorance are people like ourselves; who do it in supreme wisdom, the former Ācāryas; who surrendered in complete *bhakti* were the Āḻvārs.[77]

To worship the *arcā* is thus a religious act equally relevant to all members of the Śrīvaiṣṇava community—from the saints and scholars down to the simple man.

The doctrine of the *arcâvatāra* represents the sophisticated expression, now in a systematic and theological manner, of the conception that Viṣṇu is present in the temple. But whether formulated as part of a theological system, or, as in the Āḻvārs, implied in simple poetic expression, this conception by itself is an abstract idea. How the *bhakta* reacted to it, in which manner he tried to achieve this surrender, how it influenced his religious attitudes, and, in turn, how the theologian interpreted all this and tried to influence it in a normative manner—these points remain to be discussed. It will be here that we can see how an idea worked in society and how a whole culture grew out of it.

It is, however, essential to keep in mind that the abstract line of doctrinal developments which has been depicted so far covers a span of about a millennium. The religious response developed along with it. Thus when we ask now what impact the dogma had on society, it would be a mistake to ignore the influences which the religious response and the cultural patterns surrounding the temple cult had upon precisely the doctrinal developments. And it would equally be a mistake to assume a homomorphous character for both lines of development.

[76]*Śrīvacanabhūṣaṇam, sūtra* 40.
[77]*Ibid., sūtras* 41-43.

II. Patterns of Religious Response to Viṣṇu's Presence

Despite the modifications which Śrīvaiṣṇava doctrinal history shows with regard to the conception of Viṣṇu's presence in the *vigraha*, the idea remains fundamentally the same throughout the millennium under consideration. Viṣṇu wants to be close and available to man, to manifest the beauty of his form and arouse his love towards him. Thereby man is challenged to react; the manner in which the Tamils did this, the models their reaction adopted and the patterns it developed, and the cultural complexes that grew out of them, will have to be considered now.

We may begin by looking at some of the *normative* injunctions in which the theologian envisaged how man *ought to* react. Veṅkaṭanātha says:

> The *prapanna* (lit. "he who has surrendered himself") should adopt a behaviour [towards the *arcâvatāra*] in accordance with the type of relationship he may want to choose and with [Viṣṇu's] *paratva* and *saulabhya*, as is illustrated by the [following stanzas]: "Like a faithful wife towards her dear husband, like a mother towards her child, like a disciple towards his teacher, or like a friend towards his friend, one should show one's affection to Hari; he should always be considered as lord, friend, teacher, father, or mother."—"One should treat Bhagavān with awe, like a young king, an elephant in rut, or a dear guest who has arrived."—"One should respect Hari as if he were one's dear son."[78] [79]

This means that the devotee can orient himself in his response to the *arcā* according to various models of ordinary human interaction. Vedântadeśika lists a number of such models and divides them into two groups; those appropriate for Viṣṇu's *paratva* (e.g. the fear with which one approaches an elephant in rut) and those for *saulabhya* (e.g. like a mother treats her child). He does, however, not provide an empirically gained system which Tamil society might have developed; he simply wants to do justice to rather esoteric (Pāñcarātra) scriptural passages. In fact, he adds one further explanation in his own words to the passage just quoted, in which he says no more than "he should adopt a behaviour like that of a servant to his king."[80]

In the following three sections I shall turn to those responses which *de facto* were cultivated in Tamil society. The distinction drawn between *paratva* and *saulabhya* serves also here useful purposes; but while the first category can be illustrated by the theme "Viṣṇu as lord and king," the second category had to

[78] According to the editor: *Śāṇḍilya-smṛti* IV, 37f; 31; the third quotation has not been identified.

[79] *Rahasyatrayasāram*, chapter XV, pp. 512f.

[80] *Ibid.*, p. 514.

be broken up into two separate themes, viz. "Viṣṇu as lover" and "Viṣṇu as child."

(1) *Viṣṇu as chieftain and king.* Already on the previous pages indications were found of a symbolism by which Viṣṇu in the temple is treated like a chieftain or king. Viṣṇu "resides" as the "lord" in his "palace," he "owns" as the "master" his "village" or "town." It follows naturally from this that the *bhakta* places himself into the role of a servant and loyal subject. Historically, we are dealing here with the original connotations of the term "bhakti," viz. "loyalty, faithful service," like that of a feudal subject to his master. The new concept "prapatti" which became typical of Śrīvaiṣṇavism expands this older connotation by stressing both the protective aspect of Viṣṇu (who offers refuge) and the total surrender of the devotee. Earlier Tamil cultural history provides further aspects of this symbolism. Thus it appears to be possible to detect in the classical strata of *caṅkam* literature a specific link between the Pāṇṭiya kings and Viṣṇu[81]; this association of Viṣṇu with kingship is also well-known from other areas of Indian history. Possibly as a consequence of the collapse of traditional power structures in the South during the third century, Viṣṇu emancipated from that association, and in a now independent position enjoys the praise previously rendered to the king or chieftains. This shift manifests itself in various forms. The most obvious example is the change in meaning of the word *kōyil* (palace→temple). Moreover, the ancient bardic poetry knew of a particular slot in the structure of the poem into which a reference to the king or chieftain could be inserted. In some later *caṅkam* poems, Viṣṇu and his temple figured in this slot[82] and with the Āḻvārs it became a stereotyped pattern. Also the following feature may be used as evidence, if it is legitimate to identify the "brahmins" mentioned there as *pūjāris*: attributes of praise which had previously been used for a king or chieftain, are now applied to the Vedas and the brahmins. This results in rather incongruous expressions, e.g. "the Vedas of fame, abounding in glory,"[83] "morality protected by the brahmins of mighty strength and rich in fame."[84] A somewhat ambiguous poem in the *Cilappatikāram*[85] seems to say that in reality it is Viṣṇu who is king of the Pāṇṭiya etc. countries.

These external indications help us to understand the internal religious developments. "Service" is the logical link between Viṣṇu the king and the devotee as his servant. This service materializes itself in the acts of worship (*pūjā* in a general sense) which themselves are modelled according to the service rendered to a king or chieftain.

The phraseology employed is interesting. The most common root used is

[81]See Hardy, *op. cit.*, pp. 202-10; 664-66.

[82]Examples are *Paripāṭal* XV, *Akanāṉūru* 59, *Kalittokai* 102-6.

[83]*Paripāṭal* II, 63.

[84]*Ibid.* I, 37f.

[85]*Āycciyarkuravai*, poem 12

āḷ, which as verb means "to rule, own" and is constantly said about Viṣṇu with reference to the devotee. As a noun, denoting that which is owned—viz. "servant, labourer"—it refers to the devotee. Another word is *aṭimai* which derives from *aṭi* "foot, base, bottom" and denotes either "slavery, servitude" or "slave, servant." A third word is *toṇṭu* "slavery, devoted service" or "slave, devoted servant (in that meaning also *toṇṭar*)." This relationship is symbolically and ritually enacted by prostrating oneself before the "lord" and worshipping his feet "with one's head."[86]

We may assume that while the cult surrounding the person of honour (viz. from chieftain to king) increased in complexity, so also did the symbolism imposed on the temple god, but details illustrating this development are difficult to find. The testimony of the later Āḻvārs (c. 800 to 900 A.D.) shows however that the temple service is already differentiated and complex. Two of these later Āḻvārs were temple brahmins or *pūjāris*, Toṇṭaraṭippoṭi and Periyâḻvār. The former tells us that it was his "service (*toṇṭu*)" to prepare the *tulsī* garlands for worship. His *Tiruppaḷḷiyeḻucci* is an elaborate hymn, addressed to Viṣṇu in Śrīraṅgam and to be sung in the morning to wake up the god. It is clearly modelled on Sanskrit songs of the same purpose but addressed to a king. This developed as a poetic genre both in Tamil and in Sanskrit (called *suprabhātam*), and most Śrīvaiṣṇava temples possess now their own *paḷḷiyeḻucci* or *suprabhātam.* Other features which were adopted from the royal cult and integrated into the *pūjā* are for instance the dressing of the *vigraha*, placing ornaments on it, then holding a mirror in front of it, fanning it with a *cāmara* (a yak tail whisk) and holding a parasol over its head (both the chowrie and the parasol are royal insignia), etc. In the past, the temple god was also entertained with music, song, and dance (for details see below).

Given the complexity of the ritual, professional "servants" were essential. The distinction between these and the ordinary worshippers is marked today (I cannot comment on the earlier period) by the fact that only the *pūjāri* is allowed to enter the *garbhagṛha* of a temple where the *vigraha* is placed.

Periyâḻvār, like Toṇṭaraṭippoṭi, was such a *pūjāri*, and he provides us with some interesting information about his daily life. Thus he tells us that he is

[86]Already in *Paripāṭal* II, 72; Fragment I, 5f. Burrow/Emeneau, *A Dravidian Etymological Dictionary*, Oxford, 1966, No. 2903, connects the word *toṇṭu* with *tolil* "work"; this would suggest a common element *tol* (+tu/il) which might also be implied in $\sqrt{}$*tolu* "to worship" (Burrow/Emeneau 2904), also "to bow." However, this possible etymological connection of "work, service" with "worship" is highly speculative. To worship with one's head the feet of the *arcâvatāra* has been given an ingenious ritual expression; whether it was because of the abrasion of the *vigraha* through the constant contact with the devotees' forehead, or whether as a direct consequence of closing the *garbhagṛha* to the public, a device called *caṭakōpam* was developed. This is a bell-shaped metal object which has a pair of feet sculptured on its top. During *sevā* it is placed by the *pūjāri* for a moment on the head of the devotee, like a crown.

"a Vaiṣṇava who lives in your (=Viṣṇu's) temple"[87]; in Viṣṇu's service he finds the fulfilment of his life: "I do not desire clothes or food—I obtain them through that 'royal splendour' called 'to be your servant'. Do not doubt that I want to be taken as your slave into your service."[88] While his servitude is demonstrated by "being brand-marked, myself and everything I own, with the property sign of your discus,"[89] Viṣṇu's generosity and care as the master shows itself in this manner: he is "capable of rendering my soul pure by granting me boiled rice with ghee, the office of a royal servant, betel nuts, ornaments, rings for my ears, and sandal-paste to put on my body." The Āḻvār states: "we are servants in such manner that we wear the yellow garment which you wore and discarded, eat out of your vessels, and adorn ourselves with the *tulsī* that adorned you and which you then discarded."[90] This means in more abstract words that the *bhakta* surrenders himself and everything that belongs to him entirely to Viṣṇu, and receives in turn everything he requires, from bodily ornaments to food, as objects that purify his heart. In the context of temple ritual it means that all those objects mentioned are offered to the *arcā*, and when purified by the physical contact with Viṣṇu and thus endowed with their own purifying power, are received back as *prasādam*. If any of the objects are brought as offerings by a devotee, they will be shared by him and the *pūjāri* after the ritual.

This conception of Viṣṇu as the king in the temple had an enormous impact on Śrīvaiṣṇava thought and life. Rāmānuja took the truly revolutionary step of redefining the essence of man (his *svarūpa*) as being Viṣṇu's *śeṣa* "totally subject and dependent subject," instead of using the definition, hallowed since the time of the Upaniṣads, of man as the (potential) *jñānī*, "endowed with perfect knowledge." *Kaiṅkarya*, acts of (ritualized) service, remain essential even for the *jīvanmukta*, that means for the person who has already realized his essential nature while still living in his mortal frame, as both Piḷḷai Lokâcārya and Vedântadeśika state.[91] Moreover, even in the final state of *mukti* (defined as the full enjoyment of Viṣṇu in heaven), *kaiṅkarya* remains the basic mode of communication between the liberated soul and Viṣṇu. When the *mukta* has reached heaven, Veṅkaṭanātha says, "he will accept for as long as his soul lasts all the services which he wishes for in agreement with Viṣṇu's own desires."[92] In another place, "service is the outflow of the special love

[87] *Periyâlvar-Tirumoli* V, 1, 3.

[88] *Ibid.* 4; *aṭimai*[y] *eṉṉum akkōyiṉmaiyālē*, according to the Madras Tamil Lexicon "royal dignity; pride, as of a king." One commentator: =*puruṣârtha*.

[89] *Ibid.* V, 4, 1. Compare V, 2, 8 and I, 1, 7 where this "seal" or "brand-mark" (*ilañcaṉai, pori*) is also mentioned.

[90] *Ibid.* I, 1, 7f.—*Attāṇi cēvakam*, probably from Sanskrit *āsthāna* ("hall of audience") + *sevaka* ("servant").

[91] *Mumukṣuppaṭi* (ed. Aṇṇaṅkarâcāriyar, Kāñcīpuram, 1966), *sūtras* 165-87; *Śrīvacanabhūṣaṇam*, *sūtras* 274f; 288; etc.—*Rahasyatrayasāram*, chapter XV, pp. 509-15.

[92] *Rahasyatrayasāram*, chapter 21, p. 670.

which arises from his complete enjoyment [of Viṣṇu] in heaven."[93] Thus the service performed by the *bhakta* in the temple is a symbolic enactment of what he will continue to do in heaven.

If service to Viṣṇu is common to *bhakta* and *mukta*, to heaven and earth, one of the most fundamental premises of Hindu belief, the value-judgement made with reference to the dischotomy *saṃsāra* : *mokṣa*, was no longer totally taken for granted. Thus we hear indeed in Nammāḻvār:

> A birth on earth as Viṣṇu's slave, regardless of who one were or how lowly stationed,—is that not the splendour of heaven! [Why] should we fear our ancient deeds? Should we crave for heaven as the only thing [worth wishing for]?[94]

The theme "Viṣṇu the king" has had many other corollaries. For instance, according to present Indian law, Viṣṇu figures as a person legally entitled to own property etc. The temples and all their revenues are his property, and they are administered on his behalf by the trustees (*adhikārins*). A whole segment of society, from the *pūjāri* down to the sugar-candy supplier, finds employment and maintenance in the temples. At least in the past, this included also artists which made the temples one of the most important centers for the arts. It would be an interesting point to investigate in which manner the actual king related himself to "Viṣṇu the king" in the temple, but a systematic study of the *sthalapurāṇas* which may well contain material relevant for this point, is still a *desideratum*.[95]

(2) *Viṣṇu as lover*. The projection of all the paraphernalia of a palace culture onto the temple cult, and the *bhakta*'s treatment of Viṣṇu as chieftain or king, do not exhaust the range of what can be called the Tamil exploitation of the theme "Viṣṇu is in the temple." A second, and at least during certain periods very important, theme can be discerned which, interestingly enough, is not even mentioned by Veṅkaṭanātha:[96] Viṣṇu the lover. This theme clearly originated in the Āḻvārs in whom we can trace the developments leading up to his full exploitation. Since I have, however, dealt with this topic in great detail elsewhere,[97] a brief summary will be sufficient here.

[93] *Ibid.*, chapter 22, p. 685; compare p. 686: "exclusive service which is the outflow of experiencing (Viṣṇu in heaven)."

[94] *Periyatiruvantâti*, stanza 79. Such reflections are, however, very rare in the *Prabandham*, and I do not know of any example in the Ācāryas.

[95] On one related example see below, under III (Kāladūṣaka and the king).

[96] He does, after all, quote only three *Sanskrit* passages. In a number of instances, he himself contributed to the present theme, but his source of inspiration are the Ālvārs. See his *Navamaṇi-mālai*, *Acyutaśatakam*, and *Devanāyakapañcāśat*. Piḷḷai Lokâcārya deals, I presume, in a theoretical manner with it in his *Navavidhasambandham;* but this work has not been available to me.

[97] See Hardy, *op. cit.*

Already in the earliest strata of Tamil literature, the conception of a "hero" implies a twofold characteristic: strength, shown in defeating his enemies, in raiding their cattle, etc., and beauty with reference to women; in other words, heroic and sexual prowess. This twofold aspect becomes formalized by the poeticians in the distinction of *puram* "external" and *akam* "internal" poetry, and is borne out by two distinct poetic genres. Some centuries later, when the first Āḻvārs express their sentiments before the images of Viṣṇu, they stress not only Viṣṇu's awe-inspiring lordship which enslaves them, but also his beauty which is manifest in the *arcā*. More important: they establish a direct parallel between his descent into the temple image and into the heart of the *bhakta*. Entranced by the manifest beauty and filled with love, these Āḻvārs express a strong desire to "unite" with Viṣṇu. Nammāḻvār, who is the key-figure in the history of Southern Vaiṣṇavism, does not only extend this desire for union into mysticism, but also imposes the conventions and sentiments of the old *love* poetry onto this temple-mysticism. I believe that this combination was one of the most important achievements in Vaiṣṇava history, and proved inspiring even beyond the boundaries of Tamil Nadu But given the particular conventions of *akam* lyrics, the initial drive displayed by the early Āḻvārs to "unite" with Viṣṇu had to be modified by Nammāḻvār to a mysticism of "separation," in which the inability of the human frame, fully to grasp Viṣṇu, is stressed. All this is expressed through poetic symbolism, the central symbol being that of the "girl" who is depicted as being in love with Viṣṇu, the lord of the local temple. A similar symbolism is found in the later Āḻvārs, in Kalikaṉri and, most intensely, in Āṇṭāḷ. In order to illustrate this type of poetry, I quote one stanza from Nammāḻvār:

My mother says: "She is an absolute shame to our family" and does not let me look out for him.
When I saw the lord of TirukKuruṅkuṭi,
he filled my soul, and since then
has remained hidden in it
with his gold-like body that is surrounded
by a flood of splendour. . . .[98]

Particularly in Kalikaṉri, Viṣṇu of the local temple is envisaged as active, at least on the plane of poetry. For instance:

Was he a thief ?
He came like a big black bull and said to my daughter:
"Come ! Come !"
He took her by the hand which white bracelets adorned,

[98]*Tiruvāymoli* V, 5, 7.

and they abandoned the mother who gave birth to her.
Gone away, they must now have entered Tiruvāli
beautiful with its fields and marshy tracts.[99]

This is an altogether new type of *bhakti*; it is not the passionless *bhakti-yoga* of the Gītā, but an impassioned, often ecstatic abandon to Viṣṇu's beauty and modelled according to the love of a girl towards her lover. The further history of this new form of *bhakti* which had a very strong impact on religion in the North, falls outside the scope of the present paper; I have dealt with it elsewhere.[100] Within the Śrīvaiṣṇava tradition, the theme of "Viṣṇu the lover" continues in a rather peculiar manner. The sober Ācāryas, in spite of all their appreciation of the Āḻvārs, somehow felt embarrassed by the frank sensuality of their mysticism of separation, and in their own religious attitude concentrated on Viṣṇu the *śeṣī* who demanded complete surrender (*prapatti*) from the devotee, his *śeṣa*. When the theme of Viṣṇu the lover makes its fleeting appearance in Veṅkaṭanātha. it is perhaps no more than an academic poetic experiment with older genres.[101] These normative pressures of the Ācāryas[102] reduced the importance of the theme in the area of theology; but in more popular areas it remained operative and established a definite link of *eros* with the temple cult. The following examples will illustrate this.

One way in which the theme of Viṣṇu the lover developed in the post-Āḻvār period was by replacing the "girl" by Lakṣmī. Since the temple contains an *arcā* of her, besides that of Viṣṇu, all the love games he is supposed to play with her in heaven can be brought down to earth and ritually enacted. Particularly the *vasantôtsava*, the spring festival, is loaded with erotic sentiments.

> Hari observed the season of spring—the breeze filled with streams of fragrance, the swarms of bees and the cuckoos with sweet voices, the abundant splendour of Kāma who subdues the world. Bhagavān who resides in Śrīraṅgam had his heart captivated by all this beauty of the season of flowers, and along with his queens he went out into the park, desirous of honouring the new flowers. In the park, the whole world was informed about the arrival of Kāma by the noise from the throats of the mellifluous cuckoos.[103]

[99]*Periyatirumoli* III, 7, 1.

[100]See Hardy, *op. cit.*, pp. 554-620.

[101]See note 96 above. I am preparing a detailed study of Veṅkaṭanātha's poetry where a discussion of these themes will be found.

[102]In cases where a discussion of the theme is necessary, viz. in the commentaries on the erotic poems of the Ālvārs, an *allegorical* explanation is given to the "love symbolism"; see Hardy, *op. cit.*, p. 342 with note 91; pp. 344f with note 103. On the other hand, the Ācāryas were certainly tolerant enough not to exclude this form of religious attitude in their lists of *possible* relationships.

[103]*Divyasūricarita*, canto XV, verses 2. 4-6.

This passage represents a poetic and imaginative rendering of a ritual event: the *arcās* of Viṣṇu, Lakṣmī, etc. are taken out in procession into the temple garden, where the spring festival is celebrated with them.

Many of the Tamil poetic genres which are included under the label "*prabandham*"[104] had their origin in such ritual events When Viṣṇu and Lakṣmī are placed on the swing, songs to accompany the swinging were designed, the *ūcal*[105] Many other such poems or songs, of an erotic character, were written for such festivals in the individual temples. There are those describing the infatuating beauty of Viṣṇu seen by a girl, when he is carried in procession through the town (*ulā* or *maṭal*), and there are messenger poems addressed by the girl to the temple god (*tūtu*).[106] Larger poetic forms, like the *kalampakam*, *paḷḷu*, or *noṇṭi-nāṭakam*,[107] integrate a number of these smaller genres. It is particularly in these Tamil *prabandhams* that the erotic poetry of the Āḻvārs is developed further.

But when discussing the theme of *eros* as pervading the Śrīvaiṣṇava temple culture, one further topic cannot be avoided: the music and dance professionally cultivated by the *devadāsīs*. Whatever the historical and sociological developments may have been which led to this institution, the Śrīvaiṣṇava sources known to me are silent about it. Missionaries like the Abbé Dubois and some Westernized Indians, encountering a presumably declining stage in the development of the *devadāsī* institution, attacked it with a puritanical fanaticism which was equalled only by their complete ignorance of (or unwillingness to understand) its history and the motivation behind it. They succeeded only too well in their task: the abolition by law of the *devadāsīs* was regarded as a necessary reform of South Indian temple culture, but it also resulted in the total destruction of one major segment of that culture through which for one and a half millennia deep-rooted Southern religious sentiments ments had expressed themselves. The whole range of art that had surrounded the temple was eliminated, and even the whole issue of temple eroticism was prejudiced. This means that it would require considerable courage to explore the possibility that the stanza from the *Periyatirumoḻi* quoted above had a *realistic* basis: that the mother expresses her feelings of loss because her daughter had decided to become a servant-girl in the temple of Tiruvāli—a service which at the time of the Āḻvars may have implied none of the features which were so shocking to the modern observer. But it may be of interest to

[104]On the various genres and their themes in general Tamil literature, see K.V. Zvelebil, *Tamil Literature*,=vol. X, fasc. 1, of *A History of Indian Literature*, ed. J. Gonda, Wiesbaden, 1974, pp. 193-230.

[105]See e.g. PiḷḷaipPerumāḷ Aiyaṅkār's *Cīraṅkanāyaka-ūcal* or Veṅkaṭanātha's (lost) *Devanāyaka-ūcal*

[106]Examples are: *Tirucciruppuliyūr-ulā*; *Alakar-kiḷḷai-viṭu-tūtu; Alakar-Kuravañci.*

[107]For instance the *Teṉ-tirupPērai-Kalampakam, Kurukūr-paḷḷu, TirupPullāṇi-noṇṭi-nāṭakam.*

discuss a unique document which illustrates how *within* Śrīvaiṣṇavism the *devadāsī* institution was regarded. This is a one-act play (*bhāṇa*) in Sanskrit[108] which was written c. 1850 A.D. by Veṅkaṭâcārya and is entitled *Kandarpa-darpaṇa*.[109] It is set in Triplicane/Madras during the *vijayadaśamī* festival of the Pārthasārathi temple.

Kalahaṃsaka, the *viṭa* ("playboy") typical of this genre of drama, is in love with Kandarpasenā's daughter Kamalamañjarī. A message from her mother arrives: "Today will take place the great festival of my daughter Kamala-mañjarī's first appearance on the stage, before Śrī Pārthasārathi who is an ocean of all auspicious qualities and whose feet-lotuses are served by all gods and demons. Therefore you must make your appearance there!"[110] This means: the girl, trained as a dancer and a *devadāsī*, will give her first public display before the *vigraha* of Viṣṇu. Why Kalahaṃsaka must be there will become clear presenty. Although it is still morning, he sets out, and wandering leisure-ly through the streets of Triplicane, he describes various scenes and people. Seeing a group of temple prostitutes walking before the *arcā* of Pārthasārathi which is carried through the streets in procession, he says: "I will cast a look at Bhagavān with devotion!" Beholding him, he says with admiration: "That deity, consisting of Love's bliss,[111] honours with affection the young prostitutes who are to be his beloved ones and who skilfully perform their dance inside the courtyard which his own ornaments make radiant."[112] This sight gives him the opportunity to attack those puritanical (and since this was about 1850, Westernized?) brahmins who express their dislike for these *devadāsīs* "always delightful to watch for the Puruṣottama (pun: the greatest of males) who is the great deity of the erotic sentiment (*śṛṅgāra-rasa*)." With a charming piece of fanciful allegory he actually "proves" this statement about Viṣṇu. "Bhagavān puts behind his back the crowd of brahmins who recite the Vedas; he separates himself from those who recite the Tamil-Veda (=Nam-māḻvār's poems) by placing the prostitutes between himself and them."[113] This refers to the arrangement in the procession. When evening begins, he

[108]For a general discussion of recent *bhāṇas*, including those which are connected with Śrīvaiṣṇava temples (*i a.* Varadâcārya's *Vasantatilakam* or Raṅgâcārya's *Pañcabāṇavijaya*), see S.S. Janaki, "Le piu recenti composizioni teatrali di tipo bhāṇa" in *Atti della Accademia delle Scienze di Torino*, II—Classe di Scienze morali, storiche e filologiche, vol. 107(1972-73), pp. 459-90.

[109]The full name of the author is Tirumalai Caturveda-śatakratu Nāvalpākkam Ayyā Veṅkaṭâcārya; the *bhāṇa* has been published serially in the *Journal of the Tanjore Sarasvati Mahal Library*, vols. XIX 1/2 (1966) to XX 1 (1966), from manuscript No. 168 of that library.

[110]Lines 3-5 of prose after verse 9; p. 6.

[111]*Śṛṅgārasya rasasya daivatam*; in other words, a personification of Kāma. This may well be a play on the definition of Viṣṇu as (knowledge and) bliss.

[112]Prose after verse 41; verse 43

[113]Verse 45.

arrives at the house of Kandarpasenā. While he remains outside and watches, he sees her "carrying in her hand many different and lovely offerings for the god"[114] and leading her daughter to the stage, where Pārthasārathi has already been placed on a high seat. Kalahaṃsaka prostrates himself before the *vigraha*, and after some prayers he says: "Nectar is poured into the ears of Arjuna's charioteer (=Pārthasārathi) by the jingling noise of the dancing bracelets; he watches with excitement these women approaching, and time and again radiates forth with a gentle smile."[115] The dance performance begins, and the *viṭa* describes in detail the entrancing dance of Kamalamañjarī, while "Bhagavān is seated high up, as if eager to enjoy the abundant pleasure of her dance."[116] At Kandarpasenā's house, after the ceremony, he signs a contract called *kalatrapatrikā*[117] which gives him the privilege "to dally with her [Kamalamañjarī] until a child is conceived," while he guarantees to support her and provide her with clothes and ornaments.

The humorous character of the play should not distract our attention from the genuine religious spirit which pervades it. The author makes it clear that in his opinion Viṣṇu, present in the *arcā*, derives enjoyment from the art of the girls who are dedicated to him, just as he would enjoy the *tulsī, kuṅkuma*, camphor, etc. which are offered to him in the *pūjā*. And just as he returns these objects after the worship to the devotee, these girls are returned. Thus it seems possible to interpret Kalahaṃsaka's quasi-marital union with Kamalamañjarī, which is founded on a legally binding contract, as a special type of *prasādam*. This is perfectly legitimate and logical within the structure of Śrīvaiṣṇava temple culture, in which eros and the arts have played an important role throughout its history. Seen from the point of view of the girl, it represents the harmonious synthesis of the two themes discussed so far: she dedicates herself in surrender and service to Viṣṇu the lord, and her art, her love and passions to Viṣṇu the lover.

A similar synthesis of the two themes, in a more general manner, can be detected in Śrīvaiṣṇava parlance The Sanskrit words *sevā* and *sev*, "service" and "to serve," have acquired here, as *cēvai* and *cēvittal*, the additional meanings of "relishing the beauty of the *vigraha* with one's eyes"—in other words what in modern Indian parlance is meant by "darśan." This synthesis has also a ritual side. When the devotee visits a temple, he offers *i.a.* some camphor (thus the element of service) which is placed on a tray, lit, and used by the *pūjāri* as a lamp to illuminate the full *vigraha*. It has frequently happened during my own visits to those temples that the *pūjāri* would actually ask the

[114]Verse 204.

[115]Verse 211.

[116]Prose before verse 212.

[117]For details on this type of document (also called *nibandhanapattrikā* or *maitrīpattrikā*) see Janaki, *op. cit.*, pp. 481-83.

devotees present whether they could see the figure properly, or whether they wanted to see more of the statue.

(3) *Viṣṇu as child.* The two themes discussed so far both imply an element of awe, lordship, and remoteness. Also the girl in Āḻvār poetry remains subject to Viṣṇu's—often unpredictable—will, and this in turn explains their mysticism of separation. But Śrīvaiṣṇavism developed a further theme in which the *saulabhya* aspect of Viṣṇu plays the dominant rōle: that of Viṣṇu the child. This theme originally derives from the purāṇic treatment of Kṛṣṇa's infancy and his childhood adventures. Parakālaṉ, Kulaśekhara, and particularly Periyâḻvār adopted it in their Tamil poetry and lay the foundation for a whole new genre of Tamil literature, the *piḷḷaittamiḻ*. Today many of the *divyadeśams* have their own *prabandham* of that genre.[118] What was important in the treatment of those Āḻvārs was not so much the expansion of the purāṇic incidents, but that they related those childhood events to the local temple and that they addressed themselves to women and children. Adopting various types of folk-songs, they created a whole repertoire which mothers and children could sing as accompaniment to various games. Examples are the *cappāṇi* "clapping with the hands," *ceṅkīrai* "nodding with the head," *ammāṉai* "swing songs," or *tālēlō* "lullaby." Through these songs both the mythical events of Vṛndāvana and Viṣṇu in the local temple are infused, as it were, into the everyday life of children and mothers. Playing with her child, the mother could transform her care and love into an act of *bhakti*; she could dedicate them as a quasi-service to the local *arcâvatāra*; and she could expand her village-horizon as far as the mythical realm of Vṛndāvana. Indirectly a whole pattern of child education was thereby created by means of which a child was given not only a great deal of love and care, but was also stimulated in the use of its bodily and imaginative faculties; the earlier items in the conventional *piḷḷaittamiḻ* deal with the use of various limbs of the baby, and the latter ones concern various toys (small drums, little carts), while in the *cirril* "small houses" the child builds its own sand castles. Through the example of Yaśodā, the young mother is reminded of her duty to discipline the child and also, not to lose patience when this proves difficult. Thus the intention underlying these songs is not simply to spoil the child.

In the ritual context, this theme appears for instance in a special *vigraha*, called *santāna-Gopāla*, which represents the infant Kṛṣṇa lying in his cradle and which is found in some temples; sometimes (as in Tiruppullāṇi) it is placed in a special shrine. Worshippers may handle this *vigraha*, and men desirous of children place it on their laps.

Periyâḻvār may illustrate how this theme is integrated with the other two that have been discussed previously: after the description of Kṛṣṇa's childhood pranks he turns to the well-known *gopī* episodes with all their erotic content;

[118]For instance the *Tiruvaikuṇṭanātaṉ-piḷḷaittamil, Tiruvallikkēṉippiḷḷaimaiyiṉmai.*

the theme of Viṣṇu the lord is woven into the description of the pranks, for time and again Yaśodā is awed and even frightened by the miraculous powers Kṛṣṇa appears to possess.

These three patterns of response to Viṣṇu's *arcâvatāra* contain a twofold movement. In a "centripetal" suction, the *bhakta* and everything which constitutes his life, from food, clothing, ornaments to physical love, is drawn into the service of the *arcâvatāra* who thereby exerts his right as the *śeṣī*. But a "centrifugal" drive complements this. Viṣṇu himself, in his *līlā*, radiates his own nature into the world of phenomena. Making himself available to man and enticing him with his beauty, he allows him to participate in his *līlā* by returning to him everything that had been surrendered, to be used for his own enjoyment and pleasure. Thus the three basic models of behaving towards the *arcâvatāra* are transformed into stimuli for a culture which, seen as gift for the devotee, allowed for a full enjoyment of man's faculties which was based on a fundamentally positive attitude towards the world, the senses, and the matters of ordinary life. However, we can also see that this conception, which has been described as it manifests itself empirically in Tamil society, does not agree fully with the normative pattern. Veṅkaṭanātha tones down the theme of Viṣṇu the lover by mentioning only the model of the "faithful wife towards her husband," stressing thereby primarily the aspect of her subjugation under an all-demanding master. When Kalahaṃsaka attacks some puritanical brahmins, this may well reflect a real struggle in contemporary society.

III. THE MYTHICAL STRUCTURE OF MEANING

Viṣṇu's presence in the *arcā* is responded to in models of interpersonal relationships with a human being. Many of the mythical *avatāras* are also human beings. But there is one major difference between these two types of *avatāras*: while the mythical ones possess a human body and are therefore capable of action, which takes place in the past and on the whole in regions of India other than Tamil Nadu,[119] the *arcâvatāra* cannot move or act physically and is therefore "dependent on the officiating priest."[120] Approached as king, lover, or child, action is indeed attributed to him, but this rests entirely on poetic conceit and convention. It thus lacks the element of "reality," being a highly sophisticated construction depending on a particular poetic tradition. On a more popular level, during the later medieval period when the poetic tradition had lost some of its vitality, a new structure of meaning

[119] This applies particularly to the *Kṛṣṇâvatāra; Akanāṉūṟu* 59, 3f actually says: "on the bank of the Yamunā in the North." When *Śrīrangam* claims to be the place where Rāma rested on his way to Laṅkā, the actual *vigraha* there must nevertheless be considered to be *commemorative*, and not a perpetuation, of that event.

[120] See note 56 above.

evolved which attempted to explain the significance of the temple in mythical terms, overcoming thereby the difference in the two types of *avatāras*. Moreover, with many centuries of history behind them, these temples gave rise to a number of questions in the minds of the devotees, for which neither the doctrine formulated by the Ācāryas nor the religious attitudes created by the Āḻvārs had the answers. All this is dealt with in a new genre of literature, viz. the *sthalapurāṇas* (also called *māhātmyas*, *vaibhava*, and in Tamil *talavaralāru* "history of the temple locality"). The adjective "new" simply refers to the chronologically late appearance in Śrīvaiṣṇava tradition of an other wise and elsewhere much older genre.

These *māhātmyams* conceive of Viṣṇu as manifesting himself in that locality some time in the past, displaying all his supernatural splendour and power, acting for the benefit of a particular devotee, and then deciding to abide permanently, as the *arcā*, in that place. Thus the *arcâvatāra* is the perpetuation of the real, acting Viṣṇu in a particular temple.

I shall begin the discussion with some observations on the development of this literary genre in Śrīvaiṣṇava tradition. Probably the earliest trace of the kind of question that then stimulated the formation of Śrīvaiṣṇava *sthalapurāṇa* literature is found in this stanza: "You and the Sacred Lady (= Viṣṇu and Lakṣmī) remain from now onwards in the *iṭaikaḻi* of Kōvalūr, neither proceeding towards the entrance gate nor entering inside [the shrine]."[121] *Iṭaikaḻi* in a traditional South Indian house denotes the open verandah, covered by a roof, in front of a house, which is used as a sleeping place.[122] The stanza is difficult to interpret, but it seems to comment on the peculiar position in which the Āḻvār found the *vigrahas*. But when in the eleventh century Āḻvār hagiography begins to develop, this mysterious allusion to the "antechamber" and to the equally mysterious "from now onwards"[123] gave rise to a piece of *sthalapurāṇa* mythology. Thus we read in the *Divyasūricarita*:[124]

> On one occasion, Bhagavān brought the [three first Āḻvārs who till then had not met each other] together in the *Vāmana-kṣetra* (=Tirukkōvalūr). All of a sudden he created a "cloudless" (=artificial) rain in the night and thereby forced them to take shelter in a narrow *dehalī* (= *iṭaikaḻi*). Poykai-Āḻvār and the other two were squeezing each other in that confined space, but then they realised that apart from them another person was present,

[121] *1st Antâti*, stanza 86.

[122] Vedântadeśika translates the word as *dehalī* "threshold, antechamber"; in the temple context it probably refers to the *ardhamaṇḍapam*.

[123] Since there is a reference to Kṛṣṇa's lifting the mountain Govardhana, it might be said that the "from now onwards" stresses the permanent availability of Viṣṇu in the temple by contrasting it with "the greatness you displayed by checking the pouring rain through lifting the mountain" which was of help only to the people in Vraja.

[124] Canto II, verses 18-20. Later works have greatly expanded the story.

and separately they made lamps which revealed the manifestation of the Highest Being.

The three Āḻvārs express their experience of Viṣṇu in three poems, and then walk away on their separate ways. While the primary intention of this legend is to tell us about the circumstances which led to the composition of the three *Antâtis* of the *Prabandham, in nucleo* it also contains a *sthalapurāṇa*-like explanation of how Viṣṇu came to be present in the Kōvalūr temple, in that particular position.

Another early example may be mentioned here. The Tiruvehkā temple in Kāñcīpuram is probably the first temple referred to in *caṅkam* literature.[125] Viṣṇu there is known as Yathôktakārī (in Tamil: Coṉṉa vaṇṇañ ceyta Perumāḷ) "who acts according to the request (of the *bhakta*)." This name is "explained," that means exemplified, through a legend about Tirumaḻicai Āḻvār. The Āḻvār's disciple Kaṇikṛṣṇa was an excellent poet, but refused to employ his talents for secular purposes by composing a poem of flattery for the king of Kāñcīpuram. The king expelled him from his town; the Āḻvār decided to accompany his disciple, and requested Viṣṇu in Tiruvehkā to leave along with them When the three had left, all the splendour abandoned the town, and in remorse the king hasted after them and persuaded them to return. Back in the town, "the son of Bhṛgu (= Tirumaḻicai Āḻvār) requested Viṣṇu"—I quote again from the *Divyasūricarita*—" 'Please spread out the serpent as your couch here, and sleep in this place!' Madhava agreed, and in order to indicate his having left [the temple] and then returned to it, he rested his head on his *left* arm."[126] This legend explains two points: how Viṣṇu became known as Yathôktakārī (he accepted the Āḻvār's request to come with him), and why his head rests on his left, instead of his right hand, which conventional iconography would demand. As in the previous example, a particular iconographic feature, which struck the observant pilgrim as being out of the ordinary, is explained by reference to a local legend. Moreover, in both cases the legend is part of the Āḻvār cycle; it seems in fact quite natural that at the beginning of Śrīvaiṣṇava *māhātmya* literature Āḻvārs provided the focus of attention, who after all accounted for the sanctity of the temples by having sung about them. But soon local mythology turned to other, and we may add, by then more prestigious, areas of inspiration. This can be illustrated from that portion of the legend which precedes the "*yathôktakārī* events." The latter could not answer one important question in the mind of the worshipper, which was how Viṣṇu came to be there in the temple in the first place, before the Āḻvār asked him to leave. The answer is given in the following story which does not use Āḻvār legends but elements associated with brahmin

[125]See note 7.
[126]Canto III, verses 37f.

religion: Vedic sacrifice, Brahmā, Sarasvatī, etc. Tiruvehkā lies on the bank of the river Vegavatī; Viṣṇu inside the temple reclines on the serpent Ananta, and the massive stone couch must have reminded someone of a causeway across the river. Thus in the early *Divyasūricarita* we hear simply: "Mādhava who was reclining there *like* a dam blocking the river Sarasvatī (or: which was the goddess Sarasvatī)."[127] Another name of Viṣṇu in the same temple resulted from this flight of fancy: Vegasetu "the dam across the river Vegavatī." This is the legend which explains this highly imaginative nomenclature. Brahmā, deluded by pride about his privileged status (as creator etc.), thought that he would be able, through his own effort, to obtain a vision in *samādhi* of Viṣṇu. All his attempts, however, failed; finally, he was advised to perform an *aśva-medha* sacrifice in the holy town Kāñcīpuram. Although invited to participate in this sacrifice, his wife Sarasvatī (herself busy with performing *tapas* in the river Sarasvatī) refused, because at the time she was quarrelling with Brahmā. But when she came to know that Brahmā's other wives were taking part in the sacrifice, she became jealous and rushed in the form of a river *vegavatī* "with great vehemence" towards the place where the *aśvamedha* was being performed, in order to sweep away its altar. "But he who is his father[128] and has the serpent as his couch had compassion with the primordial Unborn (=Brahmā) and turned himself into a dam,"[129] and thereby blocked the flow of the river.

Veṅkaṭanātha's rendering of this myth is interesting for various reasons. It is a fairly unique example of a *sthalapurāṇa* presented in the literary form of a dance-play, and at the same time pervaded through and through with theological reflections worthy of the learned Ācārya. Moreover, the play as a whole deals not only with the one temple Tiruvehkā in Kāñcī, but also with a second, and probably by the author's time already much more important, temple, that of Varadarājapperumāḷ. While Vehkā is the place where Viṣṇu became the dam, Varadarāja is where he revealed himself to Brahmā in the sacrificial fire on the altar. This is the theology which Veṅkaṭanātha derives from this:

> One and the same splendour has revealed itself, through its own free will; it is visible in the middle of the Vegavatī and on the Elephant Hill (on which the Varadarāja temple is situated), as the means (*upāya*) and the final reward (*phala*,∼*upeya*).[130]

[127]Canto III, verse 18.

[128]Since Brahmā is born in the lotus growing in Viṣṇu's navel, Viṣṇu can thus be called his "father."

[129]*Meyviratamāṉmiyam*, a dance-play by Veṅkaṭanātha (ed. in Tamil and Grantha characters by A. Śrīnivāsarākavaṉ, Kumbakonam, 1937,=pp. 373-92 in vol. II of *Patiṉoru-cillarai-rahasyaṅkaḷ*), from Tamil verse 13, p. 382.—An earlier version of the legend, apparently an apocryphe portion of the *Brahmâṇḍa-Purāṇa*, is referred to by Vedântadeśika.

[130]*Ibid.*, Sanskrit verse X, p. 389.—The terms *upāya* and *upeya* denote in Śrīvaiṣṇava

This is not just a theological game; it is a rational explanation of a particular situation: that there are two Viṣṇu temples in close proximity,[131] both famous, but one of them, Varadarāja (which is hardly mentioned in the *Prabandham*[132]), has become so much more imposing and grandiose than the older Vehkā.

This consideration leads over to a discussion of the *Tañjāpurīmāhātmyam*, the Sanskrit *sthalapurāṇa* of (Vaiṣṇava) Tanjore. Apart from the Bṛhadīśvara (Śiva) temple built by Rājarāja Cōḻa, (completed 1009 A.D.), and numerous lesser shrines, there are three Viṣṇu and one Devī temple in the town; the three Viṣṇu shrines count as *one divyadeśam*.[133] Since the date of this *sthalapurāṇa* is unknown, it cannot be stated with certainty that it is later than the imposing Bṛhadīśvara temple, although it seems very likely. This is the story which interests us here. The sage Parāśara—famous as the author of the *Viṣṇupurāṇa*, the most authoritative *purāṇa* among Śrīvaiṣṇavas—has taken down with him to earth his share of the nectar which Viṣṇu obtained by churning the milk-ocean, and has poured it into the pond of his *āśrama*. During a severe drought, three demons, Tañjaka etc., arrive there along with their hordes and devastate the whole area, naturally also disturbing the *tapas* of the sages living in the *āśrama*. Paraśara turns for help to Brahmā, but he declines. Śiva is more willing to give assistance, but when he hears that this would involve dealing with Tañjaka etc., he prefers to hand over the task to Caṇḍikā. She fights indeed with the demons and seems to succeed in killing them. But because of the nectar in the pond, they come to life again. She tries hard for many days, but without success, and the sage dismisses her. Now he prays to Viṣṇu who "by the name of Nīlamegha ('black cloud') appeared before him. Displaying his black cloud-like form in the sky, he was illuminated by the lightning in the form of the lovely Śrī."[134] He can kill the bulk of the demons immediately. When he is about to fight with the three leading demons, Kalī appears and insists on having her share in the battle; Viṣṇu leaves the youngest one, Tāraka, to her. When Tañjaka cannot defeat Viṣṇu, he becomes an elephant; but Viṣṇu turns into a lion and subdues him. A Viṣṇu holds him on his lap and is about to tear him apart with his claws, he is requested by Tañjaka:

---

theology the means by which *mokṣa* can be obtained and the goal of all human religious endeavour. Just as Viṣṇu himself is the goal, he is also the agent underlying all human religious exercises, and thus is the means.

[131]In the catalogues of *divyadeśams*, in fact fourteen are mentioned for Kāñcīpuram. But Vedântadeśika restricts himself (here in the dance-play and also in his *Vegasetustotra*) to the two most important ones.

[132]There are only six, partly doubtful references.

[133]This is called Tiruttañcai; since the references in the Ālvārs do not allow us to identify three clearly distinct temples, we can only say that at least one of the Viṣṇu shrines in Tanjore goes back to the time of the Ālvārs.

[134]*Tañjāpurī-māhātmyam*, manuscript (Descriptive Catalogue No. 10480) of the Tanjore Sarasvati Mahal Library; Chapter V, verses 11f.

"That form of a man-lion (Nṛ-siṃha) which you have taken on for my sake—may you dress yourself permanently in it. Moreover, let this temple-town be called by my name, viz. Tañjapurī."[135] When the second demon sees his companion killed, he disappears into the ground and tries to escape by burrowing his way through it. Viṣṇu turns into a boar and runs above the ground ahead of the demon, so that he can kill him as soon as he surfaces again. "Before killing him he granted the demon a boon: that he would stay, in the form of a boar, on the spot where he is to kill him."[136] Also the Devī succeeds in killing Taraka, and stays there "for the protection of the town."[137]

It is not difficult to detect the rationale underlying this legend. It provides a meaningful explanation for the three Viṣṇu temples in Tañcai. Firstly, the Nīlameghapperumāḷ temple with the nectar-*tīrtha*, in which Viṣṇu is seated, facing the *ṛṣi* Parāśara and placing his foot on Tañjaka's head. Secondly, the Tañcaiyāḷinakar temple with Viṣṇu in the form of Nṛsiṃha. Thirdly, the Maṇikuṉṟapperumāḷ temple with Viṣṇu as Varāha (?).[138] Then there is the reference to the Ānandavalli Ammaṉ temple of Devī; that the legend gives her a certain credit for the killing of the demons can be connected with Śrīvaiṣṇava practice in certain places, of acknowledging Devī as a servant of Viṣṇu and considering her the guardian of his temples. Thus in Tirukkōvalūr a statue of Durga is even inside the *ardhamaṇḍapam* and is in worship. Śiva is, however, altogether discarded by the legend, probably in defense against the so much more grandiose Bṛhadīśvara temple.

We must turn now to one further feature which is typical of this genre of literature. Viṣṇu in Śrīvaikuṇṭham is locally known as Kaḷḷapirāṉ (Skt. Coranātha), "leader of the robbers." One is tempted to regard this as an allusion to Kṛṣṇa's stealing the *gopīs*' butter, but the temple *purāṇa* provides an entirely different explanation by referring to local events and not to Vraja. Once upon a time, it tells us, a thief lived in the town, Kāladūṣaka by name. He squandered away part of his stolen wealth gambling and enjoying himself with prostitutes, but half of it he would give to Vaikuṇṭhanātha in the temple. When the king of the area finally succeeded in tracking him down, he took refuge in the temple, and Viṣṇu Vaikuṇṭhanātha offered him shelter, having taken on the form of a brahmin. Viṣṇu then changed his appearance into that of the robber and went to meet the king—to be identified by the royal soldiers as the "coranātha." He gave the king a severe admonition, revealed himself to him as Viṣṇu, and praised the great *bhakti* of Kāladūṣaka. A reconciliation between the king and the robber was achieved, and the king requested Viṣṇu to become known by the name of Coranātha and to live permanently in the

[135] *Ibid.*, chapter VI, verses 21f.
[136] *Ibid.*, verse 28.
[137] *Ibid.*, verse 48.
[138] I can only infer this from the *Purāṇa;* the various guidebooks keep silent about this point, and I was unable to enter the temple during my visit to Tanjore.

Śrīvaikuṇṭha temple. "In the lovely season of spring, in the month of *caitra*, the king had a festival celebrated. Along with the leader of the robbers, he decorated the town and distributed many presents, particularly to the brahmins. They gave food to all the people. This pleased Viṣṇu, the Lord of the Universe and Leader of Robbers, and he granted *mukti* to both the king and the robber. Every year those two, king and robber, performed that festival."[139]

When we take into account that a particular caste, known as Kaḷḷar, "thieves, robbers (thus Sanskrit: *cora*)" lives in the environment of the Śrīvaikuṇṭham temple and that the chief trustee of the temple belongs to that community, it is not difficult to unravel a particular sociological situation behind this legend and interpret it as the legitimization of a particular power-structure. In the centre of attention we find the *coras*, thus Kaḷḷar, who have the Kaḷḷapirāṉ (Coranātha) as their "own" *arcā*. The brahmins appear in a secondary role, but displaying a benevolent attitude towards the Kaḷḷar who give them generous gifts. The actual struggle for authority takes place between the Kaḷḷar and the king; through divine intervention, the Kaḷḷar are instituted in their own rights and a balance of power is struck: both the king and the leader of the Kaḷḷar community together celebrated the spring festival.

Thus this piece of local purāṇic legend explains, motivates, and legitimizes the following points: the particular name of Viṣṇu, Kaḷḷapirāṉ; the responsibility for organizing and celebrating the spring festival; the exceptionally favoured socio-religious position of an otherwise "low" caste, and its relationship to the king's authority.[140] It is also remarkable that the whole argument is carried out through the medium of Sanskrit, a fact that would appear to bear out the "benevolent" attitude of the brahmins towards the Kaḷḷar.

By now we have gathered together sufficient material for a discussion of the essential features of this literary genre. We can say, firstly, that it creates a meaningful whole out of a set of elements which to us appear to be accidental, arbitrary, and disconnected, and have been brought about simply by historical circumstances. Such typical elements are: the reason for Viṣṇu's initial arrival at the *sthala*; his local name(s); the name of the temple, tank, town or *vimānam*; iconographic peculiarities (e.g. Viṣṇu facing West instead of the normal East, reclining with his head on the left hand instead of the

[139] *Vaikuṇṭhanātha-māhātmyam* (= pp. 1-20 in *Navatiruppati-māhātmyam*, ed. Śrīnivāsâcārya in Grantha characters, Śuṇḍa-ppāḷayam, 1909), chapter V, verses 48-52.

[140] On the Kaḷḷar see Thurston/Rangachari, *Castes and Tribes of Southern India*, vol. III, Madras, 1909, pp. 53-91. On pp.83-85 mention is made of another "Kaḷḷar temple," the Kaḷḷ-Alakar (=Tirumāliruñcōlai). See also L. Dumont, *Un Sous-Caste de l' Inde du Sud* (Kaḷḷar), Mouton, 1957.—Attention may also be drawn to H. Kulke's excellent study of a Śaivite *sthalapurāṇa: Cidambaramāhātmya—Eine Untersuchung der religonsgeschichtlichen und historischen Hintergründe für die Entstehung der Tradition einer südindischen Tempelstadt*, Wiesbaden, 1970 (=Freiburger Beiträge zur Indologie, Band 3).

right); that there are more than one temple in one locality; exceptional features in the temple ritual (e g. Kaḷḷapirāṉ is bathed every day in milk), administration, celebration of festivals, etc. The *sthalapurāṇa*, by utilizing the genre of the pan-Indian *purāṇa*, integrates all these disconnected elements into a coherent and therefore meaningful structure of a narrative about past events. Thus it "answers" all the questions which the observant pilgrim might ask, and establishes also for the resident devotees a definite frame of reference which they can resort to in cases of dispute over ritual, social, administrative, legal, or political matters connected with their temple. This frame of reference is definite because it is founded on past—mythical—events, and not on a set of positive-legal injunctions or on a purely "historical" explanation.

Secondly, besides providing an explanation or justification of a particular situation found in a local temple, these works turn their attention to the existence of the other *divyadeśams*. They attempt to place the sanctity and religious "effectiveness" of and the intensity of Viṣṇu's presence in their own temple over and above those of the other temples. Thus Brahmā is told that a single *aśvamedha* performed in Varadarāja carries the reward of a thousand performed in any other place. These *purāṇas* usually begin with *ṛṣis* asking which of all the *tīrthas* is the best, and a prestigious religious figure then explains why the particular temple is the best.

Thirdly, these texts are anxious to connect the local temple both with universal Vaiṣṇavism and normative Hinduism. This is illustrated by features like: a famous *ṛṣi*, or Brahmā himself, performed *tapas* in that place; Vedic sacrifices were performed; a particular tank contained part of the nectar obtained from churning the milk-ocean, etc. This could be described as a trend to align oneself with the Great Tradition (which, however, is a rather unfortunate term[141]). When a local version of the Nṛsiṃha myth is told about Nṛsiṃhapperumāḷ in Tañcai, this shows as much a desire to localize the latter as the attempt to link the local temple image with universal Vaiṣṇavism.

Altogether we can say that these *sthalapurāṇas* are very complex edifices (though usually not in terms of purely literary merit), structures of meaning and of values, which turn the village or town with its temple into a miniature cosmos.

Summary and Conclusions

I have attempted to delineate the significance of the Śrīvaiṣṇava temple by discussing three distinct and intrinsically different areas of indigenous inter-

[141] I have argued (Hardy, *op. cit.*, pp 8f) that it is essential for a proper understanding of Indian *Geistesgeschichte* to assume a whole range of *milieux* and traditions; "normative Hinduism" (explained *ibid.*, pp. 10-15) is only one of the various facets of the "Great Tradition."

pretation; due to historical constellations and a particular intermingling of two cultures, these areas, however, were fused in Tamil society. Firstly, the basic idea that Viṣṇu is present in the temple was developed by theology in the concept of the *arcâvatāra* by defining Viṣṇu's local manifestation in relation to his universal presence, transcendence, and mythical manifestations. This was achieved through a recourse to Sanskrit philosophical thought and terminology. Secondly, an emotionally loaded poetic environment was created which allowed the devotee to relate himself personally to Viṣṇu by adopting various models of human interaction and thus approaching Viṣṇu as king, lover, or child. This environment was thoroughly Tamil and was developed by the Āḻvārs on the basis of *caṅkam* culture and sentiments. Thirdly, the *sthalapurāṇas* surrounded the temple with a mythical framework, thereby partly replacing the emotional approach of the poetic environment. Through their narrative (and in a way much more "rational") account, they explain and legitimize a particular temple complex in relation *i.a.* to social matters. Their aim is also to stimulate awe, amazement, and wonder in the devotee (but not a spontaneous emotional reaction) and turn his attention from the here and now to the mythical past. We are here, in fact, on the surface of a far-reaching cultural difference between the Tamil South and normative Hinduism, between two different approaches to life: one poetic-emotional, the other mythical.

These three areas of interpretation did obviously not maintain the same relative importance in relation to each other during different historical periods and in different segments of Tamil society. But it would require a study much more extensive than the present one to explore which area was most important for whom and during which period. It seems clear, however, that the emotional-poetic approach shows considerable fluctuation during its history, its flourishing period is with the Āḻvārs, but while pushed by the Ācāryas into the background, it survives in certain strata of society (note the many *prabandhams* that exemplify it) and even in c. 1850 A.D. it maintains its position. But it would be a mistake to reduce the struggle underlying these developments to a simplistic brahmin *versus* non-brahmin opposition. That it is a struggle cutting across all segments of society is borne out for instance by Kalahaṃsaka (and naturally, by the author of the *bhāṇa* who was himself an "ācārya," viz. a Śrīvaiṣṇava brahmin), by DMK puritanism, and by the fact that brahmins are playing a considerable role nowadays in preserving whatever little is left of the once flourishing temple music and dance.

Nobody will deny the importance of the temple even in modern Tamil religion, and yet it seems to me that the dynamism which I find expressing itself in the various areas of interpretation that have been discussed above is dwindling. The reasons for this are numerous and can be found both within and outside Śrīvaiṣṇava tradition. The Devdāsī Act destroyed the function of the temple as a centre of the arts; anti-brahmin DMK propaganda severed the links between the Śrīvaiṣṇavas and the populace in general; and over the centuries an ever-increasing gulf between the Śrīvaiṣṇava scholar and the temple *pūjāri* became manifest. The arrival of a new age which is not really favourable to the idea of Viṣṇu's presence in the temple can perhaps be illustrated best by those loudspeakers which I found installed in the inner *prakāram* of the Kūṭal-Aḻakar temple in Madurai and which incessantly blared out the film music of All India Radio, Madras.

Index

[redacted]